HEROES
FROM THE BOOK OF MORMON

HEROES

FROM THE BOOK OF MORMON

BOOKCRAFT
Salt Lake City, Utah

Library of Congress Catalog Card Number: 95-79967
ISBN 0-88494-996-6

Fourth Printing, 1996

Printed in the United States of America

Contents

1 Elder Russell M. Nelson   1
Nephi, Son of Lehi

2 Bishop Merrill J. Bateman   16
Lehi's Tree and Alma's Seed

3 Elder Jeffrey R. Holland   32
Jacob the Unshakable

4 Elder John H. Groberg   47
Enos

5 Elder Neal A. Maxwell   59
King Benjamin

6 Elder Cree-L Kofford   68
Abinadi

7 Elder Joseph B. Wirthlin   79
Alma the Elder: A Role Model for Today

8 Elder L. Tom Perry   98
Alma, the Son of Alma

9 Elder Henry B. Eyring   106
Amulek: The Blessings of Obedience

10 Elder Dean L. Larsen   112
       Zeezrom

11 Elder F. Burton Howard   120
       Ammon: Reflections on Faith and Testimony

12 Elder Joe J. Christensen   128
       Captain Moroni, an Authentic Hero

13 Elder John K. Carmack   134
       Pahoran: Wartime Statesman, Defender of Freedom

14 Elder Richard G. Scott   145
       Nephi, Son of Helaman

15 Elder Andrew W. Peterson   157
       Samuel the Lamanite

16 Elder Spencer J. Condie   168
       Mormon: Historian, General, Man of God

17 Elder Cecil O. Samuelson Jr.   180
       The Brother of Jared

18 Elder Monte J. Brough   189
       The Prophet Ether: Man of the More Excellent Hope

19 President Gordon B. Hinckley   195
       Moroni

20 Elder Carlos E. Asay   201
       Golden Threads of the Book of Mormon

       Index   213

1

Elder Russell M. Nelson

Nephi,
Son of Lehi

At first blush, it seems odd that Nephi, son of Lehi—a man born approximately 615 years B.C.—should have such a contemporary and continuing influence upon my life. But he has.

When I received my call to serve as one of the Twelve Apostles, my response included a quotation from Nephi: "I will go and do the things which the Lord hath commanded, for I know that the Lord giveth no commandments unto the children of men, save he shall prepare a way for them that they may accomplish the thing which he commandeth them" (1 Nephi 3:7). Thus, in one of the most important moments of my life, I spoke the words of a man whom I had never met, but in whom I had implicit trust. Ever since Sister Nelson and I were married, we have tried to emulate Nephi's example in accepting assignments in the Church. In that same address in which I quoted Nephi's words, I said, "I have learned not to put question marks but to use exclamation points when calls are issued through inspired channels of priesthood government" ("Call to the Holy Apostleship," *Ensign*, May 1984, p. 52).

Nephi had influenced my life previously through my many years as a medical educator, researcher, and surgeon. Having grown up in a day when it was not fashionable for medical doctors to participate in religious affairs, I was determined to be different. I wanted to follow the example of Nephi, who taught that we should "liken all scriptures unto us" (1 Nephi 19:23). The concept of blending scriptural truth with academic learning and not separating the two made perfect sense to me.

I took a great deal of courage from that concept in doing research on the heart. When I graduated from medical school, it was commonly believed that one must not touch the beating heart for fear it would stop. Because of Nephi's teachings, I chose to liken the scriptures to the field of my interest in the heart. Verses from the Doctrine and Covenants that served to undergird my thinking included:

> There is a law, irrevocably decreed in heaven before the foundations of this world, upon which all blessings are predicated—
> And when we obtain any blessing from God, it is by obedience to that law upon which it is predicated (D&C 130:20–21).

> All kingdoms have a law given;
> And there are many kingdoms; for there is no space in the which there is no kingdom; and there is no kingdom in which there is no space, either a greater or a lesser kingdom.
> And unto every kingdom is given a law; and unto every law there are certain bounds also and conditions. (D&C 88:36–38.)

These scriptures helped me to understand that laws pertained to all blessings, including that of the beating heart. I felt that once we understood what the laws are that keep the heart beating, we should be able to stop a damaged heart, make required repairs, and start it again. Indeed that proved to be true. Surgeons now routinely stop and start the heart, knowing that the divine laws pertaining to that blessing are dependable and incontrovertible.

During the long years of education I spent in earning two doctoral degrees, scriptures also helped me to distinguish between learning and wisdom. I am so grateful for this counsel of Nephi, quoting his brother Jacob: "O the vainness, and the frailties, and the foolishness of men! When they are learned they think they are wise, and they hearken not unto the counsel of God, for they set it aside, supposing they know of themselves, wherefore, their wisdom is foolishness and it profiteth them not. And they shall perish. But to be learned is good if they hearken unto the counsels of God." (2 Nephi 9:28–29.)

NEPHI: MAN OF FAITH AND ABILITY

A study of Nephi's life provides inspiration as well as information.[1] To me, it is highly significant that his first scriptural
statement compliments his parents, Lehi and Sariah (see 1
Nephi 1:1). A sign of greatness then and now is the expression
of deferential honor to parents. Lehi and Sariah's family of
sons—Laman, Lemuel, Sam, Nephi, Jacob, and Joseph—and un-
named daughters are familiar to readers of the Book of Mormon
(see 2 Nephi 5:6). Though Laman and Lemuel often resisted
their father's counsel, most of Lehi's children honored him and
followed his direction. Foremost among them was Nephi.
Nephi's trials in obtaining the plates of Laban are a case in point.

Father Lehi responded to divine instruction by removing his
family from the land of Jerusalem. The group traveled south
into the wilderness adjacent to the Red Sea. Lehi was told that if
he and his family remained obedient, they would be led to a
land "choice above all other lands" (1 Nephi 2:20; 2 Nephi 1:5)—
but to preserve their faith, they needed to have the scriptures
with them. So Lehi, under inspiration, sent his sons back to
Jerusalem to obtain from Laban valuable records written on
brass plates that contained both the sacred scriptures and the
genealogy of Lehi and his ancestors. After a great deal of trouble,
the plates were obtained. Laban's servant Zoram joined with the
Nephites; the sword of Laban, a weapon of superior craftsman-
ship, was brought back to Lehi.

As Latter-day Saints, we know that story well. But we are
less familiar with the terrain and climate of that area. Sister
Nelson and I have visited Israel a number of times. When so-
journing in its southern sector, we have traveled in the comfort
of an air-conditioned vehicle—a must for us in that very hot
desert area. After an hour or two under the merciless rays of the
midday sun, we have eagerly sought a cold drink or an early return to air-conditioned accommodations.

---

1. For thoughtful reviews, see Allen E. Bergin, "Nephi, a Universal Man,"
Ensign, September 1976, pp. 65–70; Noel B. Reynolds, "Nephi," in *Encyclopedia
of Mormonism*, ed. Daniel H. Ludlow, 5 vols. (New York: Macmillan, 1992),
3:1003–5.

Although the place where Lehi issued the request for his sons to return to Jerusalem is not known exactly, we do know that it was along the eastern shore of the Red Sea. The distance they would have traveled—each way—has been estimated to be at least 250 miles. That is a long way to go without roads, cars, cold drinks, or air-conditioning. No wonder Laman and Lemuel murmured (see 1 Nephi 3:5). No wonder their mother complained (see 1 Nephi 5:2–3). But Nephi said, "I will go and do . . ." A similar response was rephrased on another occasion when he said, "If it so be that the children of men keep the commandments of God he doth nourish them, and strengthen them, and provide means whereby they can accomplish the thing which he has commanded them" (1 Nephi 17:3). When Lehi asked his sons to return to Jerusalem a *second* time, their trek through the hot desert country would also have been without the benefit of the creature comforts to which we are accustomed. I deeply respect the faith of Nephi, whose "I will go and do" statement we quote so freely. Those words bear profound meaning for me.

The depth of Nephi's determination to follow inspired counsel is again revealed in a statement made later: "If God had commanded me to do all things I could do them. If he should command me that I should say unto this water, be thou earth, it should be earth; and if I should say it, it would be done." (1 Nephi 17:50.) That kind of faith made Nephi fearless.

Nephi had other sterling qualities as well. Even more uncomfortable than sun and desert must have been the challenges of dissension within his father's family. Lehi and Sariah's colony spent a total of eight years in the wilderness. Laman and Lemuel were older than Nephi, rebellious against both him and their father, Lehi. Divine intervention was necessary on several occasions to keep those sons from thwarting the plans of their prophet-father. Shortly after Lehi's death, Laman and Lemuel and the sons of Ishamel openly rebelled against Nephi—the spiritual successor to their father—insomuch that they sought to kill him, as they had done several years previously. Nonetheless his attitude was still kind and brotherly, as when he had said, "I did frankly forgive them all that they had done." (See 1 Nephi 7:16, 21; 2 Nephi 5:2.)

Meanwhile, Nephi became the preeminent record keeper of his civilization, surpassed perhaps only by Mormon. Commanded to keep accurate records of events he would witness, Nephi formed some plates that he called the plates of Nephi (later called the large plates of Nephi), upon which he engraved the history of his people.

Nephi was an exemplary leader. He was a young man when called to be a prophet, and he established a government based on sound political, legal, economic, and religious principles. His people proclaimed him king, although he resisted this action initially. He taught them to be industrious and to provide for their needs. He prepared them to defend themselves. He built a temple and anointed his younger brothers Jacob and Joseph as priests and teachers to instruct the people and lead them in spiritual matters. (See 2 Nephi 5:10, 16, 26; Jacob 1:18.)

Before he died, he appointed a new king and appointed his brother Jacob as caretaker of religious records. "Nephi gave me, Jacob, a commandment concerning the small plates. . . . I should write upon these plates a few of the things which I considered to be most precious; . . . I should preserve these plates and hand them down unto my seed, from generation to generation. And if there were preaching which was sacred, or revelation which was great, or prophesying, that I should engraven the heads of them upon these plates, and touch upon them as much as it were possible, for Christ's sake, and for the sake of our people." (Jacob 1:1–4.)

Nephi was also a great follower. He trusted God completely. Nephi taught us that though no one can discern the purpose and meaning of all life's situations, we can rest assured "that [God] loveth his children" (1 Nephi 11:17). Nephi's great trust in Deity is typified in his statement: "My voice shall forever ascend up unto thee, my rock and mine everlasting God" (2 Nephi 4:35).

Nephi's response to the Lord's command to build a ship provides another glimpse of his remarkable faith. Through the ages, several great prophets have felt overwhelmed by tasks assigned to them by the Lord. Inexperienced Nephi easily could have wondered how to build an oceangoing ship. But his immediate response was simply, "Whither shall I go that I may find ore to molten?" (1 Nephi 17:9.) Nephi was shown how to build the ship.

Nephi was a craftsman of unusual versatility. He personally refined the ore, designed the shape, and made the metal plates on which he wrote (see 1 Nephi 19:1). When his steel bow broke, he made one of wood (see 1 Nephi 16:23). He smelted ore, fashioned tools, and built a ship of "exceedingly fine" workmanship (see 1 Nephi 17:16; 18:1–4). In the promised land he established a city, built a temple "after the manner of the temple of Solomon," and taught people to build buildings and to work in wood, iron, copper, brass, steel, gold, silver, and precious ores (see 2 Nephi 5:15–16).

Nephi's faith was buttressed by determination. We have record of a very significant oath that he declared: "As the Lord liveth, and as we live, we will not go down unto our father in the wilderness until we have accomplished the thing which the Lord hath commanded us" (1 Nephi 3:15). In those days, no man would dream of breaking such an oath. It would be the most solemn of all oaths to the Semite: "As the Lord liveth, and as I live!" Nephi swore that oath in order to pacify the struggling Zoram in an instant (see 1 Nephi 4:32, 35).

Another measure of a leader's greatness may be assessed in his foresight to prepare his successors. In his old age, Nephi anointed a man to be a king and ruler over his people. In deference to the name of Nephi, the king was called Second Nephi. Succeeding kings were called Third Nephi, and so on.

When Nephi passed away, Second Nephi became the Nephites' king; Jacob, the younger brother of Nephi, became their prophet.

NEPHI: MAN OF LETTERS

The exceptional literacy of later Nephite leaders may have been due to the fact that Nephi was such an exemplary man of letters. He was probably fluent in both Hebrew and Egyptian, having stated that he had been taught somewhat in all "the learning of the Jews and the language of the Egyptians," and of his father (1 Nephi 1:1–2).

Nephi displayed literary competence in the way he organized his writings and employed a diversity of literary devices. He used narrative, rhetoric, and poetic forms, including a psalm. He loved the writings of Isaiah and quoted them extensively (see, for example, 1 Nephi 20–21; 2 Nephi 12–24). Nephi often provided interpretations. In comparing the biblical and the Book of Mormon presentations of the Isaiah verses, we see that they are not all identical. Some important refinements occur in the Book of Mormon. For example, compare Isaiah 13:3 with 2 Nephi 23:3. No doubt many of them can be attributed to Nephi.

He began writing on the large plates soon after Lehi's group arrived in the promised land. Those plates served as the official record of the Nephites from about 590 B.C. to A.D. 385 (see 1 Nephi 19:1–4). During part of this period, they were primarily a record of secular events among the descendants of Lehi; later they contained the religious record as well (see 1 Nephi 19:4; Jacob 3:13). These plates contained "a full account of the history of [Nephi's] people" (1 Nephi 9:2; see also verse 4; 2 Nephi 4:14; Jacob 1:2–3).

He began writing on the small plates of Nephi about 570 B.C. They served thereafter as the religious record of the Nephite nation (see 1 Nephi 6:3–6; 9:4; 19:2–3, 5–6; 2 Nephi 5:29–32; Jacob 1:4).

Nephi had a penchant for plain expression. "My brethren, I have spoken plainly that ye cannot err" (2 Nephi 25:20). Nephi asserted that precious truths would be restored through written records and that they would "make known the plain and precious things which have been taken away" (1 Nephi 13:40).

Such plain and precious things included knowledge of basic ordinances of baptism and partaking of the sacrament.

Nephi established personal policies by which he decided which items to include in his sacred records. He explained: "It mattereth not to me that I am particular to give a full account of all the things of my father, for they cannot be written upon these plates, for I desire the room that I may write of the things of God. For the fulness of mine intent is that I may persuade men to come unto the God of Abraham, and the God of Isaac, and the God of Jacob, and be saved. Wherefore, the things which are pleasing unto the world I do not write, but the things which are pleasing unto God and unto those who are not of the world. Wherefore, I shall give commandment unto my seed, that they shall not occupy these plates with things which are not of worth unto the children of men." (1 Nephi 6:3–6.)

Nephi: Man of Meekness

Throughout Nephi's many activities, he was consistently opposed and threatened, even with death, by Laman and Lemuel. But in each crisis he was miraculously delivered by the power of the Lord and blessed to complete his task. He was a man with a wide range of human sensitivities, and he yearned for the welfare of those who tormented him. He had a deep love and sense of responsibility for his people, as evidenced by this expression: "But I, Nephi, have written what I have written, and I esteem it as of great worth, and especially unto my people. For I pray continually for them by day, and mine eyes water my pillow by night, because of them; and I cry unto my God in faith, and I know that he will hear my cry." (2 Nephi 33:3.)

Nephi possessed a humility not often seen among gifted men. In fact, he was quite self-deprecating: "Nevertheless, notwithstanding the great goodness of the Lord, in showing me his great and marvelous works, my heart exclaimeth: O wretched man that I am! Yea, my heart sorroweth because of my flesh; my soul grieveth because of mine iniquities. I am encompassed about, because of the temptations and the sins which do so easily beset me. And when I desire to rejoice, my heart groaneth because of my sins; nevertheless, I know in whom I have trusted." (2 Nephi 4:17–19.)

Though opposed and provoked by them, Nephi did not sever ties with his rebellious brothers until the Lord told him to start a colony of believers. He maintained his affection for them. Rebuke and exhortation were followed by love. We sense, at least to a degree, some of his sorrow when his brothers rejected the invitation to embrace the gospel of Jesus Christ.

Nephi: Man of God

Nephi, and his father, Lehi, enjoyed frequent communion with the heavens, even communing with Jehovah. They had the Melchizedek Priesthood and the fulness of the gospel. They taught the doctrines of salvation and the necessity of a spiritual rebirth for all men and women who desired to become sons and daughters of Christ. It was Nephi who affirmed by oath and testimony the pivotal role of Jesus. "For according to the words of the prophets, the Messiah cometh in six hundred years from the time that my father left Jerusalem; and according to the words of the prophets, and also the word of the angel of God, his name shall be Jesus Christ, the Son of God" (2 Nephi 25:19).

Nephi understood the importance of the Atonement that was to come. On his plates he recorded Jacob's exultant words, "O how great the plan of our God!" (2 Nephi 9:13), and he expressed pleasure in the privilege of teaching of Christ. "My soul delighteth in proving unto my people the truth of the coming of Christ; . . . and all things which have been given of God from the beginning of the world, unto man, are the typifying of him. Also my soul delighteth in the covenants of the Lord which he hath made to our fathers; yea, my soul delighteth in his grace, and in his justice, and power, and mercy in the great and eternal plan of deliverance from death. And my soul delighteth in proving unto my people that save Christ should come all men must perish." (2 Nephi 11:4–6.) Nephi knew that Jesus would be "lifted up upon the cross and slain for the sins of the world" (1 Nephi 11:33).

Later, Nephi expanded his prophecy of the forthcoming Atonement: "They [the people] will reject [Jesus], because of their iniquities, and the hardness of their hearts, and the stiffness of their necks. Behold, they will crucify him; and after he is laid in a sepulchre for the space of three days he shall rise from the dead, with healing in his wings; and all those who shall believe on his name shall be saved in the kingdom of God. Wherefore, my soul delighteth to prophesy concerning him, *for I have seen his day.*" (2 Nephi 25:12–13; emphasis added.)

In the context of the Savior's atonement, Nephi stressed the need for repentance. He also acknowledged the Lord's justice and mercy when he added: "And as one generation hath been destroyed among the Jews because of iniquity, even so have they been destroyed from generation to generation according to their iniquities; and never hath any of them been destroyed save it were foretold them by the prophets of the Lord" (2 Nephi 25:9).

Like Joseph Smith, Nephi had an avid appetite for spiritual truth, and the Lord responded by appearing to each of these great prophets. On one occasion, Nephi wrote of "having great desires to know of the mysteries of God, wherefore, I did cry unto the Lord; and behold he did visit me" (1 Nephi 2:16). He expected his contemporaries to ask God when they lacked understanding: "I said unto them: Have ye inquired of the Lord?" (1 Nephi 15:8.)

Nephi's unusual spiritual endowment may be measured by special gifts, messages, and powers that he received. As with Joseph Smith, he obtained spiritual knowledge at a young age and was given a preview of his destiny. He knew his divine calling even before he obtained the brass plates of Laban (see 1 Nephi 2:16–22).

Nephi was a mighty seer who prophesied about future events involving the Nephites and Lamanites (see 1 Nephi 12), the Jews (see 2 Nephi 25:9–20), and the Gentiles (see 2 Nephi 26:12 through 30:18). Nephi saw our day and the great work that would be accomplished in the dispensation of the fulness of times.

Nephi also received knowledge of the dispersion and later gathering of Israel. Of this he wrote, "It appears that the house of Israel, sooner or later, will be scattered upon all the face of the earth, and also among all nations" (1 Nephi 22:3). Among this group would be many of the tribe of Ephraim, who would be sought out in the final restoration to lay the foundation for the latter-day work of establishing the church and kingdom of God upon the earth.

In referring to the gathering of Israel, Nephi taught of the responsibilities that we would now have in fulfilling God's ancient promises. He informed us who we really are. Long before Christ was born in Bethlehem, Nephi foresaw our potential. To people of his day, he explained: "Our father hath not spoken of our seed alone, but also of all the house of Israel, pointing to the covenant which should be fulfilled *in the latter days;* which covenant the Lord made to our father Abraham, saying: In thy seed shall all the kindreds of the earth be blessed" (1 Nephi 15:18; emphasis added).

In addition to being a revelator, Nephi was a temple builder. "I, Nephi, did build a temple; and I did construct it after the manner of the temple of Solomon save it were not built of so many precious things; for they were not to be found upon the land, wherefore, it could not be built like unto Solomon's temple. But the manner of the construction was like unto the temple of Solomon; and the workmanship thereof was exceedingly fine." (2 Nephi 5:16.)

The means by which prophets receive revelation are known only to God and His prophets. But Nephi provided some insight with this statement: "For it came to pass after I had desired to know the things that my father had seen, and believing that the Lord was able to make them known unto me, as I sat pondering in mine heart I was caught away in the Spirit of the Lord, yea, into an exceedingly high mountain, which I never had before seen, and upon which I never had before set my foot" (1 Nephi 11:1).

Could it be that some of the things taught to him on such a mountain pertained to the temple? In any case, Nephi was "bidden that [he] should not write them" (2 Nephi 4:25). What he did write, however, was of great importance—summarized well by Elder Boyd K. Packer. He explained:

In that vision [Nephi] saw:

- A virgin bearing a child in her arms,
- One who should prepare the way—John the Baptist,
- The ministry of the Son of God,
- Twelve others following the Messiah,
- The heavens open and angels ministering to them,
- The multitudes blessed and healed,
- The crucifixion of the Christ,
- The wisdom and pride of the world opposing his work. (See 1 Nephi 11:14–36.)

That vision is the central message of the Book of Mormon.
The Book of Mormon is in truth another testament of Jesus Christ. (*Ensign*, May 1986, pp. 60–61.)

Nephi also recorded that he beheld "one of the twelve apostles of the Lamb," identifying him later as John (see 1 Nephi 14:20, 27).

In view of the remarkable prophetic powers of Nephi, it is appropriate that a song about him be in the official hymnbook of the Church. The words to that hymn bear repeating here:

To Nephi, seer of olden time,
A vision came from God,
Wherein the holy word sublime
Was shown an iron rod.

While on our journey here below,
Beneath temptation's pow'r,
Through mists of darkness we must go,
In peril ev'ry hour.

And when temptation's pow'r is nigh,
Our pathway clouded o'er,
Upon the rod we can rely,
And heaven's aid implore.

Hold to the rod, the iron rod;
'Tis strong, and bright, and true.
The iron rod is the word of God;
'Twill safely guide us through.
(Joseph L. Townsend, "The Iron Rod," in *Hymns*, no. 274.)

NEPHI: MESSENGER OF THE MESSAGE

Major writers of the Book of Mormon included Nephi, Jacob, Mormon, and Moroni. All four of them were privileged to see the Savior. Nephi testified of his experience:

> And it came to pass that I, Nephi, being exceedingly young, nevertheless being large in stature, and also having great desires to know of the mysteries of God, wherefore, I did cry unto the Lord; and behold he did visit me, and did soften my heart that I did believe all the words which had been spoken by my father; wherefore, I did not rebel against him like unto my brothers (1 Nephi 2:16).

> And now I, Nephi, write more of the words of Isaiah, for my soul delighteth in his words. For I will liken his words unto my people, and I will send them forth unto all my children, for he verily saw my Redeemer, even as I have seen him.
> And my brother, Jacob, also has seen him as I have seen him; wherefore, I will send their words forth unto my children to prove unto them that my words are true. (2 Nephi 11:2–3.)

Those personal encounters with the premortal Savior have given us the advantage of knowledge otherwise unattainable. Nephi taught that the Atonement makes available to all who have faith in Christ a liberation from sin and a spiritual redemption from the adversary. Hence, all men and women who follow the example of Christ and enter into His way through repentance and baptism will be blessed with a baptism of fire and the Holy Ghost—which brings a remission of sin and individual guidance—so that they might endure to the end in faith and receive eternal life (see 2 Nephi 31).

In his prophetic description of the churches of the last days, Nephi wrote: "Yea, and there shall be many which shall teach after this manner, false and vain and foolish doctrines, and shall be puffed up in their hearts, and shall seek deep to hide their counsels from the Lord; and their works shall be in the dark" (2 Nephi 28:9). So great would be the influence of "vain and foolish doctrines" and "wickedness, and abominations," Nephi prophesied, that "all" will have gone astray "save it be a few, who are the humble followers of Christ; nevertheless, they [the true believers in Christ] are led, that in many instances they do err because they are taught by the precepts of men" (2 Nephi 28:14).

Nephi taught that if one follows the example of his Savior—by being obedient to the commandment to be baptized by water as a sincere act of covenant—"then shall ye receive the Holy Ghost; yea, then cometh the baptism of fire and of the Holy Ghost; and then can ye speak with the tongue of angels, and shout praises unto the Holy One of Israel" (2 Nephi 31:13).

Later Nephi explained: "And now, behold, my beloved brethren, I suppose that ye ponder somewhat in your hearts concerning that which ye should do after ye have entered in by the way. But, behold, why do ye ponder these things in your hearts? Do ye not remember that I said unto you that after ye had received the Holy Ghost ye could speak with the tongue of angels? And now, how could ye speak with the tongue of angels save it were by the Holy Ghost? Angels speak by the power of the Holy Ghost; wherefore, they speak the words of Christ. Wherefore, I said unto you, feast upon the words of Christ; for behold, the words of Christ will tell you all things what ye should do." (2 Nephi 32:1–3.)

Nephi's power as a messenger of the message enabled him to instruct us in a more appropriate manner of worship. "The right way," he said, "is to believe in Christ and deny him not; for by denying him ye also deny the prophets and the law. And now behold, I say unto you that the right way is to believe in Christ, and deny him not; and Christ is the Holy One of Israel; wherefore ye must bow down before him, and worship him with all your might, mind, and strength, and your whole soul; and if ye do this ye shall in nowise be cast out." (2 Nephi 25:28–29.)

Nephi's personality comes to life as we read his closing testimony. He reveals his strengths, his perceived weaknesses, his frustrations, his delights, and, finally, his sterling commitment to obey God.

> I, Nephi, cannot write all the things which were taught among my people; neither am I mighty in writing, like unto speaking; for when a man speaketh by the power of the Holy Ghost the power of the Holy Ghost carrieth it unto the hearts of the children of men.
>
> But behold, there are many that harden their hearts against the Holy Spirit, that it hath no place in them; wherefore, they cast many things away which are written and esteem them as things of naught.
>
> But I, Nephi, have written what I have written, and I esteem it as of great worth, and especially unto my people. . . .
>
> . . . The words which I have written in weakness will be made strong unto them; for it persuadeth them to do good; it maketh known unto them of their fathers; and it speaketh of Jesus, and persuadeth them to believe in him, and to endure to the end, which is life eternal. . . .
>
> I glory in plainness; I glory in truth; I glory in my Jesus, for he hath redeemed my soul from hell.
>
> I have charity for my people, and great faith in Christ that I shall meet many souls spotless at his judgment-seat.
>
> I have charity for the Jew—I say Jew, because I mean them from whence I came.
>
> I also have charity for the Gentiles. But behold, for none of these can I hope except they shall be reconciled unto Christ, and enter into the narrow gate, and walk in the strait path which leads to life, and continue in the path until the end of the day of probation.
>
> And now, my beloved brethren, and also Jew, and all ye ends of the earth, hearken unto these words and believe in Christ; and

if ye believe not in these words believe in Christ. And if ye shall believe in Christ ye will believe in these words, for they are the words of Christ, and he hath given them unto me; and they teach all men that they should do good.

. . . Christ will show unto you, with power and great glory, that they are his words, at the last day; and you and I shall stand face to face before his bar; and ye shall know that I have been commanded of him to write these things, notwithstanding my weakness.

. . . And now, my beloved brethren, all those who are of the house of Israel, and all ye ends of the earth, I speak unto you as the voice of one crying from the dust: Farewell until that great day shall come.

. . . I bid you an everlasting farewell, for these words shall condemn you at the last day.

For what I seal on earth, shall be brought against you at the judgment bar; for thus hath the Lord commanded me, and I must obey. (2 Nephi 33:1–4, 6–11, 13–15.)

SUMMARY AND CONCLUSION

Nephi was a multifaceted genius. Endowed with great physical stature, he was a prophet, teacher, ruler, colonizer, builder, craftsman, scholar, writer, poet, military leader, and father of nations. Nephi had a sincere desire to know the mysteries of God. He became a special witness and trusted prophet of the Lord.

Nephi lived an adventurous life and faced numerous difficulties. Some of the challenges he faced included fleeing Jerusalem, building a ship, crossing the waters to the promised land, colonizing, withstanding persecution, fulfilling family and leadership responsibilities, and keeping records. Toward the end of his inspiring life Nephi wrote his concluding testimony and bore witness of the doctrine of Christ, the power of the Holy Ghost, and the truthfulness of the words he had written. Appropriately, his final testimony closed with the words that could be known as his signature: *"I must obey."*

Few have spoken so profoundly in behalf of one generation to another. Indeed, Nephi's life and mission were destined to bless us and all people of our day.

2

Bishop Merrill J. Bateman

Lehi's Tree and Alma's Seed

From the beginning, God has chosen good and faithful men to serve as prophets to the nations—His spokesmen and sentinels on earth. The Lord called Abraham in the Grand Council before the world was formed (see Abraham 3:22–23). Jeremiah was ordained a prophet before his birth (see Jeremiah 1:4–5). John the Baptist, Peter, James, and John, and modern-day prophets were all foreordained. The selection of these noble men to be prophets was based on their exceeding faith and good works before the foundation of the earth was laid. (See Alma 13:1–6.)

The major role of a prophet is to invite men, women, and children to come unto Christ; to preach righteousness; to teach men about God's character and the plan of salvation; to denounce sin and foretell its consequences. On occasion prophets foretell future events. Above all, prophets testify of the divinity of the Lord Jesus Christ, His earthly ministry in the meridian of time, His atonement in the garden and on the cross, and His resurrection three days after the Crucifixion.

LEHI AND ALMA THE YOUNGER

Lehi and Alma the Younger were two noble Book of Mormon prophets. Both were great teachers of righteousness; both invited their flocks to come to and follow the Good

Shepherd. The two prophets lived approximately five hundred years apart, as Lehi's ministry began about 600 B.C. while Alma began his ministry about ninety years before Christ's birth. Lehi's call to be a prophet is recorded in 1 Nephi 1:6–7. Later in the same chapter he is shown a vision in which he sees the destruction of Jerusalem. Subsequently, being warned by the Lord that his life is in danger, Lehi is commanded to leave the city with his family in order to preserve a branch of Israel. The family leave behind all their worldly possessions and are led by their prophet-father into the wilderness, taking only provisions and tents for the journey.

Alma the Younger with his friends were unbelievers in their youth. As an articulate young man, he went about seeking to destroy the Church, to lead people astray. Because of his father's prayers, an angel of the Lord appeared and commanded Alma and his friends to repent or be destroyed. During three days and nights, Alma wrestled with his wickedness as his body lay lifeless. Eventually, he remembered his father's teachings concerning Jesus Christ, who would atone for the sins of the world. As his mind caught hold of this thought, he cried out and appealed to the Savior for mercy. The bitterness, misery, and pain associated with his sins were turned to joy, light, and peace as he received a new birth through the power of the Holy Ghost. (See Mosiah 27; Alma 36.) Afterwards, Alma reflected on his experience and realized he was shown a vision similar to one received by father Lehi wherein both men saw "God sitting upon his throne, surrounded with numberless concourses of angels in the attitude of singing and praising their God" (1 Nephi 1:8; Alma 36:22). This vision enabled both men to become powerful witnesses of the Lord Jesus Christ.

Lehi and Alma the Younger also shared another vision—that of the tree of life. Lehi's dream is one of the most-quoted passages in the Book of Mormon and yet is only partially understood by many readers (see 1 Nephi 8, 11–15). His vision of the tree and its fruit, the rod of iron, the river, and other symbols occurred early in the family's journey. It was given for the spiritual preservation of Lehi's family—that is, to help family members understand the eternal purposes of mortality and to know to whom they should look for assistance during their trials and tribulations. The desert storms, the broken bow, childbirth in a wilderness, father Ishmael's death, the building of a ship, and the journey to the promised land provided both physical and spiritual challenges. The ultimate spiritual test was one of maintaining faith in God and His prophet in spite of the journey's difficulties. Each family member had to choose between the broad path leading to the large and spacious building on the one hand and the narrow and strait path leading to the tree on the other.

Five hundred years later, the posterity of Lehi were still benefiting from his spiritual odyssey. Alma, no doubt remembering Lehi's teachings, used the tree of life symbol to teach the Zoramites how to develop faith in Christ (see Alma 32). He taught them to plant a seed (the word of God) in their hearts. He promised that if the seed was nourished and cared for, it would mature into a tree "springing up unto everlasting life," and its fruit would be "sweet above all that is sweet, and . . . white above all that is white, yea, and pure above all that is pure" (Alma 32:41, 42). By planting the seed, the Zoramites would put themselves on the "strait and narrow path," and they would remain on the path by nourishing the seed with great care until it matured within them.

In order to more fully understand the meaning of Lehi's dream and Alma's teachings, a review and examination of Lehi's vision, of Nephi's interpretation, and of Alma's words follow. It is Nephi's explanation of the tree which gives insight into the meaning of Lehi's dream and Alma's message.

Lehi's Dream of the Tree of Life

While tarrying in the wilderness, Lehi announced to his family that he had dreamed a dream, or that he had seen a vision. In the dream, Lehi traveled through a dark and dreary wilderness for the space of many hours, led by a man dressed in a white robe. The darkness weighed on Lehi's spirit, even though he had a guide, and he prayed that the Lord would have mercy on him (see 1 Nephi 8:8). In answer to his prayer, Lehi entered a large and spacious field in which he beheld a tree "whose fruit was desirable to make one happy" (1 Nephi 8:10). The sweetness of the fruit exceeded anything he had tasted, and it was white beyond all whiteness that he had seen. The prophet partook of the fruit, which filled his soul with great joy, and he became desirous that his family should partake.

Lehi's Invitation to His Family

Lehi cast his eyes about, hoping to find his family. As he looked he saw a river which ran near the tree. At the head of the river he noticed his wife, Sariah, and two sons, Sam and Nephi. They appeared uncertain as to their direction. Lehi beckoned them with a loud voice and invited them to come to the tree and partake of the fruit. They answered his call, came, and partook. Then the prophet wanted his other two sons, Laman and Lemuel, to come and partake. Again he looked toward the head of the river to find them. Finally, they came into view and he invited them. To his dismay, they would not accept the invitation.

The Difficulties Along the Strait and Narrow Path

As Nephi records his father's dream, the prophet saw a rod of iron extending along the bank of the river, and it led to the tree. He beheld a strait and narrow path alongside the rod of iron which came to the tree. The path also led by a fountain of water to a large and spacious field.

Lehi beheld four groups of people traveling in different directions, some toward the tree and others away from it. The first group found the path and began the journey toward the tree. Along the way they encountered a mist of darkness which caused them to wander off and become lost. Others pressed forward, caught hold of the rod of iron, pressed through the mist by clinging to the rod, arrived at the tree, and partook of the fruit. Even though they tasted the sweetness of the fruit, they did not persist. They succumbed to the mocking of finely dressed people who inhabited a great and spacious building across the river. The scoffing and finger-pointing of the well-dressed caused the second group to become ashamed, and they drifted away into forbidden paths and were lost.

The third group pressed forward onto the path and caught hold of the rod. By continually holding to the rod of iron, they reached the tree, fell down, and partook of the fruit. Nephi's record of his father's vision does not elaborate more with regard to these people. However, it is obvious that these are the faithful, those who continually hold to the rod, those who are humbled by the tree and its fruit. This is the only group that falls down at the foot of the tree before partaking of the fruit.

The fourth group in Lehi's vision felt their way towards the great and spacious building. They had little or no interest in searching for the tree or the life it provides. After entering the building, they joined the others in pointing the finger of scorn at Lehi and those eating the fruit. Lehi, Sariah, Sam, and Nephi did not heed the people in the large building. But Laman and Lemuel refused to travel the path toward the tree and partake of the fruit. This upset Lehi, as he feared that the two eldest sons would be cast off from the presence of the Lord. Nephi states that after father Lehi had related all the words of the dream, he exhorted his older sons "with all the feeling of a tender parent, that they would hearken to his words" (1 Nephi 8:37).

Lehi's vision contains many symbols, including the strait and narrow path, the rod of iron, the mist of darkness, the large and spacious building, the river of water, and the tree of life. Each symbol has a special meaning, but the central message concerns the tree and its fruit. This is illustrated in 1 Nephi 11 where Nephi is asked questions concerning his belief in the tree and is taught concerning its meaning.

NEPHI'S VISION OF THE TREE AND ITS INTERPRETATION

Each time Lehi shared his spiritual experiences with his children, Nephi desired to know and understand for himself. Following Lehi's vision of Jerusalem's destruction, Nephi cried to the Lord in prayer and received an answer. Nephi records: "Behold he [the Lord] did visit me, and did soften my heart that I did believe all the words which had been spoken by my father; wherefore, I did not rebel against him like unto my brothers" (1 Nephi 2:16). Lehi's telling of the tree of life dream sparked the same desire in his righteous son. Nephi states that he (1) desired to know the things his father had seen; (2) believed the Lord would make them known to him; and (3) pondered the vision and its meaning in his heart (see 1 Nephi 11:1). As a consequence, he was carried away into an exceedingly high mountain by the Spirit of the Lord.

The Tree of Life

The Spirit questioned Nephi regarding his desires. Nephi answered that he desired to behold the things which his father had seen. The Spirit then asked: "Believest thou that thy father saw the tree of which he hath spoken?" (1 Nephi 11:3.) Nephi confirmed his belief in all his father's words. The Spirit "cried . . . : Hosanna to the Lord" (1 Nephi 11:6), blessed Nephi, and told him that what he would see would be for a sign—for after he beheld the tree which bore the fruit, he would see a man descend out of the heavens, and Nephi would become a witness of the Son of God (see 1 Nephi 11:7). Although Nephi would shortly conclude that the tree represents the love of God, we can also think of the tree as being a sign or symbol of the person through whom that love is expressed so perfectly, the Lord Jesus Christ.

The Spirit then showed Nephi the tree. Nephi gives a description of the tree which is missing in Lehi's story—at least in Nephi's record of his father's telling of the dream. Nephi describes the tree as having "beauty . . . exceeding of all beauty; and the whiteness thereof did exceed the whiteness of the driven snow" (1 Nephi 11:8). The beauty of the tree is descriptive of the Lord. The Psalmist used the same word when he desired "to behold the beauty of the Lord" (Psalm 27:4). Whiteness is a symbol of Christ's purity and cleanliness, as He lived a perfect, sinless life. It also denotes His radiance in the glorified state. Mark described the Lord's raiment on the Mount of Transfiguration as "shining, exceeding white as snow" (Mark 9:3). Nephi also exclaims that the tree is precious above all (1 Nephi 11:9).

The Love of God

Later, Nephi describes the tree and the fountain of living waters as the "love of God" (1 Nephi 11:22, 25). What is the love of God? Jesus testified to Nicodemus that "God so loved the world, that he gave his only begotten Son, that whosoever believeth in him should not perish, but have everlasting life" (John 3:16).

God's love for His children is shown by His willingness to sacrifice His only begotten Son. Also, the love of God is reflected in the Savior's obedience in voluntarily completing the Atonement.

Another indication that the "love of God" refers to Christ is the reference to the fountain. The "fountain of living water" symbol in the scriptures refers to Jehovah or Jesus. Jehovah lamented the fact that the Jewish nation had forsaken Him, "the fountain of living waters" (Jeremiah 2:13). Jesus offered living water to the woman of Samaria at the well. Not understanding, she told Him that the well was deep and that He did not have anything with which to draw. He then said: "Whosoever drinketh of this water shall thirst again: But whosoever drinketh of the water that I shall give him shall never thirst; but the water that I shall give him shall be in him a well of water springing up into everlasting life." (John 4:10–14.) The "fountain of living water" is a type of Christ as the source of life with regard to both immortality and eternal life.

The Condescension of God

At this point in the vision, the Spirit asked Nephi again what he desired. Nephi indicated that he desired to know the interpretation thereof—in other words, he wanted a more complete understanding of the vision, and particularly the meaning of the tree and its fruit. The vision unfolded further and Nephi saw Jerusalem, the city of Nazareth, and a virgin who was exceedingly fair and white. An angel then queried Nephi regarding what he had seen. Nephi reported that he had seen a virgin, most beautiful and fair above all other virgins. The angel asked if he knew or understood the "condescension of God," or in other words, God stepping down from a higher state to be with man. Nephi replied that he knew that God loves His children but that he, Nephi, did not know all things. Nephi was then told that the virgin was "the mother of the Son of God, after the manner of the flesh" (1 Nephi 11:18). He saw her carried away in the Spirit for a time, and then she returned with a child in her arms. The angel told Nephi to "behold the Lamb of God, yea, even the Son of the Eternal Father! Knowest thou the meaning of the tree . . . ?" (1 Nephi 11:21.) The birth of the Son of God to a virgin involved the condescension of both the Father and the

Son. The tree is a symbol for God's love in that the Father became the Father of the Only Begotten in the flesh, who descended to earth in order that He might live and minister to mortal men and women.

Later in the chapter, Nephi was again told to behold the condescension of God (see 1 Nephi 11:26). This time he was shown the Savior's baptism by John, the Lord's ministry, His choosing of twelve disciples, His healing power, and His crucifixion for the sins of the world. In these passages (1 Nephi 11:27–33), the condescension of God refers to the Savior's righteousness in being baptized and receiving the Holy Ghost, in His ministering to His brothers and sisters, and in performing the Atonement.

Nephi's interpretation of the tree centers on the birth of Jesus Christ and His ministry among mortals. The tree is a type or sign of the Savior.

The Fruit

If the tree typifies Christ, what is the fruit? Christ's fruit is His atonement, with all its attendant blessings and gifts. In speaking to the eleven disciples following His resurrection, Jesus said: "All power is given unto me in heaven and in earth" (Matthew 28:18). Peter stated that Jesus' "divine power hath given unto us all things that pertain unto life and godliness" (2 Peter 1:3). As the Apostle Paul stated, the fruit of Jesus' atonement is the power to change mortals into immortals, corruptible people into incorruptible beings as they are resurrected, overcoming physical and spiritual death through their faith in Christ (1 Corinthians 15:52–53, 57–58).

It is interesting to note that the words Lehi used to describe the fruit (*sweet, white, pure, most desirable*) and the effect of the fruit when eaten (filled his soul with "exceedingly great joy") are similar to the words used by Alma the Younger when he partook of the blessings of the Atonement and was born of God. In describing his conversion he said: "And oh, what joy, and what marvelous light I did behold; yea, my soul was filled with joy as exceeding as was my pain! . . . There can be nothing so exquisite and sweet as was my joy." (Alma 36:20–21.) The fruit of the tree is the Atonement and the blessings of forgiveness that come through it, its power to change hearts, its power to bestow eternal life.

Lehi's dream shows that one does not obtain eternal life by nibbling at the fruit. The second group in Lehi's dream partook of the fruit but then gave way to the mocking of people in the great and spacious building (see 1 Nephi 8:28). They became ashamed of the tree (Christ), drifted away from the source of truth, and were lost. This suggests that even if one finds the tree, he must hold to the rod (be obedient to the word of God) if he is to enjoy the fruit and reap the blessings. There are many people in mortality who find Christ but fail to internalize the principles and teachings of the gospel in their lives. Many come to the tree but do not remain faithful to the covenants they make with the Lord and therefore will not receive "the greatest of all the gifts of God" (1 Nephi 15:36), which is eternal life (see D&C 14:7).

A Prophet's Bidding

Nephi's interpretation of the dream gives meaning to Lehi's beckoning to his family. He was inviting them to come to Christ—an invitation extended by prophets to all people. It explains why he was so concerned about Laman and Lemuel. They failed to heed his bidding and followed the ways of the world. In spite of an angel appearing to them and giving them instructions, plus numerous other manifestations of the Lord's power, their pride and disbelief resulted in hard hearts that the Spirit could not penetrate. Still, Lehi never gave up on them.

An understanding of the dream also explains why the faithful (the third group in Lehi's dream) fell down when they approached the tree. When humble, faithful men and women come into the presence of the Redeemer, the natural inclination is to fall at His feet and worship Him. This occurred at the temple in Bountiful when the Lord appeared to the righteous Saints following the destruction associated with His crucifixion. As soon as they recognized Jesus, the multitude fell to the earth. (See 3 Nephi 11:12–14.)

The tree as a sign for the Savior is consistent with Nephi's statement that "all things which have been given of God from the beginning of the world, unto man, are the typifying of him" (2 Nephi 11:4). One comes to the Savior by holding fast to the iron rod, or God's word. Prophets invite men and women to come to Christ and partake of His saving powers. Lehi wanted his family to do the same.

Five hundred years after Lehi, Alma entreated the Zoramites to come to the tree as well. However, he changed the metaphor to show them how to find the strait and narrow path, how to recognize if they were still on the path once they had begun, and the endurance required in order to obtain all the blessings. What follows will also point out the relationship between the process of developing faith in Christ and the questions asked by Alma in Alma 5.

ALMA'S SEED AND THE TREE OF LIFE

In the thirty-first chapter of Alma, the prophet becomes concerned about the Zoramites, dissenters from the Nephites. At one time this people had been taught the gospel, but they had fallen into error and separated themselves from the faithful. Alma learned of their iniquity and felt a responsibility to teach the word of God to them. They worshipped idols, their hearts were set upon the riches of the world, and they had built a prayer tower inside their church upon which they thanked God for being "a chosen and a holy people." The Zoramites were anti-Christs in that they claimed to know that there would be no Christ. They practiced their religion one day in the week and then "returned to their homes, never speaking of their God again until they assembled themselves . . . to the holy stand" (Alma 31:23).

The Virtue of the Word

Alma's heart sorrowed as he saw the condition of the Zoramites. He determined to "try the virtue of the word of God," as it had a "more powerful effect upon the minds of the people than the sword, or anything else" (Alma 31:5). After considerable effort to teach the people, Alma and his companions began having success among the poor. Although the poorer Zoramites had built the churches, they were not allowed to worship in them, because their clothing did not meet the Zoramite standard. They had been excluded from worshipping in the churches because of their poverty.

Humble Hearts

As Alma taught those who had been cast out, he perceived that they had been humbled by their afflictions and that they were prepared to hear the gospel. He told them that they could worship God anywhere, not just in church. He also pointed out that faithful people worship God at all times, not just one day in the week. Then Alma began to teach them about faith—how to develop faith in God, in His name, and in His word.

Desire to Believe

Alma teaches that in the beginning faith is not a perfect knowledge, but one can come to know the truth by trying an experiment. Alma points out that one can begin the process "even if ye can no more than desire to believe" (Alma 32:27). The desire to believe is an essential first step in the process of developing faith.

The necessity of desiring to believe is illustrated by a story told by a missionary in Japan. During a zone conference, a missionary asked the instructor why his investigators did not receive answers to their prayers. They were reading the Book of Mormon and praying about it. The investigators were looking for the fulfillment of Moroni's promise that those who read the book and pray with real intent, with faith in Christ, will receive an answer. The instructor questioned the missionary regarding the prayers of the investigators. "Were they praying with real intent?" The missionary answered, "Yes, but they know they will not receive an answer!"

Alma states that unbelief causes the person to "resist the Spirit of the Lord" so that the seed is cast out before it has a chance to grow (Alma 32:28). A desire to believe is a prerequisite for an answer. Confirmations by the Holy Spirit are not given to unbelievers. They would not recognize the whisperings of the Holy Ghost. Further, praying with "real intent" implies praying with a desire to believe as well as a desire to know. As noted earlier, Nephi's vision was preceded by a *desire to know,* and a *belief* that an answer would come.

The Experiment

If a person has a desire to believe, the experiment begins by planting a seed in one's heart and nourishing it. The seed is the word of God—the scriptures and the words of the living prophets. Alma's seed is the same as Lehi's rod of iron. Missionaries follow Alma's pattern in teaching investigators. Missionaries ask the investigator to plant the seed and nourish it by doing a number of things. First, investigators are asked to read the Book of Mormon. Second, they are asked to pray. Missionaries teach the promise in Moroni 10:3–5 that if the investigator will ask God in the name of Christ if the book and its teachings are true, he or she will receive a confirmation of its truthfulness by the power of the Holy Ghost. A further step is to attend church in order to meet with the Saints and partake of the Holy Spirit as they worship God. Through the course of the missionary lessons, the investigator is also asked to repent, to begin the process of changing his or her life to conform to gospel principles.

If the experiment is followed by the investigator, the seed will swell and sprout within him. He will feel the workings of the Holy Spirit and will receive a confirmation that the Book of Mormon is true, that Joseph Smith is the prophet of the Restoration. The seed is a good seed, and he will receive a confirmation of it.

As the person feels the swelling motions within him—the stirring of a testimony—Alma asks the question: "Is your knowledge perfect?" He then answers: "Yea, your knowledge is perfect in that thing, and your faith is dormant; and this because you know, for ye know that the word hath swelled your souls, . . . that your understanding doth begin to be enlightened, and your mind doth begin to expand" (Alma 32:34). When an investigator receives a witness from the Spirit that the Book of Mormon is true, his belief turns to knowledge.

Alma then asks, "After ye have tasted this light is your knowledge perfect?" (Alma 32:35.) The answer is no, as one must continue to exercise faith. The investigator knows that the Book of Mormon is true, that the gospel has been restored, but his knowledge of the doctrine is meager and his ability to live gospel principles from which greater witnesses and knowledge comes is in its infant state. He must show his faith by being baptized and confirmed a member of the Church, and then must combine the small piece of knowledge he has with additional faith to continue the experiment.

Often a new member of the Church who has received a witness of the truthfulness of the gospel desires to share his newfound knowledge with family and friends and be of service to others. Also, his desire to study the gospel increases, and he becomes even more faithful in attending Church, fulfilling assignments, and accepting callings. His faith encourages him to pay tithing and other offerings. As he does these things, other witnesses and confirmations come regarding the correctness of the path he is traveling. He becomes spiritually sensitive to the reception of spiritual gifts such as peace of heart and increased faith and virtue. He desires to be a kinder person, more loving, patient, meek, gentle, and long-suffering. In other words, he is blessed by the fruits of the Spirit (see Galatians 5:22–23). He begins to take on the characteristics of the divine nature (see 2 Peter 1:3–8). If understood, this process provides additional witnesses that strengthen one's faith in the Lord. These additional swellings come from applying the word of God, and turn the seed into a seedling.

The Mature Tree

Alma indicates that if the process continues with diligence and patience, the person's faith will eventually turn the seed into a mature tree "springing up unto everlasting life" (Alma 32:41). By and by the owner will be able to pluck the fruit, which is "most precious, which is sweet above all that is sweet, and which is white above all that is white, yea, and pure above all that is pure; and ye shall feast upon this fruit even until ye are filled, that ye hunger not, neither shall ye thirst" (Alma 32:42). These are the rewards of endurance as one continually applies the experiment in his or her life.

In Alma's experiment, a person plants a seed in his heart, and by nourishing it continually, it grows into a tree of life within. What does this mean? If one constantly nourishes one's soul with the word of God, giving obedience to the principles of the gospel, one eventually puts off the natural man. Through the power of the Spirit and the atonement of Christ, one becomes more Christlike—"submissive, meek, humble, patient, full of love, willing to submit to all things which the Lord seeth fit to inflict upon him" (Mosiah 3:19). In Peter's terms, one becomes a partaker "of the divine nature" (2 Peter 1:4).

The Image of Christ in Your Countenance

The results of Alma's experiment give meaning to the questions asked by the prophet in Alma chapter 5. "And now behold, I ask of you, my brethren of the church, have ye spiritually been born of God? Have ye received his image in your countenances? Have ye experienced this mighty change in your hearts?" (Alma 5:14.) If one has the tree (Christ) and its fruit (the Atonement and its blessings) within oneself, one's countenance will reflect Christ's image. Through the experiment of trying the word, one is blessed by the Holy Spirit and receives the gifts of faith, love, virtue, brotherly kindness, and so on, and one experiences the mighty change of heart—one is born of God. The person becomes a new creature in Christ, as Christ is within him.

One of the beauties of the gospel is the consistency of the teachings. Lehi's tree is symbolic of the Savior. One obtains the fruits of the Atonement by holding to the rod of iron until one reaches the tree and partakes of the fruit. Alma teaches the same truths. By experimenting on the word (planting and nurturing the seed), a person's desire to believe is rewarded by a witness of the Spirit. He receives truth line upon line and precept upon precept. By diligent and patient continuance, the seed matures into a tree within a person's heart and soul. By the power of the Holy Spirit, the additional light with the person causes him to reflect the Savior's characteristics in his countenance and being. He puts off the natural man and becomes a partaker of the divine nature. He receives a new heart and experiences a new birth.

CONCLUSIONS

Lehi's dream of the tree of life was given to preserve not only his immediate family during their journey to the promised land, but also his extended family down through the centuries. The rod of iron was not only a guide along life's path for his children, but also a support during their trials and tribulations.

The central focus of the dream is the tree and its fruit. Nephi's interpretation points to Christ and His atonement. Lehi's invitation to his family to join him at the tree and partake of the fruit was an invitation to come to Christ by living the gospel and to receive eternal life. Sariah, Sam, and Nephi accepted the invitation. Laman and Lemuel did not. Still, Lehi refused to give up. For the rest of his days he encouraged his older sons with all the feelings of a tender parent.

The dream teaches that families are eternal. Lehi did not want to be alone in receiving the blessings of the Atonement. As his soul was filled with joy, he immediately thought of his family and desired to share it with them.

The dream teaches that Jesus has the atoning power to redeem mankind. He is willing to share the fruit of the Atonement with His brothers and sisters. He has the power to forgive, to cleanse, and to redeem those who exercise faith in Him. Both Lehi and Alma experienced the sweetness of forgiveness and were filled with joy through the Atonement.

Alma teaches one how to find the strait and narrow path and hold on to the rod. It begins with a desire to believe. Then the seed or the word must be planted in the heart and nourished. The nurturing of the seed comes by reading the scriptures, attending church, pondering, praying, and living in accordance with one's knowledge of the gospel. When a witness of the Spirit is received regarding the basic truths of the gospel, the journey is not complete. The experiment must continue after baptism. One may have a perfect knowledge in one thing, but not a knowledge of all things. It is not enough to taste the fruit once. Truth comes line upon line and precept upon precept; here a little, there a little.

As the tree grows inside one's soul, the image of Christ begins to appear in one's countenance. Through a person's faith in Christ, one receives additional gifts of the Holy Spirit made possible by the Atonement and becomes a partaker of the divine nature. He puts off the natural man and becomes Christlike. One is born again by the power of the Atonement and the Holy Spirit.

3

Elder Jeffrey R. Holland

Jacob
the Unshakable

For a key to the character and contribution of the Book of Mormon prophet Jacob, one might well go not to the beginning of his life but to the very end of it. The last chapter of the book which bears his name serves as something of an addendum to his earlier work, a chapter written "after some years had passed away" from the time Jacob presumably had finished his record, given his testimony, bidden all farewell, and spoken his "amen" (Jacob 6:13; 7:1).

It is here in Jacob 7 that we meet Sherem, the first of the anti-Christs to step forward in the Book of Mormon. With flattery on his lips and malice in his heart he attempted to "overthrow the doctrine of Christ," which had been so firmly established among the faithful followers of Nephi (see 2 Nephi 31). With glaring lack of imagination, Sherem went about his perverse mission and attempted his deceit principally through the approach common to all anti-Christs—the tedious assertion "that there should be no Christ" (Jacob 7:2; see also Alma 30:12–17). For this sort of nonbeliever, the thought of no Christ to come was wishful thinking elevated to the level of a feeble personal philosophy.

Unfortunately Sherem enjoyed some success. He was, Jacob said, "learned, [having] a perfect knowledge of the language of the people; wherefore, he could use much flattery, and much power of speech, according to the power of the devil" (Jacob

7:4). With an arrogance often prevalent in the deceived, he had sought many opportunities to confront no less a man than Jacob himself, the great high priest of the day and the spiritual leader of the Church. Sherem sought such an opportunity with the hope that he might, by Jacob's own admission, "shake me from the faith." But Jacob was manifestly the wrong man to confront in such a matter, and Sherem lived—or, more precisely, died—to regret his meeting with this remarkable prophet, a man who had had "many revelations . . . [and] had seen angels, and they had administered unto me. And also I had heard the voice of the Lord speaking unto me in very word from time to time; *wherefore I could not be shaken.*" (Jacob 7:5; emphasis added.)

Jacob, the believer. Jacob, the foe of the anti-Christ. Jacob, the unshakable. By definition all Book of Mormon prophets had great faith and were unyielding in their convictions. All had a deep witness of the mission and divinity of Christ. But in a life only sketchily documented (Jacob's teachings are limited to thirty-one pages in the Book of Mormon, and many of those are devoted to the quotations of other prophets), and although he considers his contribution to the Book of Mormon to be small (see Jacob 7:27), nevertheless this prophet comes to us in word and deed as absolutely rocklike, solid, invincible, unshakable.

Indeed it is Jacob, at least as much as any other in the Book of Mormon, to whom Helaman's great declaration applies: "Remember, remember that it is upon the rock of our Redeemer, who is Christ, the Son of God, that ye must build your foundation; that when the devil shall send forth his mighty winds, yea, his shafts in the whirlwind, yea, when all his hail and his mighty storm shall beat upon you, it shall have no power over you to drag you down to the gulf of misery and endless wo, because of the rock upon which ye are built, which is a sure foundation, a foundation whereon if men build they cannot fall" (Helaman 5:12).

What were the sources for Jacob's forthright behavior and the unwavering declaration of his doctrines? In a life of near-anonymity, where was the making and what are the marks of his great moral strength? Even the brief record we have gives some indications.

BORN IN TRIBULATION

In a great patriarchal/doctrinal blessing given to his fifth son, Lehi said: "Jacob, . . . thou art my first-born in the days of my tribulation in the wilderness. And behold, in thy childhood thou hast suffered afflictions and much sorrow, because of the rudeness of thy brethren. Nevertheless, Jacob, my first-born in the wilderness, thou knowest the greatness of God; and he shall consecrate thine afflictions for thy gain." (2 Nephi 2:1–2.)

Jacob was a child of the wilderness, a son born to affliction. We don't know exactly when Jacob was born, but he is first mentioned relatively late in the first book of Nephi when Lehi's group is preparing to sail to the promised land. With one short line there, Nephi introduces Jacob to the reader: "And now, my father had begat two sons in the wilderness; the elder was called Jacob and the younger Joseph" (1 Nephi 18:7).

In this portion of Nephi's record outlining the difficulties faced in traveling in the wilderness from Jerusalem to the land of Bountiful, and later on the open sea, Nephi wrote that his "parents being stricken in years, and having suffered much grief because of their children . . . were brought down, yea, even upon their sick beds" (1 Nephi 18:17). Indeed, the personal grief over the iniquity of Laman and Lemuel (and their followers) was so profound and the degree of their unrighteous behavior so great that it threatened the very life of these two "grey hair[ed]" travelers, Lehi and Sariah. Tersely the record says, "Jacob and Joseph . . . being young, having need of much nourishment, were grieved because of the afflictions of their mother" (1 Nephi 18:18–19).

Thus at a very early age Jacob's future character and unshakable faith were being forged in the furnace of affliction. One student of human behavior said of him, "In the pitched moral battle that surrounded his childhood, he committed himself" (C. Terry Warner, "Jacob," *Ensign*, October 1976, p. 26). Nephi and Sam, faithful sons of Lehi and Sariah, had known something of better times in Jerusalem. In their days of trial and deprivation they had more comfortable memories to call upon. But Jacob knew nothing of Lehi's prosperity in Jerusalem nor of the relative ease which might have attended it. He knew only the struggle of the wilderness, the challenge of the sea, and the ongoing drama of good and evil all too frequently personified in the lives of two of his own older brothers.

It seems unfortunate that one so young would be deprived of so many physical comforts and at the same time suffer such wrenching emotional and spiritual conflicts within his family. But painful as it was, this was all part of the making of a prophet.

Jacob was learning very early what his father Lehi would later confirm in that patriarchal blessing already mentioned—that in this fallen world there would be "opposition in all things" (2 Nephi 2:11), opposition without which no purpose and meaning in the great creation of God could exist, including no promise of eternal life nor any gift of unending happiness. Only in opposition and through the moral choices that opposition poses could one prove his or her faithfulness, exercising moral agency wisely and well in the face of such forces for good and evil. Jacob was an apt student of these doctrines of salvation, the essential elements of "the great plan of happiness" (Alma 42:8), from the earliest days of his life forward. And those powerful lessons, both experiential and doctrinal, helped forge an unshakable faith in Christ.

PROMISES TO THE HOUSE OF ISRAEL

One of Jacob's singular themes, and a doctrine contributing significantly to his steadfastness, was that of God's unwavering covenant with the house of Israel. In spite of their sins and sufferings, and notwithstanding their discouragements and dispersions, these children of the promise were constantly reassured by the great Jehovah that they would be gathered together again physically and restored to their ancient privileges spiritually. Jacob has only three major "sermons" attributed to him in the Book of Mormon, and two of them deal with this subject. In one instance it is examined in one of the longest single sermons recorded anywhere in scripture. The second message comes in a detailed allegory constituting the longest single chapter in all of the Book of Mormon.

The length as well as the depth of these verses suggests how important this doctrine was to Jacob. The promise of heritage, family unity, future stability, and ultimate success must have been particularly reassuring to one who was himself homeless, whose family was in confrontational disarray, and who seemed destined to wander in a foreign wilderness as other branches of Israel's family had been required to do. God's promise to Jacob of old had special meaning for this young man who, presumably, was named for that first great Israelite.

Jacob's sermon on this subject—only part of which is reported in the Book of Mormon and which was delivered on two successive days—draws heavily on the writings of the prophet Isaiah, especially chapters 49 through 52. This sermon, which so impressed Nephi that he included it in the material of his second book, was apparently assigned to Jacob by his older brother (see 2 Nephi 6:4). With that charge Jacob did what the Book of Mormon prophets invite us as readers to do—he likened the teachings of the ancient prophets to the contemporary audience before him. "For ye are of the house of Israel," he said, "and there are many things which have been spoken by Isaiah which may be likened unto you, because ye are of the house of Israel" (2 Nephi 6:5).

This sermon, which constitutes chapters 6 through 10 of 2 Nephi, introduces the covenantal promise given to Abraham, Isaac, and Jacob, specifically the promise that those who were at Jerusalem and had been carried away captive would one day be returned to the land and city of their inheritance.

It is here, in one of the great Book of Mormon sermons, that the role the Savior, Jesus Christ, plays in fulfilling this covenant is examined and explained. Jacob notes that in revelation he has been shown "that the Lord God, the Holy One of Israel," would manifest Himself to the posterity of Israel, and although they would initially harden their hearts and stiffen their necks against Him—scourging and finally crucifying Him—"nevertheless, the Lord will be merciful unto them, that when they shall come to the knowledge of their Redeemer, they shall be gathered together again to the lands of their inheritance" (2 Nephi 6:8–11). And not only will these Jews be gathered—a great promise and reassurance in its own right—but Jacob underscores the great messianic irony that this very Jesus whom they rejected will play a very personal and protective role in that process. "And behold, according to the words of the prophet, the Messiah will set himself again the second time to recover them; wherefore, he will manifest himself unto them in power and great glory, unto the destruction of their enemies, when that day cometh when they shall believe in him; and none will be destroyed that believe in him. . . . For the mighty God shall deliver his covenant people." (2 Nephi 6:14, 17.)

By extension, that sermon begun in the pages of 2 Nephi reaches its ultimate fruition in Jacob's later rehearsal of Zenos's long allegory of the tame and wild olive trees (see Jacob 5). There again he drives home—at length—the sequence and substance of God's covenantal relationship with the house of Israel, underscoring the fact that God is unfailingly loyal to these children, regardless of the degree of their dispersion or how often they may have been disobedient along the way.

But there is much more here than simply the unraveling of convoluted Israelite history. Of greater significance in this allegory is the benevolent view of God that it provides. He is portrayed here as one who repeatedly, painstakingly, endlessly tries to save the work of His hands and in moments of greatest disappointment holds His head in His hands and weeps, "What could I have done more for my vineyard?" (Jacob 5:41, 47, 49.) This allegory is a declaration of divine love, of God's unceasing effort as a father laboring on behalf of His children. As one writer has noted, "Zenos's allegory ought to take its place beside the parable of the prodigal son. Both stories make the Lord's mercy so movingly memorable." (John S. Tanner, "Jacob and His Descendants as Authors," in *Rediscovering the Book of Mormon*, ed. John L. Sorenson and Melvin J. Thorne [Provo: Foundation for Ancient Research and Mormon Studies; and Salt Lake City: Deseret Book, 1991], p. 61.)

An almost haunting declaration of this divine devotion is laced through these seventy-seven verses in the eight-fold repetition of the line "it grieveth me that I should lose this tree." This long parable does outline Israel's history, but soon enough the attentive reader senses a much more personal story coming from the printed page—the grief and the godly pain of a father anguishing over the needless destruction of His family.

Yet from this demanding doctrine Jacob draws strength. It casts greater light on agency, on moral choice, and on opposition in all things. Best of all, for those who want and will it so, there is a happy ending.

"And how merciful is our God unto us, for he remembereth the house of Israel, both roots and branches; and he stretches forth his hands unto them all the day long; . . . and . . . as many as will not harden their hearts shall be saved in the kingdom of God" (Jacob 6:4).

Like the man for whom he was named, this Jacob knows something of a family divided and dispersed. But he also knows of God's redeeming covenant and the role of the Savior of the world in fulfilling it. To that ministry he pledges his life's effort. "How blessed are they who have labored diligently in his vineyard," he says (Jacob 6:3), and by the promise given to those who so serve, he stands "unshaken."

A WOUNDED SOUL

Another element of Jacob's steadfastness is the fact that such concern for the salvation of both immediate and extended family has created in him a kind of special sensitivity to—or more accurately a deep aversion to—the temptations of the world and the serious effects of sin. His forthright response is evoked even when the people were only *beginning* to labor in sin, when their "thoughts" were unholy even though in behavior and performance they were still obedient to the commandments Jacob had given them (see Jacob 2:4–5).

As one student of Jacob has counted, of the seventeen times such phrases as "grieveth me" and "burdeneth my soul" are used in the entire Book of Mormon, eleven of those utterances are by Jacob. The word *wound* or a variant of it is used thirty-one times in the Book of Mormon, twenty-four of those referring to physical wounds. It is not surprising that the other seven uses, which apply to a "wounded soul," are all from the writings of Jacob. (See Chris Conkling, "The Gentle Power of Jacob," *Ensign*, February 1992, p. 7.)

This aversion to sin felt by a particularly sensitive soul helps explain the constant anxiety Jacob feels for his people. Because of "faith and great anxiety"—an unusual turn of phrase, though not a surprising combination of prophetic feelings—Jacob is shown some of this fate we have mentioned regarding his fam-

ily (see Jacob 1:5). That weighs him down "with much more desire and anxiety" for the welfare of their souls, a burden so great
that he pleads not to be "shaken from my firmness in the spirit,
and stumble because of my over anxiety for you" (Jacob 2:3;
4:18). Whether it be against the anti-Christ or the specter of de-
bilitating sin, Jacob remains "unshaken."

This very personal burden of pain, this special sensitivity over
the sins of his brethren, is best seen in a great sermon by Jacob
which first decries the pride and crassness so often accompanying materialistic riches, and then denounces the "grosser crime"
of unchastity. In our Book of Mormon account, in introducing this
sermon Jacob spends much of ten full verses apologizing, in effect, for the sins he must address and the language he must use in
addressing them. He notes that he does so with "soberness,"
being "weighed down with much more desire and anxiety for the
welfare of [his hearers'] souls" (Jacob 2:2–3). Knowing him as we
do, we would be surprised if he had said otherwise.

Listen to the mournful tone of these passages—literally the
grief of them—as he single-mindedly pursues what he has always been single-minded about—steadfast loyalty to God and
His commandments.

> Yea, it grieveth my soul and causeth me to shrink with shame
> before the presence of my Maker, that I must testify unto you con-
> cerning the wickedness of your hearts.
>
> And also it grieveth me that I must use so much boldness of
> speech concerning you, before your wives and your children,
> many of whose feelings are exceedingly tender and chaste and del-
> icate before God, which thing is pleasing unto God. . . .
>
> Wherefore, it burdeneth my soul that I should be constrained,
> because of the strict commandment which I have received from
> God, to admonish you according to your crimes, to enlarge the
> wounds of those who are already wounded, instead of consoling
> and healing their wounds; and those who have not been
> wounded, instead of feasting upon the pleasing word of God have
> daggers placed to pierce their souls and wound their delicate
> minds. (Jacob 2:6–7, 9.)

We are not even into the discourse per se before we sense
that, quite literally, this bold and unyielding manner of preaching

is almost as hard on Jacob as it is on the guilty ones in his audience. But perhaps that is as it should be always, and why Christ in his preaching was ofttimes "a man of sorrows." The commandments have to be kept, sin has to be rebuked. But even such bold positions must be taken compassionately. Even the sternest of prophets must preach from the depths of a sensitive soul.

Once Jacob gets past his natural reticence in such matters and rises to the ecclesiastical commission he has been given, his voice is unexcelled in the Book of Mormon pulpit, so to speak. When motivated by the Holy Spirit and enlightened by the clear-cut, either-or choice of gospel living, Jacob is as bold and unshaken a voice as we have in the entire record. In spite of his personal aversion to sin and the inherent sensitivity which makes it difficult for him even to address such subjects, nevertheless he can be very "blunt and forceful in his message." For all the sincerity in his apologetic preamble, he can be "devastatingly direct in reminding the people of their sins." (Robert J. Matthews, "Jacob: Prophet, Theologian, Historian," in *The Book of Mormon, Jacob Through Words of Mormon, To Learn with Joy* [Provo: Religious Studies Center, BYU, 1990], p. 43.)

As an example, consider this pulpit delivery: "O, my beloved brethren, remember my words. Behold, I take off my garments, and I shake them before you; I pray the God of my salvation that he view me with his all-searching eye; wherefore, ye shall know at the last day, when all men shall be judged of their works, that the God of Israel did witness that I shook your iniquities from my soul, and that I stand with brightness before him, and am rid of your blood." (2 Nephi 9:44.)

Or this: "And we did magnify our office unto the Lord, taking upon us the responsibility, answering the sins of the people upon our own heads if we did not teach them the word of God with all diligence; wherefore, by laboring with our might their blood might not come upon our garments; otherwise their blood would come upon our garments, and we would not be found spotless at the last day" (Jacob 1:19).

Someone who preaches in this manner and accepts his responsibility with such single-mindedness is bound to gain the attention of his audience—even if they do not listen with great delight to his messages. Jacob may not have been particularly popular with his congregation, but listening to him must have been an experience unlike any other.

In the sermon on chastity, it is particularly revealing that Jacob is so sensitive to the women in his audience. Whether or not that was a result of having seen his mother in anguish over the wickedness of her eldest sons we cannot know, but it is interesting that in his unflinching declaration against sexual transgression Jacob quotes a communication from heaven as follows:

I, the Lord, have seen the sorrow, and heard the mourning of the *daughters* of my people in the land of Jerusalem, yea, and in all the lands of my people, because of the wickedness and abominations of their *husbands.*

And I will not suffer, saith the Lord of Hosts, that the cries of the fair *daughters* of this people, which I have led out of the land of Jerusalem, shall come up unto me against the *men* of my people, saith the Lord of Hosts.

For they shall not lead away captive the *daughters* of my people because of their tenderness, save I shall visit them with a sore curse, even unto destruction; . . .

Ye have broken the hearts of your tender *wives,* and lost the confidence of your children, because of your bad examples before them; and the sobbings of their hearts ascend up to God against you. And because of the strictness of the word of God, which cometh down against you, many hearts died, pierced with deep wounds. (Jacob 2:31–33, 35; emphasis added.)

That is a poetic, profound, "piercing" indictment, and we have the feeling here that Jacob understood then what we unfortunately understand now—that it is usually (but not always) the woman who suffers most in the tragedy of unchastity and that usually (but not always) it is the transgressing man who causes the "sobbings of the [women's] hearts to ascend up to God."

Stylistically this sensitive but vigorous pulpit manner of one who feels wounds in the soul is revealed in the very language Jacob uses. For one example, note that in chapter 9 of 2 Nephi, Jacob soars in his declaration of the atonement of Jesus Christ with at least fourteen uses of the cry "O." For both stylistic and theological contrast, this is linked in long, rhyming vowels with at least ten references to "Wo," an exclamation used to mark the dangers of going against the doctrine of Christ.[1]

When Jacob is immersed in doctrine and underscoring his prophetic role with poetic perorations, we see him at the height of his powers—powers which give him the unshakable confidence to say:

> Would I harrow up your souls if your minds were pure? Would I be plain unto you according to the plainness of the truth if ye were freed from sin?
>
> Behold, if ye were holy I would speak unto you of holiness; but as ye are not holy, and ye look upon me as a teacher, it must needs be expedient that I teach you the consequences of sin.
>
> Behold, my soul abhorreth sin, and my heart delighteth in righteousness; and I will praise the holy name of my God.
>
> Come, my brethren, every one that thirsteth, come ye to the waters; and he that hath no money, come buy and eat; yea, come buy wine and milk without money and without price. (2 Nephi 9:47–50.)

I HAVE SEEN MY REDEEMER

In that powerful patriarchal blessing Lehi gave him, Jacob was able to receive truly remarkable promises because, even at that early age, his relationship with the Lord was one of rare privilege and sanctity. "I know that thou art redeemed," Lehi told him, "because of the righteousness of thy Redeemer; for thou hast beheld that in the fulness of time he cometh to bring salvation unto men. And thou hast beheld in thy youth his glory; wherefore, thou art blessed even as they unto whom he shall minister in the flesh." (2 Nephi 2:3–4.)

Later Nephi designates Jacob as one of the three great witnesses of the Savior positioned in the introductory pages of the Book of Mormon, saying: "Now I, Nephi, write more of the words of Isaiah, for my soul delighteth in his words. For I will

---

1. The "O," "Wo" device is yet another confirmation of the multiple authorship and stylistic distinctions which make the Book of Mormon so literarily rich. The interjection of an "O" to start a passage lets the reader know almost instantly that Jacob is the speaker. See Jacob 2 and 3 for additional examples.

liken his words unto my people, and I will send them forth unto all my children, for he verily saw my Redeemer, even as I have seen him. And my brother, Jacob, also has seen him as I have seen him . . . Wherefore, by the words of three, God hath said, . . . I will establish my word." (2 Nephi 11:2–3.)

When all else is said and done, it is ultimately this powerful personal relationship with the Savior—including the magnificence of open vision and of hearing "the voice of the Lord speaking unto me in very word, from time to time"—that makes Jacob the unshakable one. It is this that makes Jacob that "man of Christ" who is built upon "a sure foundation, a foundation whereon if men build they cannot fall" (Helaman 3:29; 5:12).

At the heart of this great reassuring theology about the redemption of the children of Israel, Jacob testifies of the atonement and resurrection of the Savior. In doing so he gives Lehi's family (and all the children of the covenant everywhere) hope, "that ye may rejoice, and lift up your heads forever, because of the blessings which the Lord God shall bestow upon your children" (2 Nephi 9:3).

Like Job—with whom Jacob on more than one occasion could identify—he promises his "brethren" and their families that although "our flesh must waste away and die; nevertheless in our bodies we shall see God" (2 Nephi 9:4; see also Job 19:26).

In that spirit of reassurance about the resurrection, Jacob gives one of the greatest sermons in all of scripture regarding the Savior, beginning with the simple declaration, "For it behooveth the great Creator that he suffereth himself to become subject unto man in the flesh, and die for all men, that all men might become subject unto him" (2 Nephi 9:5).

Noting the triumph of both body and spirit through that atonement, Jacob cries with more of those exultant O's:

> O the wisdom of God, his mercy and grace! For behold, if the flesh should rise no more our spirits must become subject to that angel who fell from before the presence of the Eternal God, and became the devil, to rise no more.
>
> And our spirits must have become like unto him, and we become devils, angels to a devil, to be shut out from the presence of our God, and to remain with the father of lies, in misery, like unto himself. . . .

O how great the goodness of our God, who prepareth a way
for our escape from the grasp of this awful monster; yea, that monster, death and hell, which I call the death of the body, and also the
death of the spirit.

And because of the way of deliverance of our God, the Holy
One of Israel, . . . the bodies and the spirits of men will be restored
one to the other; and it is by the power of the resurrection of the
Holy One of Israel. (2 Nephi 9:8–12.)

Outlining the nature of the Atonement and these promises
of the Resurrection, Jacob describes "an infinite atonement" (2
Nephi 9:7)—he being the first to use that phrase in the Book of
Mormon. This infinite aspect of that atonement is affirmed
throughout his teaching with references to the depth and
breadth of the Savior's redemption. Note this kind of inclusive
statement about the Atonement's effect on the entire human
family: "And he cometh into the world that he may save *all* men
if they will hearken unto his voice; for behold, he suffereth the
pains of *all* men, yea, the pains of *every* living creature, both
men, women, and children, who belong to the family of Adam.
And he suffereth this that the resurrection might pass upon *all*
men, that *all* might stand before him at the great and judgment
day." (2 Nephi 9:21–22; emphasis added.)

This great declaration of Christ's atonement provides a
backdrop for that series of warning "Wo's" already mentioned,
warning to those who will not consider themselves "fools before
God" and come down into the depths of humility before the
Holy One of Israel. Wo unto him that has the law given and yet
transgresseth. Wo unto the rich who despise the poor, persecute
the meek, and whose hearts are set upon their treasure. Wo unto
the deaf that will not hear. Wo unto the blind that will not see.
Wo unto the uncircumcised of heart. Wo unto the liar, the murderer, the committer of whoredoms, the worshipper of idols,
and those who die in their sins. (See 2 Nephi 9:27–38.)

The warnings are unmistakable. Again we see the un-
equivocal, straightforward, either-or aspect of Jacob's belief.
Opposition continues in all things, contrasts which he is more
than capable of making very clear. Sensitive nature and poetic
soul notwithstanding, Jacob's sermons go for the jugular.

Nevertheless there is always, even in this direct style and

uncompromised doctrinal boldness, the great reassurance which meant so much to Jacob personally and which he wants his people to cherish—that he knew that Christ (and fittingly it is Jacob who is first told, by an angel, that this would be the Savior's name in mortality—see 2 Nephi 10:3), would honor the covenant given to Abraham and redeem the children of promise. "When the day cometh that they shall believe in me, that I am Christ," the Savior said, "then have I covenanted with their fathers that they shall be restored in the flesh, upon the earth, unto the lands of their inheritance. And it shall come to pass that they shall be gathered in from their long dispersion, from the isles of the sea, and from the four parts of the earth." (2 Nephi 10:7–8.)

With the hope of temporal restoration (gathering) and eternal restoration (the resurrection) firmly in the center of his heart and his theology, Jacob testifies in some of the very phrases taught him by his father.[2]

> Therefore, cheer up your hearts, and remember that ye are free to act for yourselves. . . .
>
> Wherefore, my beloved brethren, reconcile yourselves to the will of God, and not to the will of the devil and the flesh; and remember, after ye are reconciled unto God, that it is only in and through the grace of God that ye are saved.
>
> Wherefore, may God raise you from death by the power of the resurrection, and also from everlasting death by the power of the atonement, that ye may be received into the eternal kingdom of God, that ye may praise him through grace divine. (2 Nephi 10:23–25.)

Toward the end of his life and writing to the children of the next generation Jacob explains how he can speak—and live—with such unshakable faith, revealing in the process just how much "plain and precious" doctrine about Christ has been lost from the Old Testament:

---

2. The teachings of fathers to sons is one of the great themes of the Book of Mormon. For example, Jacob remembers Lehi's teachings, and Enos, Jacob's son, will remember the teachings of his father (see Enos 1:1).

For, for this intent have we written these things, that they may know that we knew of Christ, and we had a hope of his glory many hundred years before his coming; and not only we ourselves had a hope of his glory, but also all the holy prophets which were before us.

Behold, they believed in Christ and worshiped the Father in his name, and also we worship the Father in his name. And for this intent we keep the law of Moses, it pointing our souls to him; and for this cause it is sanctified unto us for righteousness, even as it was accounted unto Abraham in the wilderness to be obedient unto the commands of God in offering up his son Isaac, which is a similitude of God and his Only Begotten Son.

Wherefore, we search the prophets, and we have many revelations and the spirit of prophecy; and having all these witnesses we obtain a hope, and *our faith becometh unshaken,* insomuch that we truly can command in the name of Jesus and the very trees obey us, or the mountains, or the waves of the sea. (Jacob 4:4–6; emphasis added.)

Jacob, the unshaken. Jacob, the unshakable. Jacob—born in affliction, refined in service, triumphant in Christ.

"Wherefore, beloved brethren, be reconciled unto [God] through the atonement of Christ, his Only Begotten Son, . . . having faith, and [having] obtained a good hope of glory in him before he manifesteth himself in the flesh. . . . Why not speak of the atonement of Christ, and attain to a perfect knowledge of him?" (Jacob 4:11–12.)

Why not, indeed.

4

Elder John H. Groberg

Enos

As I read the twenty-seven verses of the book of Enos I am impressed with the message that it is essential to put forth *great effort* to receive answers to prayers and to gain exaltation. We cannot expect that casual effort or perfunctory prayers will bring the desired results, for as Enos clearly shows, great effort is essential to exaltation.

I am also impressed with the *great persistence* Enos showed in fulfilling his calling as a prophet throughout his life. The book of Enos explains that he went again and again to the Lord to receive more instructions and to seek blessings for himself and for others. Enos was a prophet who practiced persistence.

Finally, I am impressed with the *great ability* Enos demonstrated in differentiating between the important and the vital. He knew it was important to pray, but vital to receive forgiveness. He knew it was important to teach and to testify, but vital to persist in teaching and testifying to the end of his life.

I find in this brief book a wonderful pattern, or steps which Enos followed to achieve "eternal life and the joy of the saints." I believe these steps make a perfect pattern for all who desire to have the same assurance that Enos had at the end of his life as he prepared to meet his Maker, namely: "Then shall I see his face with pleasure, and he will say unto me: Come unto me, ye blessed, there is a place prepared for you in the mansions of my Father" (Enos 1:27).

These vital steps, as I see them, are:

1. Gratitude for blessings
2. Recognition of shortcomings
3. Desire to receive forgiveness and peace
4. Willingness to put forth great effort to receive forgiveness and peace
5. Feeling wonder and amazement at receiving forgiveness and peace
6. Desire to bless others
7. Putting forth great effort to be an instrument in God's hands to bless others to the end of mortal life

I believe these qualities can be summarized under three headings which I shall call the cycle of growth, as each leads to the next in ever-expanding circles of spiritual growth.

1. Gratitude
2. Humility
3. Effort

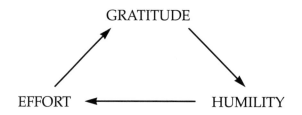

This concept helps me to understand an earlier scripture in the Book of Mormon: "Wherefore, the course of the Lord is one eternal round" (1 Nephi 10:19).

Let us study these twenty-seven verses of Enos and see if we can understand the workings of this cycle in his life and how we can apply them to our lives.

To me, the very first verse contains the key to starting anyone's spiritual growth, namely, a feeling of gratitude. Enos recognized the great blessing of having good parents who taught him correct principles, and he acknowledged this as a blessing from God.

It is interesting that this feeling of gratitude is also the first recorded expression of Nephi, and thus the actual beginning of the Book of Mormon. To my mind, this sets a very important precedent or pattern for us; that is, spiritual growth begins with gratitude. If we do not recognize that we have been blessed, or if we do not feel gratitude for our blessings, we simply cannot grow spiritually.

One of the most consistent themes in the Savior's life was His constant expression of gratitude to His Father. How often we read in the scriptures the phrase, "Father, I thank thee!"

We do not know how old Enos was as his writings begin, but we do know that at some point in his life he recognized his blessings and thanked God for them. Thus having achieved a grateful heart, he was prepared to take the next step, which I have chosen to term humility. To me, humility is seeing "things as they really are," or being fully honest. Sometimes that is hard, even painful, but it is absolutely necessary if we are to make progress and grow spiritually.

Verses 2–4 express this step very well. As Enos pondered on the blessing of having good parents who taught him correct principles, the importance of those principles "sunk deep" into his heart. The deeper they sank, the more he knew that his life must be in harmony with God in order for him to experience "the joy of the saints." Because of the humility that followed his gratitude he was able to see clearly that his life was not fully in tune with the Spirit of God and that he must do something about it.

Humility is largely a recognition of our own inadequacies as well as a recognition that we need outside help to achieve the joy that is the end of our existence, namely, eternal life. As Enos sensed this truth his soul "hungered" to achieve that goal.

I have a feeling that this was not the first time he had wondered, or prayed about these things, but his account explains that this was the time he resolved to seriously do something about it. Like so many of us, he may have offered perfunctory prayers before, but this time was going to be different. This time he was going to give his all in a powerful prayer of faith, for he was determined! Like Enos, we will only achieve our goal when we are determined enough to do whatever is necessary to reach it.

As Enos felt this spiritual hunger, he wanted with his whole soul to put his life in tune with the Lord so he could experience the joy he had heard so much about and which he now desired more than anything. He knew that the things he had done wrong, things which were contrary to the will of God, would keep him from experiencing the "joy of the saints" or "eternal life." He knew he must receive forgiveness for the things he had done wrong and have them wiped away from his life through the merits and mercy of the Lord Jesus Christ.

Because of his gratitude and his humility and his determination, he knew what he must do, so he "kneeled down before [his] Maker," and "cried unto him in mighty prayer and supplication" for the welfare of his soul (see verse 4). He was beginning the third step of the cycle of spiritual growth, that is, putting forth great effort to bring his life into tune with God's will.

We don't know specifically what his problems or sins or shortcomings were, and it doesn't matter to us. What does matter is that he openly acknowledged whatever his shortcomings were and paid whatever price was required to achieve forgiveness. I am deeply moved by Enos's willingness to continue putting forth more and more effort until he received the needed answers.

I have heard people speculate that Enos must have had a lot of things to repent of, as it took him all day and into the night to receive forgiveness. We ought never to make such judgments, but rather ask if we are willing to do whatever is required to receive forgiveness of *our* sins and thus find ourselves securely on the path to "eternal life" and the "joy of the saints." Obviously there were things Enos needed to repent of, but I wonder if much of what went on was preparing him for his calling of teaching the truth and testifying of the Savior for the rest of his life.

I marvel at the timeless message Enos gives us through his own personal experiences; namely, that to accomplish anything good takes effort, and to achieve great good takes great effort. He had the ability to tell the difference between the important and the vital and was willing to pay the price required to achieve that which was vital to him, which was to know that his life was in tune with the will of God and thus the door was open to him to be able to achieve "eternal life" and "the joy of the saints."

What an important lesson for all of us to learn! Everyone's experience in how he achieves this forgiveness and assurance of God's direction in his life will be somewhat different from that of others, but for Enos it took all day and into the night to receive the assurances and directions he so desperately desired. We know from the balance of his account that this was only the beginning, as he spent the rest of his life carrying out the promises he made to the Lord.

Enos knew it was important to pray, but he also knew it was vital to receive forgiveness of his sins and he was willing to pray as long and as intensely as needed and to pay the price required to accomplish that which to him was vital.

When I think of Enos's ability to see this difference I think of a young man in the islands who also saw clearly the difference between the important and the vital. Let me briefly relate this incident. I was not personally present when it happened, but I checked carefully with several eyewitnesses who all verified that the event took place just as explained.

A young man in Tonga by the name of Finau had heard the missionaries and believed their message and wanted to get baptized. He had a concern, however, as his father was adamantly opposed to his "becoming a Mormon." Finau was unmarried and still lived at home, even though he was old enough to be on his own. Since he was past "legal age" he did not need his father's permission to get baptized, but he loved his father and wanted to show respect for him.

Unfortunately, every time he talked to his father about getting baptized his father beat him. Even though Finau could have left home, he stayed and tried to explain to his father how he felt about the Church and how sure he was of his testimony. After several months it became evident that his father would not give his permission, so Finau felt he had no alternative but to get baptized without his father's blessing. Since he had a testimony, was of age, and had tried diligently to reason with his father, he felt good about asking the missionaries to baptize him.

The missionaries knew Finau had faith, understood the doctrines, had a testimony, and was worthy to be baptized, as they had spent much time teaching him. They checked and found that he was indeed of legal age, that he had diligently though vainly tried to get his father's blessing, so they could see no reason why they should not baptize him. Thus, after sincere prayer together, they arranged for a time and place to baptize Finau.

There was still some fear and trepidation on the part of the missionaries, as they knew of his father's anger, but as per prior arrangement they met Finau late one Friday evening on a secluded section of beach. They were all dressed in white and together waded out into the ocean to get to a spot deep enough to perform the sacred ordinance of baptism.

Even though others were not told of the time or place, in some way the word had gotten to Finau's father several hours before, and in anger or desperation or both, he told his oldest son to "teach Finau a lesson." Encouraged by his father and drunken with anger, Finau's older brother got a large stick and headed for the beach.

He arrived at the beach just as the baptism was finished and Finau and the two elders were wading back to shore. In an anger-emboldened rage he uttered a blood-curdling scream and headed straight toward the threesome, who were now in fairly shallow water.

The two elders heard the scream, looked up, saw the stick and the charging brother, and quickly ran away. They yelled at Finau to follow them, but he quietly shook his head and simply stood there, his eyes full of peace. He raised his head and looked straight at his brother. The elders reached land and took cover in some nearby bushes just before the brother reached Finau. When the brother saw that Finau would not run but waited calmly for him with a look of perfect serenity, he hesitated for a moment—but only a moment. Then with a curse of anger he took the last couple of splashing steps, lifted his large stick, and sent it crashing across Finau's back. Finau still did not move. Again and again the stick smashed into Finau's back, tearing his shirt and exposing huge red welts oozing with blood and pain. At last an extra heavy blow crumpled Finau to his knees, then another and another left him sprawled face down in the water.

An exultant cry rent the air, and a man drunken from anger staggered to shore and disappeared uncertainly down the trail. He had "taught his brother a lesson" and left a seemingly lifeless form floating partially submerged in the gently rolling ocean.

The two elders who witnessed all this came from their hiding places and, somewhat embarrassed and very concerned, ran quickly to where Finau lay in the ocean, barely moving. They were grateful to see he was still breathing. They lifted him from the water and were sickened by what they saw. Getting beaten severely enough to raise welts and blood and tear fabric is painful enough, but to have that raw flesh submerged in salty

ocean water and sand was more pain than they could comprehend. They shuddered, and wondered if Finau also had some
broken bones or other unseen injuries.

Finau could hardly move, so they each took an arm and
lifted him up and dragged him stumblingly to shore. As they
got well onto land, Finau spoke for the first time and asked
where they were going.

"To the hospital, of course," they replied. "We must get
those wounds treated and see if there are any broken bones. You
may have some serious back or rib problems."

"No," said Finau. "Not yet. I have only been baptized. I have
not received the gift of the Holy Ghost nor been confirmed a
member of The Church of Jesus Christ of Latter-day Saints—
God's kingdom on earth. See that log over there? Take me to it,
sit me down, confer upon me the gift of the Holy Ghost, and
confirm me a member of the Church. I want to be part of God's
kingdom now."

"We'll do that tomorrow. You need to get some medical
treatment now."

"No," Finau replied firmly. "Do it now. Who knows, you
may be right, there may be serious physical problems. I may not
even make it to the hospital or I may not be alive tomorrow. Of
course, I am in pain, but mostly I just feel numb. I am, however,
in full control of my feelings and I want to become a member of
God's kingdom now—please."

The two elders looked around, sensing possible danger.
They saw no one else, however, so they looked at each other,
then at Finau, who was patiently waiting. They saw such a fire
of faith and determination coming from his eyes that they sat
him down on the log, laid their hands on his head, and by the
power and authority of the priesthood of God gave him the gift
of the Holy Ghost, confirmed him a member of The Church of
Jesus Christ of Latter-day Saints, and under the inspiration of
God gave him a special blessing that no permanent physical
damage from the beating would afflict his body.

As they took their hands from his head there was calmness
in their eyes—no more furtive glances at the surrounding
bushes, only tears of gratitude for the faith of a committed
Tongan Saint in these latter days. Finally they got him to the

hospital, where he was checked, given some care, and released with the admonition: "You were lucky this time. You have no life-threatening injuries or broken bones, but don't get into a fight like that again." (The doctors and nurses were, of course, not aware of the details.)

Finau stayed with the elders that night, but the next day he wanted to return to his home. They went with him and found his father, who, still filled with bitterness and anger, commanded him to leave home and never return. Finau's brother was nowhere to be found. The missionaries made arrangements for Finau to live with a member family.

Many things happened subsequently, but in summary: Finau was eventually reconciled with his father and his family, many of whom (including both his father and his brother) later joined the Church. He became a schoolteacher and was always active in the Church. He married, raised a wonderful family, held many positions of responsibility in the Church, and proved to be a blessing to thousands of people over decades of time.

His father eventually apologized to him and sought his forgiveness, telling him that his mind had been darkened at the time. Finau willingly, even anxiously, forgave him. Finau's back carried those physical scars throughout his life; his soul, however, remained unscarred by anger or desire for revenge.

Like Enos, Finau knew the difference between what was important and what was vital. He knew it was important to get to the hospital, but he also knew it was vital that he become a member of God's true church on earth. I suspect he intuitively knew that if he took care of that which was vital, that which was important would get taken care of as well.

We know it will take great effort on our part over our whole life to achieve the goal of "eternal life and the joy of the saints." I hope we can, with Enos, sense the difference between the important and the vital and pay whatever price is required to achieve that which is vital.

Returning to Enos's account, we see that after he had paid the necessary price in effort and sincerity, he received his heart's desire, as recorded in verse 5: "And there came a voice unto me, saying: Enos, thy sins are forgiven thee, and thou shalt be blessed."

As I read the account, I believe this is where the cycle starts over again. Enos was so filled with gratitude for this assurance and so struck with amazement at the love shown him by the Lord that he asked that eternal question, "Lord, how is it done?" (Verse 7.)

The Lord explained that it was done because of his faith in Christ. That is the way all eternal blessings come to any of us. While the scripture doesn't specifically state it, I feel that Enos must have humbly asked, at least in his heart, "And what else should I do?"

President Howard W. Hunter gave additional support to this feeling when he said, "Any time we experience the blessings of the Atonement in our lives, we cannot help but have a concern for the welfare of others" (Seminar for New Mission Presidents, June 1994).

Enos's humility was rewarded with an understanding that his own family and his own people needed the same blessings he had just received, that is, a forgiveness of sins and the accompanying feeling of love from our Father in Heaven. He wrote: "I began to feel a desire for the welfare of my brethren, the Nephites; wherefore, I did pour out my whole soul unto God for them" (verse 9).

Enos now began again the third step of the cycle of growth by putting forth great effort on behalf of his brethren. He stated: "Wherefore I did pour out my whole soul unto God for them." He again had to "struggle in the spirit," and after he had done so sufficiently he received the Lord's answer: "I will visit thy brethren according to their diligence in keeping my commandments." (Verses 9–10.)

Again Enos was comforted by the Lord's answer to him and started the cycle over again. He was so full of gratitude that he humbly approached the Lord again on behalf of his brethren the Lamanites.

I am sure this was done over a period of time, as the scriptures state. "I prayed unto him with *many long strugglings* for my brethren, the Lamanites" (verse 11; emphasis added). And again, he received his answer "after [he] had *prayed and labored with all diligence*" (verse 12; emphasis added).

Now he knew that even though the Lamanites might destroy

the Nephites, the Lord "would preserve the records . . . and . . . bring them forth unto the Lamanites in his own due time" (see verses 13–16).

Here is another important pattern which is followed by the prophets and which we must follow also:

1. First praying for the welfare of our own souls and doing what is necessary to achieve that.
2. Then praying for the welfare of our family and friends and doing what is necessary to help them.
3. Then praying for the welfare of all others, including those who some may term our enemies, and doing all we can to help them.

If we cannot honestly follow this pattern we still have a distance to go to be as God would have us be and feel and love as He would have us feel and love. After all, He is the one who admonished us to pray for others as well as for our friends: "But behold I say unto you, love your enemies, bless them that curse you, do good to them that hate you, and pray for them who despitefully use you and persecute you" (3 Nephi 12:44).

Who knows how long all of this took? At some point, however, Enos was prepared to go about his mission, for his "soul did rest" (verse 17) and he "went about among the people of Nephi, prophesying of things to come, and testifying of the things which [he] had heard and seen" (verse 19).

Not only did he work with his own people, but also he and others did what they could to preach to their "enemies." "And I bear record that the people of Nephi did seek diligently to restore the Lamanites unto the true faith in God. But our labors were vain." (Verse 20.)

His labors may have seemed vain to him and the other Nephite missionaries, but any honest effort put forth in proclaiming the truth is never in vain. First of all, this diligent effort obviously brought great blessings to Enos and his fellow workers; and second, through his faith and the faith of many others the record of the Book of Mormon was preserved and is now having a marvelous influence for good not only among the Lamanites but also among all peoples of the earth.

It is obvious that Enos wasn't the only one teaching and testifying, as verse 22 states "there were exceedingly many prophets among us." I am interested in his statement that the Nephites "were a stiffnecked people, hard to understand" (verse 22)—yet he kept preaching and working with them. It is amazing how human nature remains the same over the centuries. I am sure many missionaries encounter people today who they feel are "stiffnecked," and many parents (especially those with teenagers) relate to Enos's statement that they are "hard to understand." Yet, just as he kept trying, so must we.

How can we feel gratitude? Through faith in the Lord Jesus Christ. How do we gain faith in the Lord Jesus Christ? Through sincere prayer, diligent scripture study, honest listening to the Lord's prophets and leaders (including parents), through obedience to God's commands and through diligent effort to help and serve and bless others. How can we feel humility? By doing all of the above. How can we feel the desire to put forth great effort in doing good? Again, by doing all of the above. What a marvelous eternal round as we feel gratitude, humility, and a desire to put forth great effort all through faith on the Lord Jesus Christ, which is gained by sincere prayer, diligent scripture study, honest listening to the Lord's prophets and leaders (including parents), and on and on—round after increasing round, until we find ourselves able to feel as Enos did as his life began to draw to a close, as he said: "And I have declared [the word— the gospel] in all my days, and have rejoiced in it above that of the world" (verse 26). What an example for us to follow!

As we near the end of his account we realize Enos was near the end of his life, but he knew where he was going. "And I soon go to the place of my rest, which is with my Redeemer; for I know that in him I shall rest. And I rejoice in the day when my mortal shall put on immortality, and shall stand before him; then shall I see his face with pleasure, and he will say unto me: Come unto me, ye blessed, there is a place prepared for you in the mansions of my Father." (Verse 27.)

Yes, we can learn much from the prophet Enos. In these brief twenty-seven verses we see how he put forth great effort, how he persisted in that effort all of his life, and how clearly he understood the difference between the important and the vital and unwaveringly did what was necessary to see that the vital was achieved.

We can see that over his whole life he followed the cycle of growth from gratitude to humility to effort to greater gratitude, greater humility, and greater effort, and on and on until eventually he could say with deep assurance, "Then shall I see his face with pleasure."

I hope we can all learn the lessons Enos so beautifully and succinctly teaches us.

5

Elder Neal A. Maxwell

King Benjamin

King Benjamin, a remarkable prophet and king, received and deserved the accolades "a holy man" who "reigned in righteousness," indeed, a "just man before the Lord" (Words of Mormon 1:17; Omni 1:25). Earlier in his ministry it took these qualities, plus laboring "with all the might of his body and the faculty of his whole soul," to "establish peace" in the land "once more" (Words of Mormon 1:18).

Benjamin was a special king. His successor son, Mosiah, wished "ye could have men for your kings who would do even as my father Benjamin did for this people" (Mosiah 29:13). Clearly, Benjamin's own outstanding father had taught him well. In turn, King Benjamin taught his own sons well, including the younger Mosiah who later succeeded him, including training them "in all the language of his fathers" (Mosiah 1:2).[1] Benjamin also stressed the importance of the teachings contained on the carefully preserved plates of which he was custodian (see Mosiah 1:6–7). He desired to preserve this precious and sacred, spiritual

---

1. Contrast such excellent fatherhood—tutorial and loving—with the sad circumstances of so many children in our time in America when "about 40 percent of U.S. children will go to sleep in homes in which their fathers do not live. More than half of our children are likely to spend a significant portion of childhood living apart from their fathers. . . . Fatherlessness is . . . the engine driving our most urgent social problems, from crime to adolescent pregnancy to domestic violence." (David Blankenhorn, "Life Without Father," *USA Weekend*, 24–26 February 1995, p. 6.)

memory. This desire to preserve and impart doubtless intensi-
fied especially as Benjamin "waxed old" (Mosiah 1:9).[2]

When the time for succession arrived, aging King
Benjamin's proclamation assembled all the people so that he
might install as king his son, Mosiah, and, more important from
our perspective, give his people a mighty valedictory sermon.
Because of their great love for King Benjamin the people came in
great numbers to an event which may also have coincided with
a ritual celebration (see *Encyclopedia of Mormonism*, 1:189, concerning "Year Rite" and coronation parallels).

The throngs pitched their many tents round about the first
Bountiful temple, "every man according to his family" while facing the tower, especially built so that as many as possible might
hear King Benjamin's voice. To further accommodate and communicate with the people he loved so deeply, Benjamin had his
words written down and sent forth among the people. After he
had concluded speaking, Benjamin, ever meekly concerned with
communicating effectively, sent out among the people to see if
they really had believed on his words (see Mosiah 5:1).

King Benjamin observed in his sermon that he could no
longer serve as the *teacher* or the *king* of the people, hence the
need to install his son Mosiah. Significantly, Benjamin noted his
role as a teacher *before* noting his role as a king.

Given his understanding of the importance of sacred records
and plates, King Benjamin would have been painfully aware of
how quickly a people, bereft of inspiring and informing records,
can cease believing in Jesus and in the resurrection.[3] It had happened before the time of Benjamin, when predecessors had
"their language . . . corrupted; and they had brought no records
with them; and they denied the being of their Creator" (Omni
1:17). Spirituality can be lost even within a single generation; an
untaught generation can become an unbelieving generation, as
later happened among the Nephites: "Now it came to pass that
there were many of the rising generation that could not under-

---

2. Many of us, like Lehi, when "filled" with "exceedingly great joy," become very "desirous" that our "family should partake" of the fulness of gospel
fruit (see 1 Nephi 8:12).

3. Some plates, for instance, proved crucial as verifiers and persuaders in
Ammon's later missionary work among the Lamanites (see Alma 37:9).

stand the words of king Benjamin, being little children at the time he spake unto his people; and they did not believe the tradition of their fathers. They did not believe what had been said concerning the resurrection of the dead, neither did they believe concerning the coming of Christ." (Mosiah 26:1–2. See also Judges 2:10.)

With worldly pressures so great, Latter-day Saint parents should strive valiantly to help the rising generation to be worthy spiritual successors, not a generation whose faith fades.

Benjamin's sermon was held in such high esteem that it was quoted for years: "O remember, remember, my sons, the words which king Benjamin spake unto his people; yea, remember that there is no other way nor means whereby man can be saved, only through the atoning blood of Jesus Christ, who shall come, yea, remember that he cometh to redeem the world" (Helaman 5:9).

Benjamin's great sermon included a meek disclaimer: he was no more "than a mortal man," afflicted with the usual infirmities of body and mind. Though not by way of boasting, he nevertheless reminded his people that during his administration there had been no dungeons and no slavery. Nor had Benjamin laden them with grievous taxes. His people had been a commandment-keeping people, so they knew what Benjamin said to them was, in fact, true, hence the authenticity of the words of this great leader.

In meek deference, modest Benjamin also said, if the people felt to thank him (which they obviously were doing by their very presence), "Oh, how ye ought to thank your heavenly King" (Mosiah 2:19). When we keep the Heavenly King's commandments, He immediately blesses us, said Benjamin. Therefore, given all that God has provided for us, even when we serve Him well we are "unprofitable servants." Why? Because we have been given so very much! Hence, even when we are diligent, God's promises and blessings so far exceed our performances and obligations that the "return" from each of us is clearly not remotely comparable to Heavenly Father's investment in us. However, God is surely pleased when we keep His commandments, and He delights to honor those who serve Him in righteousness (see D&C 76:5).

Even given his remarkable public and prophetic service, Benjamin also meekly said he had "only been in the service of

God" (Mosiah 2:17), and so it should be with us too. The word *only*, by the way, should not be taken to mean "merely." Instead, *only* may have been intended to convey the intensity and keen focus of his service.

There are the understandable warnings in the famous sermon, such as how Benjamin's people were "eternally indebted to your Heavenly Father, [therefore] render to him all that you have and are" (Mosiah 2:34). Our time, talent, and treasure are to be given, certainly, but also ourselves! Some among us today certainly share their time and talents but nevertheless hold back some of themselves, indicating a lack of full consecration and an unwillingness to "give away" certain small sins.

King Benjamin further warned that when people transgress, the Spirit of the Lord withdraws, and thus has "no place in you to guide you in wisdom's paths" (v. 36). We live in an age when, as prophesied, "every man walketh in his own way" (D&C 1:16), and wisdom's path is the least traveled by. How keen is our need for the guiding Spirit of the Lord!

Those who die unrepentant will be awakened "to a lively sense of [their] own guilt" (Mosiah 2:38). The transgressor is actually in an "awful situation," King Benjamin further taught, compared to the "happy state" of commandment keepers who "hold out faithful to the end" (Mosiah 2:40, 41).

The Christocentricity of King Benjamin's sermon is repeatedly evident by its focusing on Jesus' character, His atonement, and His suffering (see Mosiah 3:7, 15–19). For instance, given the records he possessed, King Benjamin would have been aware of how the voice of the Father was once heard to testify of His Son's integrity and faithfulness but also to stress the importance of enduring: "And I heard a voice from the Father, saying: Yea, the words of my Beloved are true and faithful. He that endureth to the end, the same shall be saved." (2 Nephi 31:15.)

This exquisite stress on enduring is in line with Nephi's earlier counsel of which King Benjamin, who had endured much, would have also been keenly aware: "Wherefore, ye must press forward with a steadfastness in Christ, having a perfect brightness of hope, and a love of God and of all men. Wherefore, if ye shall press forward, feasting upon the word of Christ, and endure to the end, behold, thus saith the Father: Ye shall have eternal life." (2 Nephi 31:20.)

Significantly, King Benjamin spoke according to that which was given to him by an angel (see Mosiah 4:1). Of course, even angelic communication ultimately comes from the Holy Ghost—because even angels speak by the power of the Holy Ghost (see 2 Nephi 32:3).

For instance, the angel revealed to Benjamin that, decades later, Jesus would "suffer temptations and pain of body, hunger, thirst, and fatigue, even more than man can suffer, except it be unto death; for behold, blood cometh from every pore, so great shall be his anguish for the wickedness and the abominations of his people" (Mosiah 3:7).

This anguish was confirmed by the Lord's own words in modern revelation. "But if they would not repent they must suffer even as I; which suffering caused myself, even God, the greatest of all, to tremble because of pain, and to bleed at every pore, and to suffer both body and spirit—and would that I might not drink the bitter cup, and shrink" (D&C 19:17–18).

Angels are marvelous correlators as well as providers of communications, including across the centuries. The angel likewise spoke to King Benjamin about the birth of the Savior:

> And he said unto me: Awake, and hear the words which I shall tell thee; for behold, I am come to declare unto you the glad tidings of great joy.
>
> For the Lord hath heard thy prayers, and hath judged of thy righteousness, and hath sent me to declare unto thee that thou mayest rejoice; and that thou mayest declare unto thy people, that they may also be filled with joy.
>
> For behold, the time cometh, and is not far distant, that with power, the Lord Omnipotent who reigneth, who was, and is from all eternity to all eternity, shall come down from heaven among the children of men, and shall dwell in a tabernacle of clay, and shall go forth amongst men, working mighty miracles, such as healing the sick, raising the dead, causing the lame to walk, the blind to receive their sight, and the deaf to hear, and curing all manner of diseases.
>
> And he shall cast out devils, or the evil spirits which dwell in the hearts of the children of men.
>
> And lo, he shall suffer temptations, and pain of body, hunger, thirst, and fatigue, even more than man can suffer, except it be unto death; for behold, blood cometh from every pore, so great shall be his anguish for the wickedness and the abominations of his people.

And he shall be called Jesus Christ, the Son of God, the Father of heaven and earth, the Creator of all things from the beginning; and his mother shall be called Mary. (Mosiah 3:3–8.)

King Benjamin lamented of Jesus that, nevertheless, people would "consider him a man." Worse still, that "he hath a devil, [and they] shall scourge him and shall crucify him" (Mosiah 3:9). Alas, today many likewise so regard Jesus merely as "a man," judging him "to be a thing of naught" (1 Nephi 19:9). This diminished sense of Jesus' divinity is so pervasive in our time.

In stressing the atoning mission of Jesus Christ, Benjamin observed that Christ's blood atones for the sins of all those who repent or of those who have ignorantly sinned. Personal accountability depends on how much we know about the gospel. Those who "have died not knowing the will of God concerning them, or who have ignorantly sinned" is a categorical distinction carefully drawn by King Benjamin in his great sermon. (See Mosiah 3:11–13.)

Following King Benjamin's sermon, his people, in unison and fully persuaded, pleaded for God to "apply the atoning blood of Christ that we may receive forgiveness of our sins" (Mosiah 4:2).

And they all cried with one voice, saying: Yea, we believe all the words which thou hast spoken unto us; and also, we know of their surety and truth, because of the Spirit of the Lord Omnipotent, which has wrought a mighty change in us, or in our hearts, that we have no more disposition to do evil, but to do good continually. . . .

And we are willing to enter into a covenant with our God to do his will, and to be obedient to his commandments in all things that he shall command us, all the remainder of our days, that we may not bring upon ourselves a never-ending torment, as has been spoken by the angel, that we may not drink out of the cup of the wrath of God. (Mosiah 5:2, 5.)

With this "mighty change" in their hearts, King Benjamin even gave his covenant people a name, "the children of Christ," to distinguish them. Christ's name is the only name, Benjamin stressed, "whereby salvation cometh." (Mosiah 5:2, 7–8.) Benjamin's people thus witnessed that they were willing to keep

God's commandments and took upon them the name of Christ, and promised to "retain the name written always [in their] hearts" (Mosiah 5:5–12).

Because Benjamin's is such a powerful valedictory sermon, we see in it the things that mattered most to him. He lived only three years after his remarkable sermon.

How thrilling it must have been for King Benjamin to be so carefully instructed by an angel! How he must have rejoiced in the insights given to him centuries before those very things actually occurred and, likewise, over the spiritual responsiveness of his people. There was a great response to a great sermon!

One of the outstanding contributions of the King Benjamin sermon is his insight and emphasis concerning "the natural man." This teaching is particularized in the sermon in a way that provides us, as members of The Church of Jesus Christ of Latter-day Saints, with the single best description of what it means to become saintly: "For the natural man is an enemy to God, and has been from the fall of Adam, and will be, forever and ever, unless he yields to the enticings of the Holy Spirit, and putteth off the natural man and becometh a saint through the atonement of Christ the Lord, and becometh as a child, submissive, meek, humble, patient, full of love, willing to submit to all things which the Lord seeth fit to inflict upon him, even as a child doth submit to his father" (Mosiah 3:19; see and compare with Matthew 18:3).

The Apostle Paul speaks similarly of the limitations of the natural man, who regards spiritual things as "foolishness" (1 Corinthians 2:14). Putting off "the old man" was a priority for Paul as for Benjamin (see Colossians 3:9).

President Brigham Young frequently referred to the natural man[4] and how we are to put him off, doubtless reflecting President Young's great attachment to the Book of Mormon, which he studied so carefully before and after he came into the Church (see, for examples, *Journal of Discourses* 1:2–3; 2:248; 5:53, 75).

---

4. He lamented that "the natural man ... comprehends nothing more than that which he sees with the natural eye" (Brigham Young, in *Journal of Discourses* 1:2).

King Benjamin's sermon is having an even greater influence in the dispensation of the fulness of times, especially given the sheer numbers of today's Church members.

Another reason for this relevancy is Benjamin's attitude toward poverty. We must be slow to judge, he said, why individuals find themselves in poverty. It is not appropriate for us to reason casually or indifferently that "the man has brought upon himself his misery," since we are all, finally, beggars in terms of our dependence upon God (Mosiah 4:17–23). Benjamin would not have wanted the poor to covet either, but neither should the rest of us be insensitive to them. Benjamin even went so far as to say that giving to the poor is essential if we intend to retain our remission of sins and to walk guiltless before God (see Mosiah 4:26). We cannot even expect our own petitions to be heard if we neglect others "who stand in need" (Alma 34:28).

Benjamin's successor, Mosiah, had been deeply influenced by his father, and he caused that the message of his father be carried forward, as when Ammon and fifteen other representatives from Zarahemla went to the land of Nephi. They found the Nephite king, Limhi, and his people in bondage to the Lamanites, and King Benjamin's words were "rehearsed" by Ammon to these people (see Mosiah 8:3).

The Christocentricity of King Benjamin's ministry and sermon lived on long after him, to say nothing of the influence of Benjamin on millions of us today who are blessed with his words. He was a model king; but, even more important, he was the model of a disciple for all of us.

In conclusion, Nephi, Benjamin's great predecessor, would surely want us to "liken" Benjamin's words unto ourselves (see 1 Nephi 19:23). Such likening would include focusing on quality parenting, which prepares children to overcome the world; making extra efforts to communicate with others, including verifying that they have understood us and we them; valuing the scriptures by searching them; striving for meekness and modesty in our personal lives; putting off the natural man and woman; applying Jesus' great atonement to our own lives; and living so as to merit the regular guidance of the Holy Ghost to keep us in "wisdom's path."

By so doing not only will we enjoy King Benjamin's sermon but we will also apply it. This is what Benjamin would want us to do.

His challenge to his people was to be worthy to "be called the children of Christ, his sons, and his daughters" (Mosiah 5:7). This challenge is the same for us today. How can we live so as to be thus known and deserving of the designation? Benjamin tells us plainly: "Therefore, I would that ye should be steadfast and immovable, always abounding in good works, that Christ, the Lord God Omnipotent, may seal you his, that you may be brought to heaven, that ye may have everlasting salvation and eternal life, through the wisdom, and power, and justice, and mercy of him who created all things, in heaven and in earth, who is God above all. Amen." (Mosiah 5:15.)

To be "steadfast and immovable" disciples of Christ "abounding in good works" is our task, and to achieve this in a world in which so many consider Christ to be a mere man. Benjamin's mighty words can help, and so can the enduring eloquence of his example.

6

Elder Cree-L Kofford

Abinadi

Few names in the scriptures have the power to stir the vision and touch the soul in the same way as does the revered name of Abinadi. Perhaps that is why this ancient prophet stands high on my list of all-time favorites. Even though his life as known to us is recounted in less than twelve pages of the Book of Mormon, and the total length of the messages delivered by him can be read in less than twenty-five minutes, he was a man of such tremendous power and impact as to leave an indelible impression upon any who come to know him.

In his poem *Sohrab and Rustum* the great poet Matthew Arnold had Sohrab pose a question of deep meaning to Rustum, with whom he was locked in mortal combat, not realizing that Rustum was his father: "Who art thou then, that canst so touch my soul?" I find myself thinking these very words whenever the name of Abinadi is mentioned.

As you read the account of Abinadi, as recorded in Mosiah 11–17, you too may well find yourself wanting to know more about this hero from the past. Remember that Abinadi's story is part of the record of Zeniff, which is placed in the book of Mosiah essentially in a "flashback" mode, the record of Zeniff beginning about the year 200 B.C., immediately following the eighth chapter of Mosiah, which is set at about 121 B.C.

We first hear of Abinadi in King Limhi's brief review of his people's history from Zeniff's day down to his own:

And a prophet of the Lord have they slain; yea, a chosen man of God, who told them of their wickedness and abominations, and prophesied of many things which are to come, yea, even the coming of Christ.

And because he said unto them that Christ was the God, the Father of all things, and said that he should take upon him the image of man, and it should be the image after which man was created in the beginning; or in other words, he said that man was created after the image of God, and that God should come down among the children of men, and take upon him flesh and blood, and go forth upon the face of the earth—

And now, because he said this, they did put him to death. (Mosiah 7:26–28.)

The name Abinadi, and the man to whom the name was given, both step boldly onto the pages of the Book of Mormon in the twentieth verse of the eleventh chapter of Mosiah. He comes without fanfare or introduction. With almost disarming simplicity the holy record simply says, "And it came to pass that there was a man among them whose name was Abinadi."

In general terms it may be said that the recorded portion of Abinadi's life and his dealings with King Noah and his people may be conveniently broken down into the following:

1. His introduction into the citizenry and his dramatic calling of the people to repentance.
2. His disappearance for a space of two years.
3. His return, this time to face King Noah and his court, where he would teach various sublime gospel truths and again call to repentance those engaged in wickedness.
4. His arrest, his appearance before King Noah and his priests (some would say his trial), and his condemnation.
5. His martyrdom.

What is there that is so special about Abinadi? Perhaps it was his total obedience as he went, presumably alone, among those whom he must have known would take his life, to deliver the word of the Lord and to cry repentance to the people. Perhaps it is the very fact that we know so little about him, or perhaps it was simply the way with which he faced the adversities which came into his life in such a straightforward, "square-to-the world" way. Whatever the reason, Abinadi was and is special. His life, lived so long ago, still has the power to excite the mind and cause the pulse to pound.

To better understand why, imagine yourself standing in the crowd watching Abinadi converse with the priests of King Noah. If you can, you will hear him say: "Are you priests, and pretend to teach this people, and to understand the spirit of prophesying, and yet desire to know of me what these things mean? I say unto you, wo be unto you for perverting the ways of the Lord! For if ye understand these things, ye have not taught them; therefore, ye have perverted the ways of the Lord." (Mosiah 12:25–26.)

You will also see how deftly he moves from the role of witness to that of interrogator, when he says: "Ye have not applied your hearts to understanding; therefore, ye have not been wise. Therefore, what teach ye this people?" (Mosiah 12:27.)

One can almost hear the priests' rejoinder, which I imagine to have been said with some degree of self-righteousness: "We teach the law of Moses." And then this lone representative of the Lord, standing on the very threshold of losing his life, responds as would only a true servant: "If ye teach the law of Moses why do ye not keep it? Why do ye set your hearts upon riches? Why do ye commit whoredoms and spend your strength with harlots, yea, and cause this people to commit sin, that the Lord has cause to send me to prophesy against this people, yea, even a great evil against this people?" (Mosiah 12:30.)

As we continue our imaginary watch we observe that, having been confounded by the word of God's servant and following the command of their king, the wicked priests of Noah attempt to lay their hands on him that they might slay him. At this critical moment in the life of this great man, when his life hangs in the balance, his words reach out to us over a span of more than two thousand years. You can almost see his shoulders square noticeably as he draws himself to his full height and majestically proclaims: *"Touch me not, for God shall smite you if ye lay your hands upon me, for I have not delivered the message which the Lord sent me to deliver"* (Mosiah 13:3; emphasis added).

Can you feel the electricity of that moment? Can you begin to understand now why Abinadi is such a special prophet? Words like *heroic, courageous, obedient, fearless, powerful, dynamic,* and *faithful* all come flooding into your mind as you replay that moment in Abinadi's life over and over in your mind; and as you do, Abinadi rises to the very heights of what a servant of God should be.

Go with me also to a later moment in his life, when he has been condemned to death by Noah and his priests. It seems clear that King Noah had mixed emotions about what to do with this holy man. For whatever reason, it does appear that King Noah pondered the possibility of releasing Abinadi and perhaps sought a politically expedient way to do so. Consider the scene, again witnessed from our mythical vantage point, when Abinadi is brought before King Noah and his priests to hear these words: "Abinadi, we have found an accusation against thee, and thou art worthy of death. For thou hast said that God himself should come down among the children of men; and now, for this cause thou shalt be put to death unless thou wilt re-call all the words which thou hast spoken evil concerning me and my people." (Mosiah 16:7–8.)

In all probability, having been in prison, Abinadi has been brought before the king and his priests in some form of physical restraint to minimize the possibility of escape. He has just heard the supreme authority of the land pronounce the death sentence upon him. Without attempting to impart emotions to Abinadi, consider yourself in that same circumstance. Would there not have been a flood of emotion pour over your body? Would there not have been, if only for a moment, a touch of panic, a desire to flee, a hope that the heavens would open and rescue would come? Now, having placed yourself in that frame of mind, would you not then have seized upon the words "unless thou wilt recall all the words which thou has spoken evil concerning me and my people" as the hoped-for route of escape? Would not most of us have sought to find some manner of taking advantage of that opportunity to avoid the sentence of death? Under circumstances such as that, it would not seem too difficult to clothe in respectability the desire to live by simply considering all of the good which you could continue to do if your life were prolonged, and contemplating how you might "recall all the words" in such an equivocal way as to still leave intact the teachings which you had sought to impart.

Certainly most of us would be susceptible to some form of thinking along those or similar lines. And now, once again, we get a rare glimpse into the heart and mind of Abinadi, for the record states simply: "Now Abinadi said unto him: *I say unto you, I will not recall the words which I have spoken unto you concerning this people, for they are true*" (Mosiah 17:9; emphasis added).

He then underscored with this addendum the faith with which he faced that moment: "I will suffer even until death, and I will not recall my words, and they shall stand as a testimony against you" (Mosiah 17:10).

While his martyrdom, described as having been "death by fire," would undoubtedly have been a physically painful experience, it is my thought that Abinadi's moment of supreme triumph occurred in those moments when he formed the phrase: "I will not recall the words which I have spoken."

As an aside, one almost has to wonder how someone like Abinadi would feel if he were to hear some of the excuses we use for failing to do what the Lord has asked. Can you see yourself trying to explain to him why it is that you haven't been able to share the gospel with others? Why you are less than totally obedient? Or how, having taken the covenants of marriage, you can justify treating your husband or wife in less than a loving and nurturing way? Obviously, the list could go on and the examples be compounded, but perhaps in understanding yourself in these and other areas you will begin to catch a glimpse of why Abinadi has such a power to "stir my soul."

TEACHINGS OF ABINADI

The teachings of Abinadi are preserved for us in the pages of the book of Mosiah, by virtue of the fact that Alma (the father of Alma the Younger), who was converted to a belief in the words of Abinadi, "did write all the words which Abinadi had spoken" (Mosiah 17:4). As I have previously commented, all of the words spoken by Abinadi as recorded in Mosiah could well have been delivered in under twenty-five minutes. It seems, however, that in reality his preaching took a good deal longer than this and that Mormon did not carry all of Abinadi's words forward to the gold plates. (See, for example, Mosiah 12:8, 19.)

As you will see from reading the messages of Abinadi, he touches upon a great number of gospel subjects, including the law of Moses and most of the Ten Commandments. However, to me his teachings on the coming of the Savior, the Atonement, and the Resurrection stand paramount in all that he taught. It is against this backdrop that Abinadi discusses the law of Moses and points out to the priests of King Noah that the law of Moses alone cannot save. To those who would slavishly follow the law of Moses, Abinadi appropriately begins his teachings by reciting what is now the fifty-third chapter of Isaiah. That chapter contains a poetic prophecy of the coming of the Son of Man.

Incidentally, for any who have trouble in understanding Isaiah, may I suggest a learning technique that has proven very successful for me. I try to read the *thoughts* or *ideas* presented by Isaiah more than reading each individual word. I have found that in doing that I have been able to capture the spirit of what Isaiah is saying, and that spirit is confirmed by a greater understanding of his message. Typically, when I attempt to read Isaiah in the same way that I would read a manual on operating a computer, I find that a sequence of individual words can often be confusing or sometimes seemingly contradictory. When I rise above that approach and seek an understanding of what is taught, Isaiah becomes not only comprehensible but extremely enjoyable.

You will also want to read the fifteenth chapter of the book of Mosiah, where Abinadi discourses on Christ, His sojourn upon the earth, His temptation, His crucifixion, and His resurrection. You will find the ninth verse very instructive on the issue of justice and mercy.

However, it is on the issue of Christ being both the Father and the Son that I believe Abinadi is at his doctrinal best. I know of no other single place in the standard works where the principles surrounding the concept of Christ being the Father and the Son are so lucidly taught in such a short space. As you read the fifteenth chapter of Mosiah you may find it profitable to re-read the ninety-third section of the Doctrine and Covenants, particularly verses 2 through 5.

Abinadi's teachings say:

> And because he dwelleth in flesh he shall be called the Son of God, and having subjected the flesh to the will of the Father, being the Father and the Son—
>
> The Father, because he was conceived by the power of God; and the Son, because of the flesh; thus becoming the Father and the Son—
>
> And they are one God, yea, the very Eternal Father of heaven and of earth. (Mosiah 15:2–4).

The issue of how the son, Jesus Christ, also known as Jehovah, is additionally the Father is one of extreme importance and is found by many to be difficult to understand. In fact, the 1988 Gospel Doctrine manual refers to verses 1–5 of chapter 15 as "some of the most difficult verses in the Book of Mormon."

The challenge comes in understanding Abinadi's teachings in view of the separate and distinct identities of the Father and the Son and the Holy Ghost, as taught in The Church of Jesus Christ of Latter-day Saints.

Almost everyone can readily understand Abinadi when he says that Jesus Christ is the Son. That part of his teachings seems to fit neatly into the doctrines most of us have understood since the beginning of our gospel study. It is when Abinadi gets to the Father and the Son being one ("and they are one God, yea, the very Eternal Father of heaven and of earth") that we tend to become confused. If that happens to be your particular situation, don't be discouraged. It was enough of a challenge for many others that the First Presidency, on June 30, 1916, issued a statement on how Christ was the Father and the Son. (This statement is reproduced in Appendix 2 of the James E. Talmage book *The Articles of Faith*, published by the Church.)

Generally, it may be said that Christ is the Father in at least three separate ways:

1. He is the Father of heaven and earth in the sense that, acting under God the Father, He created all things.
2. He becomes the Father of those who experience a rebirth of the spirit and a change of heart such that, like King Benjamin's people (see Mosiah 5:7), they accept the teach-

ings of Jesus Christ and follow Him in a course of life which will allow them to return to live with our Heavenly Father in the highest degree of the celestial kingdom. That is to say, Christ becomes their "spiritual Father." They thus become part of Christ's family by obedience to His commandments, and thus are able to avail themselves of every benefit of the Atonement.

3. Jesus Christ sometimes speaks as if He were the Father. This is when He is representing Heavenly Father under the principle of the divine investiture of authority, when He is acting in Elohim's stead. In this situation, when Jesus uses the first person "I," to all intents and purposes it is His Father who is speaking. I observe that this is not without some parallel in our present world. For example, in the law there is a well-established principle called agency, which simply means that a party may convey authority to an agent to act on the first party's behalf and to represent the first party in a particular matter. When that authority exists, the agent speaks for and is able to bind the first party in the same way as if the first party were present personally. In a rough sort of way this illustration approximates the heavenly principle of divine investiture of authority.

Abinadi's teachings on the subject of the resurrection may need some clarification, especially to the beginning student of the gospel. To assist you in your understanding, it might be well to comment briefly upon these teachings:

> And there cometh a resurrection, even a first resurrection; yea, even a resurrection of those that have been, and who are, and who shall be, even until the resurrection of Christ—for so shall he be called.
>
> And now, the resurrection of all the prophets, and all those that have believed in their words, or all those that have kept the commandments of God, shall come forth in the first resurrection; therefore, they are the first resurrection.
>
> They are raised to dwell with God who has redeemed them; thus they have eternal life through Christ, who has broken the bands of death.

And these are those who have part in the first resurrection; and these are they that have died before Christ came, in their ignorance, not having salvation declared unto them. And thus the Lord bringeth about the restoration of these; and they have a part in the first resurrection, or have eternal life, being redeemed by the Lord.

And little children also have eternal life.

But behold, and fear, and tremble before God, for ye ought to tremble; for the Lord redeemeth none such that rebel against him and die in their sins; yea, even all those that have perished in their sins ever since the world began, that have wilfully rebelled against God, that have known the commandments of God, and would not keep them; these are they that have no part in the first resurrection.

Therefore ought ye not to tremble? For salvation cometh to none such; for the Lord hath redeemed none such; yea, neither can the Lord redeem such; for he cannot deny himself; for he cannot deny justice when it has its claim. (Mosiah 15:21–27.)

At first glance it might seem that the teachings of Abinadi are at variance with the doctrines of the resurrection accepted by the Church. That seeming contradiction disappears when we carefully examine Abinadi's counsel. You will note that Abinadi has established a special set of definitions by which his teachings are to be understood. Specifically, he defines the first resurrection in terms of the period during which the person being resurrected lives or has lived (those who lived before the resurrection of Christ), noting that the wicked have no part in that first resurrection. That resurrection being long since over, in these latter days we normally use the term *first resurrection* to refer to that which will begin at Christ's second coming, which also is linked to worthiness (see D&C 29:13). But we have to understand that Abinadi made no effort to teach concerning the various degrees of glory. That being the case, the term *eternal life*, which we currently understand to mean life in the highest degree of the celestial kingdom, must be understood as being used by Abinadi in a much broader and more inclusive way. Read with this understanding, Abinadi's instruction is both informative and enlightening.

One other doctrinal subject treated by this ancient sage compels a brief observation. In Mosiah 15:10–12, Abinadi discourses on the "spiritual seed" of Christ, or alternatively, the children of Christ by adoption:

> And now I say unto you, who shall declare his generation? Behold, I say unto you, that when his soul has been made an offering for sin he shall see his seed. And now what say ye? And who shall be his seed?
>
> Behold I say unto you, that whosoever has heard the words of the prophets, yea, all the holy prophets who have prophesied concerning the coming of the Lord—I say unto you, that all those who have hearkened unto their words, and believed that the Lord would redeem his people, and have looked forward to that day for a remission of their sins, I say unto you, that these are his seed, or they are the heirs of the kingdom of God.
>
> For these are they whose sins he has borne; these are they for whom he has died, to redeem them from their transgressions. And now, are they not his seed?

His words are both cautionary and profound. As the reading reveals, Abinadi first poses the question: Who shall be his seed? In answer to this question, Abinadi succinctly states that all those who have hearkened to the words of the holy prophets, and believed that the Lord would redeem His people, and look forward to that day for remission of their sins, are the seed of Christ.

A casual reading of Abinadi's teachings might lead the uninitiated to the conclusion that a mere intellectual belief in the words of the prophets and in the redemptive power of the Lord Jesus Christ is sufficient. That of course is not the meaning intended by Abinadi, nor is it in harmony with the teachings of the restored gospel.

To hearken to the words of the prophets means not only to hear them and seek to spiritually understand them but also to guide our lives, our conduct, and our thoughts by them. Someone who hearkens to the words of the prophets follows those words, adheres to those words, and obeys those words. Companion requirements are fairly set forth in the Articles of Faith and include the requirement of faith in the Lord Jesus Christ and the conviction that through His atoning sacrifice all mankind may be saved.

Thus, to become the seed of Jesus Christ requires not only faith in the Lord Jesus Christ and His atoning sacrifice but also obedience to the laws and ordinances of the gospel. As we harmonize our lives with these teachings, we qualify for the reward of those who are the seed of Christ. We become those for whom He has borne our sins, those for whom He has died to redeem us from the effects of our transgressions, and those who are heirs to the kingdom of God.

Perhaps, after all else has been said, it is most appropriate to conclude with the thought that Abinadi's greatest contribution lies in the fact that he lived so as to qualify to be the seed of Jesus Christ. His life and death establish a standard by which we might gauge our own progress. While it is doubtful that most of us will ever be called upon to die for our faith in the Lord Jesus Christ, it is very clear that each day we will be called upon to live for our faith in the Lord Jesus Christ.

As to the great prophet Abinadi, it seems befitting of his stature to observe that he stepped onto the passages of the Book of Mormon with obedience, courage, and faith, and he roared across its history like a meteor lighting up the sky and sealed his outstanding life with a martyr's death.

7

Elder Joseph B. Wirthlin

Alma the Elder:
A Role Model for Today

The valiant, exemplary life and powerful teachings of Alma the Elder provide us with a wealth of spiritual insight. A careful study of his conversion and subsequent labors as both a spiritual and a temporal leader reveals a number of practical guidelines and concepts that, if applied in our own lives today, can help us live more wisely and productively and, thus, more joyfully.

In my lifelong continuing study of the Book of Mormon, Another Testament of Jesus Christ, I have always sought to follow Nephi's approach to scripture study and teaching. Nephi's singular focus and ever-present objective in his teaching and writing was to "more fully persuade [his listeners and readers] to believe in the Lord their Redeemer" (1 Nephi 19:23). He made it repeatedly clear that he was anxious to bear testimony of the Savior and to teach future generations of the saving power of Christ's atonement. Nephi wrote: "We are made alive in Christ because of our faith. . . . We talk of Christ, we rejoice in Christ, we preach of Christ, we prophesy of Christ, and we write according to our prophecies, that our children may know to what source they may look for a remission of their sins." (2 Nephi 25:25–26.) Nephi also explained that in teaching his people he sought always to "liken all scriptures unto us, that it might be for our profit and learning" (1 Nephi 19:23).

In what I have written here I have sought to emulate Nephi. As we look together at a portion of what Alma can teach us, I want to "more fully persuade [you] to believe in the Lord [your] Redeemer." As we deepen our understanding of what the Book of Mormon tells us about how Alma the Elder came unto Christ through humble repentance and how by strict obedience he became a mighty man of righteousness, I want to "liken . . . unto us" his example of how the saving power of the Atonement can miraculously transform our lives. I want to leave you with some lasting ideas that will be for your "profit and learning" (1 Nephi 19:23).

As members of the Savior's church we struggle with the challenges of living in "a world set on a course which we cannot follow" (Boyd K. Packer, "The Father and the Family," *Ensign*, May 1994, p. 21). While yet a young man, Alma lived and worked in the court of the wicked King Noah as one of the king's appointed priests (see Mosiah 17:1–2). His life in an evil society presented Alma with many of the same temptations that afflict us today. His position of considerable authority in a corrupt government also confronted him with life-threatening conflicts once he embraced the gospel. Understanding how he turned his back on temptation, overcame sin, and stood fearlessly for righteousness can help us deal with our own challenges as we struggle to choose the right.

ALMA THE PENITENT

The simple yet sublime foundation of the gospel of Jesus Christ is repentance through faith in His atonement. The scriptures repeatedly remind us that the Savior was sent by our Father to redeem all mankind. In His own words, the Lord stated the essence of His gospel when He taught the Nephites during His New World ministry: "Now this is the commandment: Repent all ye ends of the earth, and come unto me and be baptized in my name, that ye may be sanctified by the reception of the Holy Ghost, that ye may stand spotless before me at the last day" (3 Nephi 27:20). Similarly, speaking through the Prophet Joseph Smith, the Lord said: "And this is my gospel—repentance and baptism by water, and then cometh the baptism of fire and the Holy Ghost, even the Comforter, which showeth all things, and teacheth the peaceable things of the kingdom" (D&C 39:6).

This is the gospel which Alma heard the prophet Abinadi preach. Having been commanded of God to proclaim the gospel, this unwavering prophet courageously raised his voice against the evils and abominations of King Noah and his people. Abinadi testified of the resurrection, final judgment, and eternal life. He preached repentance to the sinful leaders and to the people who had been "deceived by the vain and flattering words of the king and priests" (Mosiah 11:7).

In one of the most significant doctrinal discourses in the Book of Mormon, Abinadi prophesied of the coming of Christ and expounded on the vital role of the Messiah in God's plan of redemption. Abinadi taught that "God himself shall make [an atonement] for the sins and iniquities of his people" (Mosiah 13:28), "that God himself shall come down among the children of men, and shall redeem his people" (Mosiah 15:1). He taught that the righteous will be "raised to dwell with God who has redeemed them; thus they have eternal life through Christ" (Mosiah 15:23). He exhorted his listeners, Alma among them, to "remember that only in and through Christ ye can be saved," and that "redemption cometh through Christ the Lord" (Mosiah 16:13, 15).

As one of the king's priests, Alma knew firsthand "concerning the iniquity which Abinadi had testified against them" (Mosiah 17:2). As a leader of the people, Alma knew that he was guilty of the evils Abinadi had laid bare. Despite his transgressions, Alma possessed a "heart to perceive, and eyes to see, and ears to hear" (Deuteronomy 29:4). As he listened to the prophet and afterwards wrote down all that Abinadi had taught, Alma felt profoundly and personally the transforming power of the gospel of Jesus Christ. He repented, and he turned with full purpose of heart to do the work of the Lord.

Unlike King Noah and the other priests, Alma did not harden his heart. He listened carefully to the preaching of Abinadi. Alma "believed the words which Abinadi had spoken . . . therefore he began to plead with the king" to control his anger and not "cause that [Abinadi] should be put to death" (Mosiah 17:1, 2). Alma's bold intercession on Abinadi's behalf earned him the king's wrath, and he was cast out of Noah's palace. The infuriated king "sent his servants after him that they might slay him" (Mosiah 17:3). Alma fled from his pursuers and went into hiding. Even though he knew that his life was at risk if he should be found, Alma was so moved by Abinadi's testimony that during his "many days" of concealment he concentrated his energies on writing down "all the words which Abinadi had spoken" (Mosiah 17:4).

The bold and powerful testimony of Abinadi turned Alma away from evil. With a humble heart, with integrity and courage, he "repented of his sins and iniquities" (Mosiah 18:1) through faith in the Lord Jesus Christ. He freely confessed his guilt, that he had been "caught in a snare, and did many things which were abominable in the sight of the Lord, which caused [him] sore repentance." The miracle of forgiveness did not come until "after much tribulation." (Mosiah 23:9–10.) Alma's change of heart is a powerful example of how repentance through faith in the atonement of the Savior can transform our lives if we are willing to do whatever is necessary, to pay whatever price is required, to fully accept the Lord's invitation to "Come, follow me" (Matthew 16:24; 19:21).

"Having put his hand to the plough," Alma devoted himself to righteous living to make himself "fit for the kingdom of God" (Luke 9:62). From what we know of his life, he apparently never looked back upon his wicked past. He dedicated himself wholeheartedly to living the gospel and to leading others to the penitent peace he had found through faith in the Savior.

ALMA THE MISSIONARY

After Abinadi was put to death by King Noah and his wicked priests, Alma "went about privately among the people, and began to teach the words of Abinadi . . . concerning . . . the redemption of the people, which was to be brought to pass through the power, and sufferings, and death of Christ, and his resurrection and ascension into heaven." Alma shared the gospel of repentance with anyone who would listen, even at the peril of his own life. "He taught them privately, that it might not come to the knowledge of the king. And many did believe his words." (Mosiah 18:1–3.)

As more people came to believe his words, Alma resorted to

a place called Mormon which was in the borders of the land and safely away "from the searches of the king." Those who believed went there to hear Alma "preach unto them repentance, and redemption, and faith on the Lord." (Mosiah 18:5, 7.) Even though the king and his priests still sought Alma's life, he did not shrink from sharing the joy of the gospel that he had found through his own repentance.

As in Lehi's vision of the tree of life, once Alma had partaken of the fruit of the gospel he was "desirous that [others] should partake of it also" (1 Nephi 8:12). As it was with Alma, so it was with Enos also. Once Enos had obtained forgiveness for his own sins, he "began to feel a desire for the welfare of [his] brethren" (Enos 1:9). This same concern for others is powerfully expressed in Mormon's description of the missionary motivation of the four sons of Mosiah. They sought permission from their father to preach to the Lamanites because "they were desirous that salvation should be declared to every creature, for they could not bear that any human soul should perish; yea, even the very thoughts that any soul should endure endless torment did cause them to quake and tremble" (Mosiah 28:3).

Alma's loving desire to share the redeeming joy of the gospel with others without regard to his own life is an example of obedience to the Lord's admonition that we deny our selfish desires and lose ourselves in His service (see Matthew 10:38–39; 16:25; Mark 8:35–36; Luke 9:23–25; JST Luke 9:24–25; D&C 98:13; 103:27–28). Peace, happiness, and a comforting sense of meaning and fulfillment in our lives are the promised blessings that we receive if we are true to our covenants and are willing to live our lives for the Savior's sake by serving others and by sharing the gospel.

"Now, there was in [this place called] Mormon a fountain of pure water" where Alma invited those who believed in the gospel of Jesus Christ to be "baptized in the name of the Lord, as a witness before him that [they had] entered into a covenant with him, that [they would] serve him and keep his commandments" (Mosiah 18:5, 10). In Mosiah 18:8–10 we read Alma's discourse on the terms and conditions of the baptismal covenant, a comprehensive yet succinct listing of what living the gospel truly means. Alma clearly explains what it means to be a true follower of the Savior, a true disciple of the Master (see H. Burke Peterson, "Our Responsibilites to Care for Our Own," *Ensign*, May 1981, pp. 81–83), as he enumerates the qualifications, obligations, and blessings of membership in the Church of Jesus Christ:

Qualifications
Desire   to come into the fold of God
         to be called His people

Obligations
Willing to bear one another's burdens
         to mourn with those that mourn
         to comfort those that stand in need of comfort
         to stand as witnesses of God at all times
         to serve the Lord and keep His commandments

Blessings
May   be redeemed of God
         be numbered with those of the first resurrection
         have eternal life
         have the Lord pour out His Spirit more abundantly upon you

I have always found it thrilling to read about how these faithful people responded to Alma's teaching. Once they clearly understood the comprehensive nature of this covenant and its sure promises, "they clapped their hands for joy." In response to Alma's invitation to be baptized, they "exclaimed: This is the desire of our hearts." (Mosiah 18:11.) Alma took one of the believers, named Helam, down into the water, pronounced a prayer and blessing upon him, and buried both Helam and himself in the water. "They arose and came forth out of the water rejoicing, being filled with the Spirit." On that day, at Alma's invitation, "about two hundred and four souls . . . were baptized in the waters of Mormon, and were filled with the grace of God." (Mosiah 18:14, 16.) I have noted throughout my life that when people come to fully understand the blessings and the power of their baptismal covenant, whether as new converts or as lifelong members of the Church, great joy comes into their lives and they approach their duties in the kingdom with contagious enthusiasm.

ALMA THE PROPHET, FOUNDER OF THE CHURCH

In Mosiah 23:16 and again in the concluding verse of the book of Mosiah (29:47), Alma is recognized as the founder of the Church among the people of Nephi. Starting with the Nephite descendants of Zeniff in the land of Lehi-Nephi, then continuing his labors among the main body of the Nephite people in Zarahemla, Alma worked to reestablish and strengthen the church of God. Writing in 3 Nephi, Mormon recognizes Alma as the prophet who "did establish the church among the people." As "the founder of their church," Alma performed a great service for the Nephites that was, in some ways, similar to the mission of the Prophet Joseph Smith in our day. After a period of apostasy among the descendants of Zeniff, Alma was an instrument in the hands of God to restore the gospel and organize the Church among the people of Nephi, "the first church which was established among them after their transgression" (3 Nephi 5:12).

As with the Prophet Joseph Smith, when the truth was presented to him in unmistakable clarity Alma hearkened to the word of God and devoted himself completely to the work of building the kingdom and preaching the gospel of repentance. He vigorously taught the powerful, prophetic messages that he received and carefully recorded. He taught the truths of the gospel, despite great opposition and at the peril of his own life, to those relative few who were receptive.

He taught the meaning of sacred covenants and baptized the believers. He ordained priests to minister to their needs and instructed them to preach "nothing save it were repentance and faith on the Lord" (Mosiah 18:20). Alma organized the small community of believers to form "the church of God, or the church of Christ" and "commanded them that there should be no contention one with another, but that they should look forward with one eye, having one faith and one baptism, having their hearts knit together in unity and in love one towards another" (Mosiah 18:17, 21; see also Ephesians 4:3–5). He commanded them to keep the Sabbath day holy, to meet together often, and to care for the poor by imparting of their substance one to another.

He taught that their priests "should labor with their own

hands for their support. . . . The priests were not to depend upon the people . . . but for their labor they were to receive the grace of God, that they might wax strong in the Spirit, having the knowledge of God, that they might teach with power and authority from God." (Mosiah 18:24, 26.) And so it is with so many of our devoted leaders in the Church today. Supporting themselves by their own labors, they are not a burden but a blessing to their people. With "the grace of God" as their only compensation for their selfless service in the Church, they "wax strong in the Spirit" which enables them to teach "with power and authority from God" as they generously minister to the needs of their people.

Like the Prophet Joseph (and like his successor, Brigham Young), Alma led the members of the Church safely away from persecutions and encouraged them through difficult trials. Through hardship, the faithful were tried and tested, but under Alma's steady leadership they remained stalwart, living righteously even while in bondage to the Lamanites. Finally, the believers escaped from Lamanite domination and found freedom, protection, and open arms to receive them in Zarahemla.

Upon joining the main body of the Nephites in Zarahemla, Alma, at the direction of King Mosiah, organized the Church and worked tirelessly to establish faith and obedience among the people there. In Zarahemla, Alma was faced for the first time in his ministry with dissension, transgression, and persecution within the Church. He sought the Lord's will in knowing how to deal with this new challenge. When Alma's prayer for guidance was answered with revelation that he was to forgive the repentant and blot out the names of those who "would not confess their sins and repent of their iniquity," he wrote down the Lord's words "that he might have them, and that he might judge the people of that church according to the commandments of God." (Mosiah 26:33, 36.) As with Alma, so it was with Joseph Smith. Most of the revelations in the Doctrine and Covenants were given to the Prophet Joseph in response to concerns and new challenges that he faced in the early days of the modern Church.

Alma's leadership over the Zarahemla Church sets a good example for all of those who are called to labor in the Lord's church today. He always sought the will of the Lord in guiding the affairs of the Church, and he always kept the needs of the members foremost in his mind. As a caring, concerned shepherd of the Lord's flock, he worked constantly to see to the spiritual and temporal well-being of his people even in the face of stiff opposition from unbelieving persecutors. "Alma and his fellow laborers . . . who were over the church, walk[ed] in all diligence, [taught] the word of God in all things, [and] suffer[ed] all manner of afflictions, being persecuted by all those who did not belong to the church of God" (Mosiah 26:38).

They admonished and strengthened each other according to their sins and weaknesses, "being commanded of God to pray without ceasing, and to give thanks in all things" (Mosiah 26:39). Alma successfully petitioned the government of King Mosiah to declare a law of religious liberty to grant Church members protection from the unbelieving persecutors. To prevent internal dissension and conflicts, he also issued "a strict command throughout all the churches that there should be no persecutions among them, that there should be an equality among all men; that they should let no pride nor haughtiness disturb their peace; that every man should esteem his neighbor as himself" (Mosiah 27:3–4).

ALMA: LEGACY OF THE LONE CONVERT

Because of Alma's ceaseless labors, the work initiated by Abinadi to redeem the people through faith in the Savior bore good fruits. For over three hundred years, Abinadi's lone convert and his descendants provided spiritual leadership to the Nephite nation. As noted above, Alma started a religious revival among his own people, then established churches throughout all the land of Zarahemla. Later, Alma's son, also called Alma, succeeded his father as the religious leader of the people and became the first chief judge over the Nephite nation. Other descendants of Alma also became great religious leaders: his grandson Helaman; his great-grandson Helaman, the son of Helaman; his great-great-grandson Nephi, the son of Helaman; and his great-great-great-grandson, Nephi the second, who became the chief disciple of the resurrected Jesus Christ (see Daniel II. Ludlow, *A Companion to Your Study of the Book of Mormon* [Salt Lake City: Deseret Book Co., 1976], p. 187). Abinadi's courageous missionary work among an evil, worldly society, though it resulted to our knowledge in only one conversion, can hardly be said to have been in vain. Though Abinadi had only one single convert, that convert, Alma the Elder, had a truly singular impact on countless others of his people. And today, through the miracle of the Book of Mormon, Alma's Abinadi-inspired legacy blesses millions of lives.

If Alma had not been faithful, a great deal of Nephite history would be different. Certainly their spiritual history would not be the same if the life and labors of Alma the Elder were absent. While we cannot determine all the elements of Nephite history that would change in the absence of Alma's ministry, we can say that the Book of Mormon, Another Testament of Jesus Christ, would have a different name.

If Alma had not preached, baptized, and organized the Church in the land of Mormon, the sacred record of God's dealings with the ancient inhabitants of the Americas would have a different title. Mormon, the prophet-compiler-abridger-editor who did so much to prepare the ancient records that today bear his name and that are known throughout the world as the Book of Mormon, received his name from that sacred place where Alma founded the Church. The name of the prophet Mormon and, hence, the title of the Book of Mormon have come to us because of Alma's ministry in the land of Mormon where "all were gathered together that believed on his word" (Mosiah 18:7), where he "formed a church of God through the strength and power of God" (Mosiah 21:30).

In 3 Nephi 5:12, Mormon himself tells us the origin of his now renowned name: "And behold, I am called Mormon, being called after the land of Mormon, the land in which Alma did establish the church among the people."

In the land of Mormon, Alma preached boldly and organized the baptized believers into "a church of God," a church wherein he established priesthood-directed programs of teaching and education, fellowship and worship, and sacrificial service to meet the needs of others. As the record of Alma's ministry in the land of Mormon concludes, we read this moving description of the place made sacred by Alma's labors, a place whose name is borne today by a record that stands for all the world as Another Testament of Jesus Christ:

And now it came to pass that all this was done in Mormon, yea, by the waters of Mormon, in the forest that was near the waters of Mormon; yea, the place of Mormon, the waters of Mormon, the forest of Mormon, how beautiful are they to the eyes of them who there came to the knowledge of their Redeemer; yea, and how blessed are they, for they shall sing to his praise forever (Mosiah 18:30).

Just as the land of Mormon became beautifully sacred to those "who there came to the knowledge of their Redeemer," so the Book of Mormon becomes divinely sacred to those millions of people who come "to the knowledge of their Redeemer" as they study, ponder, and pray about its powerful testimony of Jesus Christ.

I hope, as we pay appropriate tribute to Mormon, Moroni, and Joseph Smith for their great work in preparing and bringing forth the Book of Mormon, that we will also remember the part Alma the Elder played in giving us the sacred name of the book. Whenever you think of the Book of Mormon or hear the name Mormon, I hope you will remember not only Alma the Elder but also the sacred significance of a holy place, a place sanctified by the Spirit, which burned in the hearts of "them who there came to the knowledge of their Redeemer" and which made the waters, and the forest, and the place of Mormon eternally beautiful to their eyes. How marvelous that the Book of Mormon, the most powerful instrument upon the face of the earth today for bringing all who will heed its message to "the knowledge of their Redeemer," should bear the name of this hallowed place!

How marvelous too that the name Mormon should remind us of the great blessing we have and can offer to others to come "to the knowledge of [our] Redeemer" through the fulness of the gospel that we possess. When our church is referred to by its nickname, the Mormon church, and when we as members are referred to as Mormons, it should remind us of the beautiful land of Mormon, of the stalwart life and ministry of Alma the Elder, of the great service of the prophet Mormon, of the miracle of the Book of Mormon, and of the power and authority of The Church of Jesus Christ of Latter-day Saints to bring all of our Heavenly Father's children across all generations of time "to the knowledge of their Redeemer."

ALMA THE GOVERNOR

Schooled and skilled in the ways of government as a member of King Noah's court, Alma proved his mettle again and again as a just and diplomatic leader of his people. When he was falsely accused of "stirring up the people in rebellion against" King Noah, Alma's acumen and wise judgment were apparent as he led his small band of 450 believers away from the land of Mormon into the wilderness and safely away from the pursuing army of King Noah.

In the land of Helam, "a very beautiful and pleasant land, a land of pure water," Alma and his faithful followers built a prosperous community. "And the people were desirous that Alma should be their king, for he was beloved by his people." Alma wisely denied his people's offer of kingship and taught them to treasure their liberty and freedom, especially their freedom "from the bonds of iniquity" into which King Noah and his wicked priests had led them. "Even so," he said, "I desire that ye should stand fast in this liberty wherewith ye have been made free." (Mosiah 23:4, 6, 13.) Alma's caution to his people applies to all of us today. We must be ever vigilant to ensure that our government leaders serve us well in protecting our liberty and freedom, including our freedom "from the bonds of iniquity."

When a marauding Lamanite army threatened the peace and prosperity that Alma's people had found in Helam, Alma calmed his people by exhorting them "that they should remember the Lord their God and he would deliver them." Alma's timely, inspiring exhortation "hushed their fears," and his people "began to cry unto the Lord." Their prayers that the Lord "would soften the hearts of the Lamanites, that they would spare them, and their wives, and their children," were answered. (Mosiah 23:27–28.)

Alma's negotiations with the roaming Lamanite army prevented any bloodshed. The Lamanites promised that they would grant Alma and his people "their lives and their liberty" (Mosiah 23:36) in exchange for directing the lost army back to the land of Nephi. Even when the Lamanites betrayed them and brought them under oppressive captivity, Alma persistently reminded his people to patiently endure their hardships by placing their faith and trust in the Lord.

Before coming upon Alma and his people in Helam, the Lamanite army, while lost in the wilderness, had encountered King Noah's wicked priests. Through wily persuasion, Amulon, the leader of the priests, curried favor with the Lamanite king. "And the king of the Lamanites had granted unto Amulon that he should be a king and a ruler over [the] people, who were in the land of Helam" (Mosiah 23:39). Amulon, like King Noah, was a wicked man who ruled by the exercise of "unrighteous dominion" (see D&C 121:39).

Amulon held the same anger in his heart against Alma that King Noah had felt, and he now vented his anger against Alma and his people by persecuting them. He even caused "that his children should persecute their children." Amulon "put tasks upon them, and put taskmasters over them." The people of Alma prayed "mightily to God" to escape their oppressive afflictions. Even when Amulon commanded them to "stop their cries and . . . put guards over them to watch them, that whosoever should be found calling upon God should be put to death," the people did not lose faith, "but did pour out their hearts to [the Lord their God]; and he did know the thoughts of their hearts." (Mosiah 24:9–12.)

God answered the prayers of their hearts even though they could not speak them aloud. He comforted Alma and his people by covenanting with them to "deliver them out of bondage." The Lord also promised to ease the burdens Amulon had placed upon them. "And this will I do," the Lord said, "that ye may stand as witnesses for me hereafter, and that ye may know of a surety that I, the Lord God, do visit my people in their afflictions." (Mosiah 24:13–14.)

And the Lord kept his covenant. Alma's people were strengthened "that they could bear up their burdens with ease, and they did submit cheerfully and with patience to all the will of the Lord." The Lord blessed Alma and his people and, eventually, delivered them from bondage. After escaping their oppressors, the people "poured out their thanks to God. . . . [They] lifted their voices in the praises of their God." (Mosiah 24:15, 21–22.)

Despite life-threatening persecutions, Alma's people were faithful. They listened to his exhortations and remained steadfast even in the face of heavy oppression. How often do we waver in our faith when faced with difficulty or opposition? We would do well to remember the example of Alma and his people, who stand as witnesses that the Lord will always "visit [his] people in their afflictions." The Lord will ease our burdens if we will "submit cheerfully and with patience to all the will of the Lord." And when we are blessed, let us not forget to humbly and joyfully acknowledge our thanks for God's blessings.

Once he was in Zarahemla, Alma continued to lead the Church and was a close adviser and confidant to King Mosiah. When King Mosiah's sons refused to succeed him on the throne, Alma's teachings to keep in remembrance the suffering of the people under King Noah were reflected in King Mosiah's treatise on the perils of kingship (see Mosiah 29:5–36). King Mosiah persuaded his people to accept changes in their government that led to the institution of the reign of the judges over the people of Nephi, a democratic government in which the voice of the people prevailed. It was a tribute to Alma's governing skill and to his influence among the people that his son, Alma the Younger, was chosen as the first chief judge.

ALMA THE PERSEVERING PARENT

Even when his namesake-son was lost among the evils of the day and went about persecuting the believers he loved so dearly and worked so hard to strengthen and to protect, Alma fervently and faithfully prayed for the redemption and salvation of his wayward son. Although we don't know what caused the son to stray from his father's teachings, we do know that Alma's son became truly evil. We read that "he became a very wicked and an idolatrous man." "A man of many words," he "did speak much flattery to the people" and "led many . . . to do after the manner of his own iniquities. And he became a great hinderment to the prosperity of the church of God." Along with the four sons of King Mosiah, "he did go about secretly . . . seeking to destroy the church, and to lead astray the people of the Lord." (Mosiah 27:8–10.)

In answer to the prayers of Alma the Elder, as his son and the four sons of Mosiah were going about their mischief "rebelling against God" (Mosiah 27:11), they were accosted by an angel of the Lord. Alma the Younger was overcome and collapsed into unconsciousness. He later testified that it was only when his beleaguered mind caught hold upon the teachings of his father that he found comfort, faith, and eventual forgiveness. "Behold," he said, "I remembered also to have heard my father prophesy unto the people concerning the coming of one Jesus Christ, a Son of God, to atone for the sins of the world" (Mosiah 36:17).

When his "mind caught hold upon this thought," Alma the Younger "cried within [his] heart" for the Lord to have mercy on him. When he regained consciousness after three days in that condition, he declared, "I have repented of my sins, and have been redeemed of the Lord; behold I am born of the Spirit." (Mosiah 36:18; 27:24.) He explained to his listeners that the Lord had taught him that all people everywhere "must be born again; yea, born of God, changed from their carnal and fallen state, to a state of righteousness, being redeemed of God, thus becoming his sons and daughters" (Mosiah 27:25). Years later, he would tell his son that through repentance he experienced soul-racking pain and anguish as he came to recognize how "great had been [his] iniquities." But he also experienced soul-soothing joy as he came to know that through the atonement and mercy of the Redeemer he had been forgiven of his sins. "My soul was filled with joy as exceeding as was my pain!" (Alma 36:14, 20.)

Alma the Younger's conversion was brought about by his father's persevering faith. Despite the profound depths of worldly wickedness into which his son had sunk, Alma did not give up on the son he loved. Here is a case where a righteous man surely loathed the sin, but dearly loved the sinner. He diligently, hopefully, fervently prayed for his son. The angel messenger who visited Alma the Younger told him that he had "come to convince [him] of the power and authority of God, that the prayers of his servants might be answered according to their faith." The angel said to the younger Alma, "Alma, who is thy father . . . has prayed with much faith concerning thee that thou mightest be brought to the knowledge of the truth" (Mosiah 27:14).

Alma, upon hearing what had happened to his son and his companions, "rejoiced, for he knew that it was the power of God." Ever the teacher of his people, Alma "caused that a multitude should be gathered together that they might witness what the Lord had done for his son." Alma asked the priests of the

Church to come together in fasting and prayer to restore his son's strength, not only for his son's sake but also "that the eyes of the people might be opened to see and know of the goodness and glory of God." (Mosiah 27:20–22.)

When we are faced with the pain of wayward children or of other loved ones who stray from the gospel path, let us remember the persistent faith of Alma. Remember that the prayer of the righteous availeth much (see James 5:16). In fervent, faithful prayers of our own we can seek the Lord's help in reaching out to grasp the hands of loved ones who have lost their grip on the iron rod.

ALMA THE TEACHER

Almost without exception, great leaders are also skilled teachers. They must be persuasive advocates of their ideas in order to win the allegiance of their people. The influence of great leaders is best exemplified by those who willingly follow out of a personal conviction that they are being led aright, according to correct principles. As is made plain time and again in what we have seen of Alma's ministry, he was a master teacher.

He was always sensitive to perceive both the needs of his audience and the mind and will of the Lord. Through the Spirit he knew what his people needed to hear, and he delivered his teachings in a timely, convincing manner. When the Lamanite army was threatening to attack them in the land of Helam, Alma quickly gathered his people to give them the reassuring comfort and inspiration that they needed in a time of crisis to encourage them to exercise their own faith to call upon the Lord for protection. Even when his son lay dumb and without strength in his limbs, Alma was mindful of how he could use the opportunity to teach his people "of the goodness and glory of God" (Mosiah 27:22).

Alma's teachings prepared his son not only for repentance but also for his impressive, exemplary service as a great leader of the Nephites, both temporally as the first chief judge and spiritually as the high priest over the Church. President Spencer W. Kimball emphasized that many of the world's ills could be cured by righteous, *teaching* parents (see *Ensign,* July 1973, p. 17, and November 1974, p. 110). President Kimball wanted us to understand that it's not enough for righteous parents to quietly live their own lives according to the commandments. We must be *teaching* parents who diligently explain and reinforce gospel principles to our children and grandchildren. Indeed, unless we are teaching our children "the doctrine of repentance, faith in Christ the Son of the living God, and of baptism and the gift of the Holy Ghost" (D&C 68:25), we are not truly keeping the commandments and cannot deservedly claim to be living righteously. President Gordon B. Hinckley has repeatedly credited the loving, diligent teaching of his parents as the primary source of his testimony and of the firm devotion to living gospel principles that he developed early in his life.

While "racked with torment, while . . . harrowed up by the memory of [his] many sins" (Alma 36:17), Alma the Younger caught hold upon the teachings of his father regarding the atonement of Jesus Christ. His father's teachings gave him faith to desire, to seek, and to receive forgiveness. The Book of Mormon is replete with examples of righteous, teaching parents. We know that Nephi was "born of goodly parents . . . [and] taught somewhat in all the learning of [his] father" (1 Nephi 1:1). Even though Laman and Lemuel were rebellious, Father Lehi did not give up trying to teach them "with all the feeling of a tender parent" (1 Nephi 8:37). From the words of his son, Enos, we learn that Jacob, the younger brother of Nephi, was a teaching parent. Enos tells us that his father taught him "in the nurture and admonition of the Lord" and that it was "the words which [he] had often heard [his] father speak concerning eternal life, and the joy of the saints, [which] sunk deep into [his] heart" and motivated him to seek "a remission of [his] sins." (Enos 1:1–3.)

In Alma chapters 36–42 we read of Alma the Younger's teachings to his three sons as he gave "unto them every one his charge, separately, concerning the things pertaining unto righteousness" (Alma 35:16). The stripling warriors of Helaman "had been taught by their mothers, that if they did not doubt, God would deliver them" (Alma 56:47). Mormon did not cease to teach his son, Moroni, even when they were apart. One of

Mormon's letters to Moroni opens with these moving words of faith-filled love: "My beloved son, Moroni, I rejoice exceedingly that your Lord Jesus Christ hath been mindful of you, and hath called you to his ministry, and to his holy work. I am mindful of you always in my prayers, continually praying unto God the Father in the name of his Holy Child, Jesus, that he, through his infinite goodness and grace, will keep you through the endurance of faith on his name to the end." (Moroni 8:2–3.) Like Alma the Elder and like so many other loving parents in the Book of Mormon, the prophet Mormon was certainly a righteous, teaching parent.

As noted earlier, Alma's influence as a teaching parent spanned at least five generations of his own direct descendants. His influence as a stalwart teacher of gospel truth is felt today among millions who know of his life and teachings through the miraculous power of the Book of Mormon, Another Testament of Jesus Christ. Alma was fearless in his teaching, defying and, when necessary, confronting the unrighteous who persecuted him and who even threatened his life. He was never distracted or dissuaded from his purpose of "preaching unto the people repentance and faith on the Lord" (Mosiah 25:15). "As many as would hear his word he did teach" (Mosiah 18:3). Alma was adamant in his efforts to declare repentance because, like Nephi, his bold teaching was motivated by "the Spirit of the Lord which was in him, which opened his mouth to utterance that he could not shut it" (2 Nephi 1:27).

ALMA THE WORTHY EXAMPLE

Before performing his first baptism at the waters of Mormon, Alma prayed, "O Lord, pour out thy Spirit upon thy servant, that he may do this work with holiness of heart" (Mosiah 18:12). In all that he did, Alma sought always to do the will of the Lord. He became chief among his people because he was such a faithful, selfless servant, forgetting himself in their service. (See Matthew 10:38–39; 16:25; 20:27; Mark 8:35–36; Luke 9:23–25; JST Luke 9:24–25; D&C 98:13; 103:27–28.)

After his repentance he was stalwart, enduring all things with humility, patience, and perseverance. After coming to a knowledge of his Redeemer, he boldly proclaimed the gospel of Jesus Christ to bring others to that same knowledge. Alma founded the Church to preserve faith and obedience among the believers, and he governed his people with love, righteousness, and justice. He was an exemplary, loving parent and a master teacher.

We know that the Book of Mormon was written, compiled, preserved, and brought forth as a beacon to guide us in our day to "come unto Christ, and be perfected in him" (Moroni 10:32). The account of Alma and his ministry was included not by happenstance but as part of a divinely designed labor to give us the insight and wisdom we need to hold to the iron rod while living in "a world set on a course which we cannot follow" (Boyd K. Packer, "The Father and the Family," *Ensign*, May 1994, p. 21). Our Heavenly Father has given us the record of Alma's life and teachings to be a strength to us. We must avail ourselves of that providential guiding strength through careful, prayerful study of all that Alma can teach us.

In the revelation the Lord gave to Alma to guide him in judging the rebellious Church members in Zarahemla, the Lord commends Alma for his faithful labors and also blesses the members of the Church, saying, "Yea, blessed is this people who are willing to bear my name; for in my name shall they be called; and they are mine" (Mosiah 26:18). We who are baptized as members of the Lord's church bear His name. We are His. I pray that we will always live true to our baptismal covenants to "serve him and keep his commandments, that he may pour out his Spirit more abundantly upon [us]" (Mosiah 18:10). In the same revelation, the Lord also promises that Alma's enduring service will merit the blessing of eternal life: "Thou art my servant; and I covenant with thee that thou shalt have eternal life" (Mosiah 26:20). If we will live as Alma lived, if we will be diligent and faithful in all things, then we may look forward with joy to that day when the blessings of eternal life, "which gift is the greatest of all the gifts of God" (D&C 14:7), will be ours.

8

Elder L. Tom Perry

Alma,
the Son of Alma

Brigham Young counseled us to read the scriptures this way: "Do you read the Scriptures, my brethren and sisters, as though you were writing them a thousand, two thousand, or five thousand years ago? Do you read them as though you stood in the place of the men who wrote them? If you do not feel thus, it is your privilege to do so, that you may be as familiar with the spirit and meaning of the written word of God as you are with your daily walk and conversation." (*Discourses of Brigham Young,* comp. John A. Widtsoe [Salt Lake City: Deseret Book Co., 1954], p. 128.)

I try to read the Book of Mormon this way. It brings life into the acquaintanceships I have with the great characters of this book. It helps in understanding their feelings as they recorded their experiences and associations.

I have always been partial to the missionaries of the scriptures, and Alma the Younger has been a special favorite of mine. I guess the reason is that he was such a great missionary.

The scriptures record that he was a wayward youth:

> Now the sons of Mosiah were numbered among the unbelievers; and also one of the sons of Alma was numbered among them, he being called Alma, after his father; nevertheless, he became a very wicked and an idolatrous man. And he was a man of many words, and did speak much flattery to the people; therefore he led many of the people to do after the manner of his iniquities.

And he became a great hinderment to the prosperity of the church of God; stealing away the hearts of the people; causing much dissension among the people; giving a chance for the enemy of God to exercise his power over them. (Mosiah 27:8–9.)

Imagine the influence he had on other young people. He was the son of the head of the Church, and his companions were the sons of the king. They were talented young men with the appeal to attract many followers. Imagine the pride in Alma's heart as many followed him, doing "after the manner of his iniquities." Because of the power of his words and his ability to attract many, it would have been difficult for him to change the course he was pursuing to the course the Lord would expect, without a real earth-shaking event. Of course, the Lord had a major event in mind for him. The scriptures record it this way: "And as I said unto you, as they were going about rebelling against God, behold, the angel of the Lord appeared unto them; and he descended as it were in a cloud; and he spake as it were with a voice of thunder, which caused the earth to shake upon which they stood" (Mosiah 27:11).

Is it any wonder that their astonishment was so great that they fell to the earth? The angel commanded: "Alma, arise and stand forth, for why persecutest thou the church of God? For the Lord hath said: This is my church, and I will establish it; and nothing shall overthrow it, save it is the transgression of my people." (Mosiah 27:13.)

The angel reminded Alma that there had been many prayers for his soul and that his father had also prayed with much faith concerning him, that he might be brought to a knowledge of the truth. It was for this reason that the angel appeared unto Alma and the sons of Mosiah, that they might be convinced of the power and authority of God, that the prayers of His servants would be answered according to their faith. The angel then continued: "And now I say unto thee, Alma, go thy way, and seek to destroy the church no more, that their prayers may be answered, and this even if thou wilt of thyself be cast off" (Mosiah 27:16). Again, continuing the scripture: "And now the astonishment of Alma was so great that he became dumb, that he could not open his mouth; yea, and he became weak, even that he could not move his hands; therefore he was taken by those that were with him, and carried helpless, even until he was laid before his father" (Mosiah 27:19).

The father's action was most interesting as his son was placed before him. His son could not speak. He could not move, and Alma the Elder rejoiced because he understood that only the Lord could have put his son in this situation. At last he knew that there was hope for his son. What did he do?

> And he caused that a multitude should be gathered together that they might witness what the Lord had done for his son, and also for those that were with him.
>
> And he caused that the priests should assemble themselves together; and they began to fast, and to pray to the Lord their God that he would open the mouth of Alma, that he might speak, and also that his limbs might receive their strength—that the eyes of the people might be opened to see and know of the goodness and glory of God.
>
> And it came to pass after they had fasted and prayed for the space of two days and two nights, the limbs of Alma received their strength, and he stood up and began to speak unto them, bidding them to be of good comfort:
>
> For, said he, I have repented of my sins, and have been redeemed of the Lord; behold I am born of the Spirit. . . .
>
> My soul hath been redeemed from the gall of bitterness and bonds of iniquity. I was in the darkest abyss; but now I behold the marvelous light of God. My soul was racked with eternal torment; but I am snatched, and my soul is pained no more.
>
> I rejected my Redeemer, and denied that which had been spoken of by our fathers; but now that they may foresee that he will come, and that he remembereth every creature of his creating, he will make himself manifest unto all. (Mosiah 27:21–24, 29–30.)

It had been a bitter course correction for Alma. He had suffered untold pain and eternal torment. But he was willing to change his life.

We see in Alma's conversion the basic elements required to make a change from a life of sin to a path that follows the Lord's plan.

The process of change usually requires a person to go through several stages. First, he must recognize that he is on the wrong path. He must desire a different course for his life. Second, it usually requires physical and/or spiritual suffering. Third, he must confess his sins; and fourth, he must forsake them.

President Spencer W. Kimball has said this about the process of repentance:

> In the process of repentance we must restore completely where possible, otherwise restore to the maximum degree attainable. And through it all we must remember that the pleading sinner, desiring to make restitution for his acts, must also forgive others of all offenses committed against him. The Lord will not forgive us unless our hearts are fully purged of all hate, bitterness and accusation against our fellowmen. . . .
>
> . . . The Lord says:
>
> . . . I the Lord cannot look upon sin with the least degree of allowance;
>
> Nevertheless, he that repents and *does the commandments of the Lord* shall be forgiven. (D&C 1:31–32. Italics added.)
>
> This scripture is most precise. First, one repents. Having gained that ground he then must live the commandments of the Lord to retain his vantage point. This is necessary to secure complete forgiveness. (*The Miracle of Forgiveness* [Salt Lake City: Bookcraft, 1969], pp. 200–202.)

Alma certainly followed this pattern. Now we find him to be a changed man trying to making restitution for the things he has done to others by his teachings and his seeking to destroy the Church. The scriptures record:

> And now it came to pass that Alma began from this time forward to teach the people, and those who were with Alma at the time the angel appeared unto them, traveling round about through all the land, publishing to all the people the things which they had heard and seen, and preaching the word of God in much tribulation, being greatly persecuted by those who were unbelievers, being smitten by many of them. . . .
>
> And they traveled throughout all the land of Zarahemla, and among all the people who were under the reign of king Mosiah, zealously striving to repair all the injuries which they had done to the church, confessing all their sins, and publishing all the things which they had seen, and explaining the prophecies and the scriptures to all who desired to hear them.

And thus they were instruments in the hands of God in bringing many to the knowledge of the truth, yea, to the knowledge of their Redeemer. (Mosiah 27:32, 35–36.)

The Savior surely taught during His ministry that once conversion takes place, there is another action that must follow: "And the Lord said, Simon, Simon, behold, Satan hath desired to have you, that he may sift you as wheat: But I have prayed for thee, that thy faith fail not: and when thou art converted, strengthen thy brethren." (Luke 22:31–32.)

After conversion and a course correction comes the responsibility and obligation to share the knowledge received. Alma's life changed and he became one of the greatest of all missionaries in carrying the word of the Lord to our Father in Heaven's children. He rose in prominence among the people. He became high priest over the Church and also chief among the judges who ruled in the land. The press of the obligations of both positions weighed heavily on him, and it reached the point where he had to make a decision—whether he would continue with the great secular responsibility of judging the people, which seemed to occupy much of his time; or whether he would do the spiritual, forsake the judgeship and go forth among the people to teach them the gospel. In his fully converted state, he selected that which was best for our Father in Heaven's children. We read this account:

> And now it came to pass that Alma, having seen the afflictions of the humble followers of God, and the persecutions which were heaped upon them by the remainder of his people, and seeing all their inequality, began to be very sorrowful; nevertheless the Spirit of the Lord did not fail him.
>
> And he selected a wise man who was among the elders of the church, and gave him power according to the voice of the people, that he might have power to enact laws according to the laws which had been given, and to put them in force according to the wickedness and the crimes of the people.
>
> Now this man's name was Nephihah, and he was appointed chief judge; and he sat in the judgment-seat to judge and to govern the people.
>
> Now Alma did not grant unto him the office of being high priest over the church, but he retained the office of high priest unto himself; but he delivered the judgment-seat unto Nephihah.

And this he did that he himself might go forth among his people, or among the people of Nephi, that he might preach the word of God unto them, to stir them up in remembrance of their duty, and that he might pull down, by the word of God, all the pride and craftiness and all the contentions which were among his people, seeing no way that he might reclaim them save it were in bearing down in pure testimony against them. (Alma 4:15–19.)

He gave up the powerful seat of chief judge so that he could spend his time in bringing people to salvation. Imagine what a difficult decision it was for him to give up the judgment seat. The judges had placed him in the highest position in the land. He had great power and authority over the people. From this position he could require obedience to the law. Giving up that position left him with the power only to teach correct principles, but left compliance to the individual and each one's own free agency. Alma understood the doctrine that man was not to be compelled, for growth would come only when he exercised his own free will to choose the right. So he made his choice to go among the people and teach them correct principles. This was the most difficult of the two assignments, for we find him struggling as he goes forward to teach.

An example of Alma's struggles is when he came to the city of Ammonihah. He began to preach the word of God to them. But Satan had hold upon the hearts of the people of this city and they would not hearken unto his words. He labored with all of the power he could muster that he might teach them correct principles. The people responded this way:

Nevertheless, they hardened their hearts, saying unto him: Behold, we know that thou art Alma; and we know that thou art high priest over the church which thou hast established in many parts of the land, according to your tradition; and we are not of thy church, and we do not believe in such foolish traditions.

And now we know that because we are not of thy church we know that thou hast no power over us; and thou hast delivered up the judgment-seat unto Nephihah; therefore thou art not the chief judge over us. (Alma 8:11–12.)

They cast him out of the city. Downtrodden, he left with a very heavy heart. But he was not to have the easy route, for an angel appeared unto him and told him to return to the city and to preach again unto the people, declaring unto them that except they would repent, they would be destroyed. His assignment became even more difficult. But what did he do? He returned speedily to the land of Ammonihah and entered the city another way. Thus he continued his teachings.

He went forward, city by city, suffering much tribulation and discouragement, and also having many successes as he taught and bore pure testimony to the people. The more he taught, the more he was thrilled and excited about the opportunity to bear the message of the gospel to those he taught.

We find him so caught up in the ministry that he wishes he had power beyond his normal ability. He declares:

> O that I were an angel, and could have the wish of mine heart, that I might go forth and speak with the trump of God, with a voice to shake the earth, and cry repentance unto every people!
>
> Yea, I would declare unto every soul, as with the voice of thunder, repentance and the plan of redemption, that they should repent and come unto our God, that there might not be more sorrow upon all the face of the earth.
>
> But behold, I am a man, and do sin in my wish; for I ought to be content with the things which the Lord hath allotted unto me. . . .
>
> I know that which the Lord hath commanded me, and I glory in it. I do not glory of myself, but I glory in that which the Lord hath commanded me; yea, and this is my glory, that perhaps I may be an instrument in the hands of God to bring some soul to repentance; and this is my joy. (Alma 29:1–3, 9.)

It is this great lesson of service I have learned from reading and studying about Alma. Our leaders from the beginning of time have continually emphasized the soul satisfaction which comes from giving service. President J. Reuben Clark Jr. said: "There is something very remarkable about what we have to give under the gospel plan. No matter how much we give of truth, of good example, of righteous living, our stores, our blessings increase, not decrease, by that which we give away." (In Conference Report, October 1946, p. 85.)

Likewise, it was President Kimball who said:

> Service to others deepens and sweetens this life while we are preparing to live in a better world. It is by serving that we learn to

serve. When we are engaged in the service of our fellowmen, not only do our deeds assist them, but we also put our own problems in a fresher perspective. When we concern ourselves more with others, there is less time to be concerned with ourselves. In the midst of serving, there is the promise of Jesus that by losing ourselves, we find ourselves! (*President Kimball Speaks Out* [Salt Lake City: Deseret Book Co., 1981], p. 39.)

As we take the time to study the scriptures, it would be my hope that we would attempt to walk in the shoes of those who have walked the paths of gospel service. There is so much we can learn from them. By so doing, we will find ourselves on that straight and narrow path that will lead us back to His eternal presence.

9

Elder Henry B. Eyring

Amulek: The Blessings of Obedience

Ve meet Amulek in the Book of Mormon on the day he makes a choice which will change his life forever. We can imagine him dressed in fine clothes because his industry had brought him wealth, smiling because he was on his way to visit a member of his family, and returning greetings to people on the streets of Ammonihah because he was well known, with many friends. And then an angel of God appeared to him.

The angel told him to turn around, go home, and feed a holy man of God he had never met. He wasn't struck down as was Saul of Tarsus or as was Alma the Younger, who was the man he was to meet. Amulek was simply given an instruction. And with it he was given a promise. Here is the account Amulek gave later:

> As I was journeying to see a very near kindred, behold an angel of the Lord appeared unto me and said: Amulek, return to thine own house, for thou shalt feed a prophet of the Lord; yea, a holy man, who is a chosen man of God; for he has fasted many days because of the sins of this people, and he is an hungred, and thou shalt receive him into thy house and feed him, and he shall bless thee and thy house; and the blessing of the Lord shall rest upon thee and thy house. (Alma 10:7.)

We don't have Amulek's account of why he obeyed so promptly. We do know that his choice to be obedient broke the pattern of a lifetime. Here is how he described what he had been like before he made the choice to obey:

Nevertheless, after all this, I never have known much of the ways of the Lord, and his mysteries and marvelous power. I said I never had known much of these things; but behold, I mistake, for I have seen much of his mysteries and his marvelous power; yea, even in the preservation of the lives of this people.

Nevertheless, I did harden my heart, for I was called many times and I would not hear; therefore I knew concerning these things, yet I would not know; therefore I went on rebelling against God, in the wickedness of my heart, even until the fourth day of this seventh month, which is in the tenth year of the reign of the judges. (Alma 10:5–6.)

That day changed the life of Amulek not just because he saw an angel but because he obeyed God. The account of what happened to him after that choice teaches you and me the certainty and the nature of the blessings which flow from choosing to submit to the will of a loving and all-knowing God, whose ways are not our ways.

One of the great lessons from what we know of Amulek is that once God knows we will obey, He will try to give us the greatest of all blessings: sanctification and hope of eternal life. The process of receiving that may take more pain and loss than we would think to seek. But with that mighty change God blesses us with the spiritual sight to see value which dwarfs the loss, the trials, and the adversity. The story of Amulek's life after that day is a sobering yet hopeful lesson for all of us.

First, by the power of the gospel of Jesus Christ, Amulek was transformed from someone who resisted the word of God into a powerful preacher of righteousness. And it took only days, not months or years. The record says that Alma stayed in Amulek's home for "many days" (Alma 8:27). During that time Alma taught Amulek. And an angel, perhaps the one who first commanded Amulek to receive Alma into his home, came to him to confirm what Alma taught. Amulek stated, "And again, I know that the things whereof he hath testified are true; for behold I say unto you, that as the Lord liveth, even so has he sent his angel to make these things manifest unto me; and this he has done while this Alma hath dwelt at my house" (Alma 10:10).

By obeying Christ's authority through His servants, Amulek was blessed with the power to lead others to eternal life in ways he could not have seen in advance. He was given immediately the gift to teach people to feel a compelling need to have all their sins washed away. As you listen to his voice in his first sermon, take hope that God could bless you and me with such a mighty change.

Remember that before Amulek said these words, he had already been given the gift to discern the heart and evil intent of the lawyer, Zeezrom; had rebuked him with power despite the reviling and threats of the people; and then was able to declare this testimony of the Savior with such power that even Zeezrom began to feel the need to be forgiven of his sins:

> And he shall come into the world to redeem his people; and he shall take upon him the transgressions of those who believe on his name; and these are they that shall have eternal life, and salvation cometh to none else.
>
> Therefore the wicked remain as though there had been no redemption made, except it be the loosing of the bands of death; for behold, the day cometh that all shall rise from the dead and stand before God, and be judged according to their works.
>
> Now, there is a death which is called a temporal death; and the death of Christ shall loose the bands of this temporal death, that all shall be raised from this temporal death.
>
> The spirit and the body shall be reunited again in its perfect form; both limb and joint shall be restored to its proper frame, even as we now are at this time; and we shall be brought to stand before God, knowing even as we know now, and have a bright recollection of all our guilt.
>
> Now, this restoration shall come to all, both old and young, both bond and free, both male and female, both the wicked and the righteous; and even there shall not so much as a hair of their heads be lost; but every thing shall be restored to its perfect frame, as it is now, or in the body, and shall be brought and be arraigned before the bar of Christ the Son, and God the Father, and the Holy Spirit, which is one Eternal God, to be judged according to their works, whether they be good or whether they be evil.
>
> Now, behold, I have spoken unto you concerning the death of the mortal body, and also concerning the resurrection of the mortal body. I say unto you that this mortal body is raised to an immortal body, that is from death, even from the first death unto life, that they can die no more; their spirits uniting with their bodies, never to be divided; thus the whole becoming spiritual and immortal, that they can no more see corruption.

Now, when Amulek had finished these words the people began again to be astonished, and also Zeezrom began to tremble. And thus ended the words of Amulek, or this is all that I have written. (Alma 11:40–46.)

The life of Amulek teaches us not only that obedience brings the inspiration of God, but that with that inspiration will come the power to accept the testing and the trials it will take to sanctify us. Amulek could not have foreseen the testing and the sacrifice ahead of him. You sense that when he says in his first sermon that the angel's promised blessing on his house and family had already been delivered. He seemed to think the blessings were delivered and assured when he verified Alma's prophetic calling this way: "Behold, he hath blessed mine house, he hath blessed me, and my women, and my children, and my father and my kinsfolk; yea, even all my kindred hath he blessed, and the blessing of the Lord hath rested upon us according to the words which he spake" (Alma 10:11).

We don't know what Amulek thought those blessings had been, but we do know what became of his house and his family. He lost them all. We know that after he taught with such power as the companion of Alma in his own city, Ammonihah, his father and kindred repudiated him: "And it came to pass that Alma and Amulek, Amulek having forsaken all his gold, and silver, and his precious things, which were in the land of Ammonihah, for the word of God, he being rejected by those who were once his friends and also by his father and his kindred . . ." (Alma 15:16).

Amulek may have lost even his wife and his children. We know that after their mission to Ammonihah, Alma took Amulek to his own home in Zarahemla to comfort him in his loneliness and loss: "Now as I said, Alma having seen all these things, therefore he took Amulek and came over to the land of Zarahemla, and took him to his own house, and did administer unto him in his tribulations, and strengthened him in the Lord" (Alma 15:18).

The fact that Amulek seemed to be completely alone suggests that he lost all his family, including his wife and his children. If they had rejected the gospel of Jesus Christ they would have been killed in the prophesied destruction of Ammonihah. An invading army took the life of every soul in a single day. If

Amulek's wife and children had made and kept covenants of the gospel, they would have been among the martyrs Alma and Amulek were forced to see die in the flames. The words Amulek spoke to Alma were touched with an anguish justified by seeing the horrible suffering of those they had converted, but this anguish would have been for his own wife and children had they accepted the gospel and remained faithful:

> And when Amulek saw the pains of the women and children who were consuming in the fire, he also was pained; and he said unto Alma: How can we witness this awful scene? Therefore let us stretch forth our hands, and exercise the power of God which is in us, and save them from the flames.
>
> But Alma said unto him: The Spirit constraineth me that I must not stretch forth mine hand; for behold the Lord receiveth them up unto himself, in glory; and he doth suffer that they may do this thing, or that the people may do this thing unto them, according to the hardness of their hearts, that the judgments which he shall exercise upon them in his wrath may be just; and the blood of the innocent shall stand as a witness against them, yea, and cry mightily against them at the last day.
>
> Now Amulek said unto Alma: Behold, perhaps they will burn us also.
>
> And Alma said: Be it according to the will of the Lord. But, behold, our work is not finished; therefore they burn us not. (Alma 14:10–13.)

Whatever the extent of his loss and pain, Amulek was given the blessing to see the goodness and fairness of God in even so horrible a tragedy. Those who wrote of the slaying of the faithful of the people of Anti-Nephi-Lehi were given that same blessing of spiritual sight, to see for a moment as God sees tragedy: "And it came to pass that the people of God were joined that day by more than the number who had been slain; and those who had been slain were righteous people, therefore we have no reason to doubt but what they were saved. And there was not a wicked man slain among them; but there were more than a thousand brought to the knowledge of the truth; thus we see that the Lord worketh in many ways to the salvation of his people." (Alma 24:26–27.)

Amulek's life teaches us again what it means to be promised blessings for obedience by a Savior who said to His Father and our Father, "Thy will be done," as He endured the pain of our sins.

The blessings of greatest worth are often more difficult to receive because they are intended to exalt us and those we love. Blessings on our home and our families are limited not only by our faith but by the faith and obedience of others, which neither we nor God can compel. Amulek was delivered by God from the powers of the adversary as a blessing for his obedience, but God would not compel his loved ones to obey. But He granted Amulek the blessing that they might hear the word of God and choose for themselves.

Amulek's life was heroic, not tragic. At the end of the account we know only that he had served a second mission, to Melek with the converted Zeezrom as his companion, and then a third to the Zoramites, called again by Alma as one of his companions. He had, as far as we know, no family left. Alma says nothing more of him, so we can only picture him as the missionary companion trusted of Zeezrom, of Alma, and trusted of God. We do know that he was blessed with the sure blessings of obedience: the transforming of his life by the power of the atonement of Jesus Christ, the gift to give others the chance to choose that blessing, and the trust which God extends to those He knows will hear, will obey, and then will endure as doers of the word to the point of sacrifice, and beyond. Amulek was blessed with all of that, as we will be if we choose to obey.

10

Elder Dean L. Larsen

Zeezrom

Zeezrom does not rank among the great prophet leaders in the Book of Mormon, but his story is one of the fascinating sidebars to the lives of the principal characters in the Nephite record. He appears on the historical scene during a time of great challenge to the Church and to the stability of the government among the Nephite people.

During the closing years of King Mosiah's life, a significant alteration occurs in the government. Frustrated in his attempts to install one of his sons as his successor, Mosiah implements a system of judges to govern the people. These judges are elected by popular vote. A chief judge is appointed as the presiding figure in this new system. Alma the Younger is chosen to fill this role, in addition to his responsibilities as the head of the Church.

Alma is soon faced with troubles in the Church, as the people begin "to wax proud" (Alma 4:6). As a result of this pride, the unity of the Nephite people begins to dissolve. In this crisis Alma is faced with a critical decision. He resigns as the chief judge of the land and determines to focus his full energies upon bringing about a spiritual renewal among the people.

Launching into his committed course with full energy and faith, Alma visits the cities and villages of the land, counseling the people and calling them to repentance. In due time his mission takes him to the city of Ammonihah, where he finds the people in almost total rebellion.

After experiencing ridicule and total rejection, Alma is finally cast out of the city. The Lord, however, directs Alma to return to Ammonihah and guides him to Amulek, a prominent citizen, who accepts Alma as a prophet. Together, the two go among the people, preaching repentance and warning of the direful consequences that will come to the inhabitants if they persist in their willful disobedience.

It is in this scenario that Zeezrom appears. While the description of conditions in Ammonihah is not given in great detail, it is not difficult to fill in the pieces of the political, moral, and social mosaic from the recorded account. Corruption and dishonesty in official circles have become endemic. Grasping for material riches, the people have clamored to gain advantage one over another. Judges have become corrupt, susceptible to bribes and yielding advantage to those who can show favors.

This litigious environment has spawned the need for many of those who can plead cases successfully before the courts. Numerous lawyers have emerged, skilled not only in the law but also in exploiting the devious legal system for the potential benefit of themselves and their clients.

It is a group of these lawyers that confront Alma and Amulek. Undoubtedly they hold some hope of profiting from feeding the controversy that has developed from the preaching of the two men. Additionally, lawyers, nimble of speech, are thought to have the best prospect of confounding the Lord's servants.

It is significant that Zeezrom presents himself as the chief spokesman for these legalists. "Now he was the foremost to accuse Amulek and Alma, he being one of the most expert among them, having much business to do among the people" (Alma 10:31).

We learn much about Zeezrom from this capsule profile. Not only is he acknowledged by his peers as one of the leaders in his craft, he is well known among the people generally, and apparently is one of the foremost to whom they look for legal assistance. This would indicate that he also has a comfortable relationship with the judges in the city.

The account of the dialogue between Zeezrom and Alma and Amulek in the eleventh chapter of the book of Alma provides additional insight into Zeezrom's worldly self-assurance. He has an audience to play to, and he intends, with his practiced sophistry and cunning, to make a game of his denegration of the two missionaries. After all, the audience is completely prejudiced in his favor, and he relishes the opportunity to add to his reputation among his peers. His questions to Alma and Amulek reflect his courtroom skills. They are designed for entrapment.

Zeezrom, however, is completely unaccustomed to dealing with those who have the spirit of inspiration and revelation working in their favor. His motives are transparent to Alma and Amulek.

Zeezrom's offer to pay the missionaries six onties of silver if they will deny that there is a Supreme Being exposes his conviction that everyone is as corruptible as himself. It is a revealing demonstration of the debauched condition into which the people have fallen. Zeezrom obviously expects no disapproval from his fellow lawyers or the people for his proffered bribe. It is a practice to which they are accustomed.

It is when Zeezrom's scheming is powerfully rebuffed by Amulek, and Amulek begins to testify of basic gospel truths, that Zeezrom senses something different about these two men. His arrogant self-confidence begins to falter. "Now, when Amulek had finished these words the people began again to be astonished, and also Zeezrom began to tremble" (Alma 11:46).

Alma, sensing that the power of the Spirit has begun to work upon the heart of Zeezrom and upon some of his listeners, takes up the attack that Amulek has begun:

> Now the words that Alma spake unto Zeezrom were heard by the people round about; for the multitude was great, and he spake on this wise:
>
> Now Zeezrom, seeing that thou hast been taken in thy lying and craftiness, for thou hast not lied unto men only but thou hast lied unto God; for behold, he knows all thy thoughts, and thou seest that thy thoughts are made known unto us by his Spirit;
>
> And thou seest that we know that thy plan was a very subtle plan, as to the subtlety of the devil, for to lie and to deceive this people that thou mightest set them against us, to revile us and to cast us out—
>
> Now this was a plan of thine adversary, and he hath exercised his power in thee. (Alma 12:2–5.)

The effect of Alma's rebuke upon Zeezrom is dramatic:

Now when Alma had spoken these words, Zeezrom began to tremble more exceedingly, for he was convinced more and more of the power of God; and he was also convinced that Alma and Amulek had a knowledge of him, for he was convinced that they knew the thoughts and intents of his heart (Alma 12:7).

It is at this point that a remarkable change begins to take place in the demeanor of Zeezrom. He becomes the earnest in-quirer—the learner. The change is the more remarkable because it occurs in the presence and full view of the people to whom he has been appealing with his inquisition. "And Zeezrom began to inquire of them diligently, that he might know more concerning the kingdom of God" (Alma 12:8).

We must pause at this point in our consideration of Zeezrom's situation to ask ourselves the question, why was this arrogant, sophisticated demagogue so susceptible to the influence of the Spirit? Other rebels in the Book of Mormon record were similarly confronted by spiritual leaders but persisted in their debauchery. Nehor, although rebuked by Alma, had no change of heart (see Alma 1), nor did Amlici (see Alma 2) or Sherem (see Jacob 7). Korihor stubbornly refused to repent (see Alma 30). What was there in the soul of Zeezrom that pressed him toward such a remarkable change?

The answers to some of these questions must be left to spec-ulation.

It is interesting, however, to contemplate the abrupt changes that occurred in the lives of others who had initially been ene-mies to the Lord's work and his people, and who reversed their life's course to become champions of the gospel plan. Alma him-self, along with the sons of King Mosiah, underwent such a re-direction. Ammon, Mosiah's son, when reflecting upon the re-markable missionary successes that he, Aaron, Omner, Himni, and their brethren had enjoyed among the Lamanite people over a fourteen-year period of unusual hardship and sacrifice, recalls the days of their rebellion: "Behold, we went forth even in wrath, with mighty threatenings to destroy his [the Lord's] church" (Alma 26:18). He then wonders, "Oh then, why did he not consign us to an awful destruction, yea, why did he not let the sword of his justice fall upon us, and doom us to eternal de-spair?" (Alma 26:19.)

Why, indeed?

Anti-Nephi-Lehi, the converted Lamanite king, acknowledges his dark past when he persuades his people to willingly lay down their lives rather than resist the threatened onslaught by their unconverted brethren: "And behold, I also thank my God, that . . . we have been convinced of our sins, and of the many murders which we have committed" (Alma 24:9).

It appears that the "light that shineth in a dark place" to which Peter referred (2 Peter 1:19) is difficult to extinguish completely in the souls of men. For those who have basked in that light and then have willfully turned against it, the regeneration process appears to be more difficult and unlikely. Such seems to have been the case with Sherem, who confessed before he died, "I fear lest I have committed the unpardonable sin, for I have lied unto God; for I denied the Christ, and said that I believed the scriptures; and they truly testify of him" (Jacob 7:19).

An important lesson seems to emerge from the experiences of Zeezrom and the other repentant transgressors who have been mentioned. It is never safe for us to judge a person to be beyond the reach of the Lord's merciful hand. Even those whose lives have been tainted by corruption and apparent rebellion against the things of God can, through sincere repentance, become forces for great good in the accomplishment of the Lord's purposes.

We do know that Zeezrom's life was dramatically redirected. It appears that in spite of his having yielded to the influence of the environment in which he had gained notoriety, a spark of spiritual light must have endured in his soul. While some of those who listen to the exchange between Zeezrom and the missionaries react in a positive way, the majority are angry and are determined to destroy Alma and Amulek. A mob spirit inflames them. They bind the two men with strong cords and take them before the chief judge, where the men are accused of reviling against the law and against the people of the land.

In the midst of this turmoil, Zeezrom attempts to come to the defense of Alma and Amulek:

> And it came to pass that Zeezrom was astonished at the words which had been spoken; and he also knew concerning the blindness of the minds, which he had caused among the people by his lying words; and his soul began to be harrowed up under a con-

sciousness of his own guilt; yea, he began to be encircled about by the pains of hell.

And it came to pass that he began to cry unto the people, saying: Behold, I am guilty, and these men are spotless before God. And he began to plead for them from that time forth; but they reviled him, saying: Art thou also possessed with the devil? And they spit upon him, and cast him out from among them. (Alma 14:6–7.)

It is apparent that in attempting to stop the destruction of Alma and Amulek, Zeezrom risks his own life. The fury of the mob turns in some measure upon him. They cast him out from among them, casting out as well all those who believe in the words of Alma and Amulek. They then gather together the wives and children of the believers and cause them to be burned, along with their sacred records. It is not difficult to imagine the agony that fills Zeezrom's soul as he witnesses the holocaust that his taunting has precipitated.

Along with the other believers who have been cast out of Ammonihah, Zeezrom finds refuge among the people of Sidom. He is found there by Alma and Amulek, who barely escaped from the city with their lives after the Lord miraculously delivered them from the hands of their tormentors. Undoubtedly the two missionaries had witnessed the futile attempt of their former antagonist to quell the wrath of the mob. They find him in dire circumstances:

Zeezrom lay sick at Sidom, with a burning fever, which was caused by the great tribulations of his mind on account of his wickedness, for he supposed that Alma and Amulek were no more; and he supposed that they had been slain because of his iniquity. And this great sin, and his many other sins, did harrow up his mind until it did become exceedingly sore, having no deliverance; therefore he began to be scorched with a burning heat. (Alma 15:3.)

When Zeezrom learns that Alma and Amulek have made their escape and are in Sidom, he pleads for them to come to him. The two companions respond immediately. With a profoundly repentant spirit, Zeezrom begs Alma and Amulek to heal him. This request in itself is reflective of the faith that has begun to take root in Zeezrom's heart.

> And it came to pass that Alma said unto him, taking him by
> the hand: Believest thou in the power of Christ unto salvation?
>
> And he answered and said: Yea, I believe all the words that
> thou hast taught. . . .
>
> And then Alma cried unto the Lord, saying: O Lord our God,
> have mercy on this man, and heal him according to his faith which
> is in Christ. (Alma 15:6–7, 10.)

Alma's administration is instantly effective. Zeezrom leaps
to his feet, healed not only physically but spiritually as well. The
report of this incident is spread throughout Sidom.

One cannot reflect upon this episode without recalling the
conversion of Saul of Tarsus in New Testament times. Saul, who
had been a tormentor of the Christians and had condoned
Stephen's martyrdom (see Acts 8:1), requires a similarly dramatic conversion experience. His sightlessness is healed under
the hands of Ananias. He is brought to a recognition and ac-
knowledgement of his folly in attempting to thwart the Lord's
work. In a flood of repentant anguish he makes a dramatic re-
versal in the course of his life. His fervor and energy are redirected to promulgate and sustain the work he has previously
sought to destroy.

So it is with Zeezrom. He is baptized by Alma, and, just as
was the case with Paul, he immediately begins to preach among
the people, later becoming a trusted companion of Alma and
Amulek. It is perhaps not adding too much to reality to suppose
that Zeezrom's healing, his conversion, and his testifying of
Christ contribute much to the missionary success enjoyed by
these three servants of the Lord. The record tells us that the
people "did flock in from all the region round about Sidom, and
were baptized" (Alma 15:14).

That Zeezrom proves himself in the eyes of his mentor,
Alma, is confirmed by the fact that he regularly appears in the
accounts of Alma's ministry as one of his most trusted and reli-
able companions and fellow servants. Years after the events in
Ammonihah and Sidom, when Alma undertakes one of the
most difficult challenges of his life's ministry—the conversion of
the Zoramites—Zeezrom is chosen along with Ammon, Aaron,
Omner, Amulek, and two of Alma's sons to be a part of this sea-
soned missionary force (see Alma 31:6).

That some of Zeezrom's testimony and teachings find their way into the permanent Nephite record is confirmed in the book of Helaman. Nephi and Lehi, the sons of Helaman, are engaged in a missionary effort among the Lamanites. They are captured and imprisoned by those they have sought to convert. In a miraculous manifestation of the Lord's power, Nephi and Lehi are encircled by a fire that preserves rather than consumes them. The Lamanites are frozen in wonderment at this spectacle. They become overshadowed by a cloud of darkness, and a voice commands them to repent. They then see Nephi and Lehi conversing with angels. Aminadab, a Nephite dissenter who had once been a believer, seizes this moment to confirm that these miracles are occurring through the Lord's power. He cries to those who are witnessing this event, "You must repent, . . . even until ye shall have faith in Christ, who was taught unto you by Alma, and Amulek, and Zeezrom" (Helaman 5:41).

Perhaps the most convincing evidence we have of the love and esteem that Zeezrom comes to enjoy among his fellow Christians is that one of the principal Nephite cities is given his name (see Alma 56:14).

Much can be learned from the story of Zeezrom: the tragedy of corruption among a people who reject Christ and sacrifice moral principle to pride and self-interest; the anguish and torment that sin produces in an individual life.

Perhaps the most significant lesson to be learned from Zeezrom's experience is that the redeeming power of Christ's love can bring about the miracle of spiritual regeneration in the vilest of sinners when they fully turn to the Savior and give themselves to the accomplishment of His purposes. In Zeezrom's story, all of us who are imperfect find hope for forgiveness, and hope in reaffirmation of the Savior's infinite love for those who reject evil and give their hearts to Him.

11

Elder F. Burton Howard

Ammon:
Reflections on Faith
and Testimony

From my earliest childhood, I held the full-time missionaries in special esteem. This, in the beginning, was due to my
mother, who taught me to pray for them. Before I could read,
she read me stories about the missionary experiences of Wilford
Woodruff, Parley P. Pratt, John Taylor, and Ammon. As a result,
my association with missionaries has always been positive and
uplifting. The most enjoyable sacrament meetings of my youth
were the homecomings and farewells of those who were coming
or going to the mission field. The example of missionaries past
and present has thrilled me from then till now.

Inspirational experiences of a more recent vintage have had
the same effect and have served to keep the missionary heritage
of the Latter-day Saints in the foreground of my life. Many a
young person has had the course of his or her life changed by the
acceptance of a mission call. I was such a one. The enlarged hori-
zons, the compassion for others, the ordering of life's priorities
which come to a missionary, can come in no other way.
Sometimes these changes are painful. They were to me. Time has
revealed previously unexpected dimensions to the missionary
experience. It is now seen as multifaceted and never ending.

My release as a full-time missionary did not signal an end to
my missionary activity. Since that time many years ago, I have
continued to associate with the work as a shepherd, coach,
player, and referee. It has been an exciting and satisfying time.
Increased maturity has also brought me an increased apprecia-

tion for the great missionaries of the past. Lessons which were perceived only dimly, if at all, now are seen more clearly. Characteristics and attributes of some of my childhood heroes are now more evident.

When I was young, the thing that impressed me most about Ammon was that he bravely defended the flocks of King Lamoni and cut off the arms of renegade Lamanites who tried to scatter those flocks. That was the kind of story that personified what I thought a missionary or great religious leader should be. But the fact that people perform brave acts or achieve victory in battle does not impress me now as much as it did before. There are more far-reaching lessons to be learned. Ammon remains one of my heroes, even though I see him with different eyes. Today, I see heroism as being something different from bravery. It is that quality which makes one courageous when it matters. It is doing what one must do when temptation, or discouragement, or illness, or personal inconvenience suggest otherwise. It is always predicated on faith.

As Moroni abridged the writings of Ether and prepared to bury the plates which became the Book of Mormon, he had occasion to look back on the record his father had written, as well as all that he knew about the history of his people. He felt impressed to talk about those who had demonstrated great faith. In the twelfth chapter of Ether, he set forth his own gallery of heroes. One of them was Ammon. Moroni said, "It was the faith of Ammon and his brethren which wrought so great a miracle among the Lamanites" (Ether 12:15). And so to me a hero is one who is and does more than we commonly expect of someone by exceeding the normal limitations of virtue, faith, valor, and excellence. He or she inspires others to exceed them as well. A hero "reminds us of what lies unrecognized and unused in ourselves" (Henry Fairlie, "Too Rich for Heroes," *Harpers*, November 1978, p. 40).

A careful study of the life of Ammon teaches lessons that cannot be learned as well anywhere else.

After their miraculous conversion, the sons of Mosiah determined to go their several ways to declare the word of God to the Lamanites. The twenty-sixth chapter of Alma tells us about this experience and their many years in the mission field. Speaking about his mission afterwards, in a setting comparable to a modern missionary homecoming, Ammon tells about his decision to go on a mission and the blessing it is to be an instrument "in the hands of God" (verse 3). He talks about how his friends gathered around to give him a scornful, mocking farewell. They laughingly asked if he supposed he could bring the heathen "to the knowledge of the truth," or if he supposed he could "convince the Lamanites of the incorrectness of the traditions of their fathers" (verse 24).

His friends reminded him that the Lamanites were difficult—that they delighted in shedding blood, that their days had been spent in grossest iniquity, and that their "ways [had] been the ways of a transgressor from the beginning" (verse 24). They suggested that they would be better off taking up arms against the Lamanites and destroying them, lest they should someday overrun the Nephites (see verse 25).

Notwithstanding this kind of negative peer pressure, Ammon went on a mission with the hope that, as he put it, he "might save some few of their souls" (verse 26). And scripture details the story of his mission. Let me highlight a few elements of that story.

The Book of Mormon tells us that he was depressed after entering the mission field and was "about to turn back" (verse 27). However, the Lord comforted him and said, "Go amongst thy brethren, the Lamanites, and bear with patience thine afflictions, and I will give you success" (verse 27). Ammon says that he did go forth and that he was patient in his sufferings; and that he suffered every privation and traveled from house to house relying upon the mercies of the world, and also upon the mercies of God.

He states that he entered into their houses and taught them, and taught them in their streets, and taught them upon their hills; and entered into their temples and their synagogues and taught them. He reports that he and his brothers were cast out and mocked, spit upon, smote upon their cheeks, stoned, bound with strong cords, and cast into prison. Through the power and wisdom of God they were delivered again (verse 29). Two verses portray in a majestic way the reward of all missionary service:

> And we suffered all manner of afflictions, and all this, that perhaps we might be the means of saving some soul; and we sup-

posed that our joy would be full if perhaps we could be the means of saving some.

Now behold, we can look forth and see the fruits of our labors; and are they few? I say unto you, Nay, they are many; yea, and we can witness of their sincerity, because of their love towards their brethren and also towards us. (Alma 26:30–31.)

Ammon's brother Aaron had previously rebuked him as he related his success in the mission field, stating, "I fear that thy joy doth carry thee away unto boasting" (verse 10). Ammon's response constitutes some of the most beautiful language in literature:

> Now have we not reason to rejoice? Yea, I say unto you, there never were men that had so great reason to rejoice as we, since the world began; yea, and my joy is carried away, even unto boasting in my God; for he has all power, all wisdom, and all understanding; he comprehendeth all things, and he is a merciful Being, even unto salvation, to those who will repent and believe on his name.
>
> Now if this is boasting, even so will I boast; for this is my life and my light, my joy and my salvation, and my redemption from everlasting wo. (Alma 26:35–36.)

A testimony of the gospel usually consists of two things. It consists of the bright moment of realization when, touched by the Holy Ghost, we first sense that the gospel is true. A testimony is also evolutionary. It is a gradual, growing awareness based on experience and prayer that one's initial testimony was incomplete because there are many facets to the gospel, each of which is true.

I cannot remember a time when I did not know that the Book of Mormon was true. I had studied it before I went on my mission. There I read it many times. After my mission, I had the privilege of teaching early morning seminary for seven years. The subject each year was the Book of Mormon. Again I read it each year, followed the outline, assimilated the lessons, and testified of its truthfulness. But after all of this, one day in preparing to teach a lesson my testimony of the Book of Mormon was fortified and the Holy Spirit touched my heart in a way that causes me to remember the moment even now after many years.

I was reading again the twenty-sixth chapter of Alma and the story of Ammon's mission. I read out loud, as I sometimes do, trying to put myself in the position of the characters in the book, imagining that I was saying or hearing the words, that I was there. Once more I went over the report, and, with a clarity which cannot be described and which would be difficult to comprehend by one who has not experienced it, the Spirit spoke to my soul, saying, *Did you notice? Everything that happened to Ammon happened to you.*

It was a totally unexpected sentiment. It was startling in its scope; it was a thought that had never occurred to me before. I quickly reread the story. Yes, there were times when my heart had been depressed and I had thought about going home. I too had gone to a foreign land to teach the gospel to the Lamanites. I had gone forth among them, had suffered hardships, had slept on the floor, endured the cold, gone without eating. I too had traveled from house to house, knocking on doors for months at a time without being invited in, relying on the mercies of God.

There had been other times when we had entered houses and talked to people. We had taught them on their streets and on their hills. We had even preached in other churches. I remembered the time I had been spit upon. I remembered the time when I, as a young district leader assigned by the mission president to open up a new town, had entered, with three other elders, the main square of a city that had never had missionaries before. We went into the park, sang a hymn, and a crowd gathered.

Then the lot fell upon me, as district leader, to preach. I stood upon a stone bench and spoke to the people. I told the story of the restoration of the gospel, of the boy Joseph going into the grove and the appearance of the Father and the Son to him. I remembered well a group of teenage boys, in the evening shadows, throwing rocks at us. I remembered the concern about being hit or injured by those who did not want to hear the message.

I remembered spending time in jail while my legal right to be a missionary in a certain country was decided by the police authorities. I didn't spend enough time in prison to compare myself to Ammon, but I still remember the feeling I had when the door was closed and I was far away from home, alone, with only the mercies of the Lord to rely on for deliverance. I remembered enduring these things with the hope that "we might be the means of saving some soul" (Alma 26:30).

And then on that day as I read, the Spirit testified to me again, and the words remain with me even today: *No one but a missionary could have written this story. Joseph Smith could never have known what it was like to be a missionary to the Lamanites, for no one he knew had ever done such a thing before.*

And so Ammon is one of my heroes, and part of my testimony of the Book of Mormon is based on the fact that I have had experiences similar to his own, and I know them to be true.

Moroni said that "it was the faith of Ammon and his brethren which wrought so great a miracle among the Lamanites" (Ether 12:15). Missionaries are noted for their faith, and because of Ammon's faith, as well as the faith of many among whom he labored, many miracles accompanied his ministry. The single-handed defeat of the robbers at the waters of Sebus was indeed miraculous. The scripture says that notwithstanding their numbers, Ammon could not be slain (see Alma 18:3). The converting of King Lamoni as a result of spiritual promptings which told Ammon what to do and say was another great miracle. The Spirit bearing witness of the divinity of the Savior to the queen was another. Ammon's rescue of his imprisoned brethren was still another, as was the conversion of thousands of the people of Anti-Nephi-Lehi. Even though the Anti-Nephi-Lehies had committed great iniquity, they were able to take advantage of the redeeming power of the Atonement, they renounced war, and they determined to be perfectly honest and upright in all things and to be firm in the faith of Christ even to the end. This was perhaps one of the greatest of all the miracles. And it was the great faith of Ammon and his brethren, combined with the faith and receptive spirit of the people, that accomplished it.

In speaking about faith, Moroni tells us that faith is things which are hoped for and not seen, and that no miracle can occur until after the trial of our faith (see Ether 12:6, 12). In addition, it has always seemed to me that faith is the power which enables us to venture beyond the limits of our own experience. It is the power that pierces the walls of certainty that surround us just enough so that we can see beyond them and slip through to a brighter realm that we have not known before. This is the legacy of Ammon. He is the personification of faith. What he did and learned as a result of going where no man had gone before will stand forever as an example to us all.

Ammon learned about missionary work, and through him the entire Church has learned about it. Ammon learned that missionary work is contagious and gratifying, that it is impossible not to be profoundly changed as a result of participating in it. He learned that those who trust in the Lord don't turn back when they encounter difficulty. He learned that there is a difference between being disappointed and being discouraged. He learned that missionaries pray and work, that they are at peace with themselves, that anyone who repents and exercises faith and accepts the gospel is given to know the mysteries of God, including a personal witness of the truthfulness of the work. He learned that one of the great blessings that men and women can aspire to is to be instruments in the hands of God. He learned of the love which exists between missionaries and converts. He learned of the joy which none receive "save it be the truly penitent" (Alma 27:18).

Ammon lived on the bright edge of the Spirit. There is no record that he ever fully comprehended the transcendent change which came into his own life. Nevertheless, his life was a miracle. He was not motivated by a hope of reward or the expectation of position. He served because he had become so close to the work that it was part of him and he was part of it. He was the kind of missionary able to be used by the Lord in any place to do any thing. He was the kind of member of the Church who caused things to go better when he was there. He sensed his responsibility to care for those who had been converted, to fellowship them and integrate them into his society. He was trusted by the Lord, with all that this implies, and was therefore able to be used as an instrument.

I suspect that Ammon came to know that the Lord often calls people to positions because of blessings He wants to give them. Not all blessings are pleasant; some are painful. Some require growth, patience, and perspective to be fully appreciated. Ammon learned that sometimes the Lord prepares His servants for future callings and that often the real value and purpose of the preparation is not revealed until a later time. Ammon is a genuine hero. He is an example to all who are laboring in that field which is white, already to harvest, and to all who ever have or who ever will do so.

His story encourages us, each and every one of us, to ask what it would be like after a lifetime of doubt to find certainty, after a period of pride and rebellion to wondrously discover God. Ammon drifted aimlessly for years before he found a purpose to his creation. He was in the dark and found light; he despaired and found hope. After a frantic, friendless search for pleasure, he found peace. He learned what it was like to leave mistakes behind and begin again. He learned to know the love of Christ, to hear the still, small voice for the first time. He learned the joys of service. He learned to receive answers to prayer.

Imagine what it would be like to have the experiences that Ammon had. Imagine what it would be like to bring these priceless gifts to others.

12

Elder Joe J. Christensen

Captain Moroni, an Authentic Hero

It is of interest to note that approximately one out of every ten pages of the Book of Mormon deals with the life and times of Captain Moroni, which we read in Alma chapters 43–63. Given the number of people and events described in the Nephite writings, have you ever wondered why so much of what we have in the Book of Mormon is dedicated to this individual and the experiences that surrounded his life?

Apparently, the prophet Mormon had many of the Nephite records available to him from which he made his abridgement. With divine guidance he selected and included those portions of the records that would be most valuable to us in our day. What are the messages from Captain Moroni and his time that have applicability to us at the present time?

First, in Captain Moroni we are provided with an authentic hero. For many, we live in a world devoid of genuine heroes. It is "a cynical age [which] now accepts the tarnished coin of celebrity in place of heroic virtue" (Pete Axthelm, "Where Have All the Heroes Gone?" *Newsweek*, 6 August 1979, p. 44).

Young people today are in much greater need than they realize to have authentic heroes. William J. Bennett writes about the lack thereof among the young:

> In a recent survey of 1,200 junior-high-school children, the most popular response to the question: "Who is your hero?" was "None." Nobody. Other answers far down the line in this and

other polls have revealed the devaluation of the hero, at least. Students today cite rock musicians, Evel Knievel and the bionic man and woman. This suggests—and my own informal poll and the reports of friends of mine who are teachers have confirmed my suspicion—that heroes are out of fashion. For some reason, perhaps for no reason, many of us think it is not proper to have heroes; or worse, that there aren't any—or only shabby ones.

Such a fad is dangerous because it puts children's ideals, aspirations and their notions of self-worth in jeopardy. Children need to know what deserves to be emulated and loved and nurtured, but knowing these things is not transmitted by their genes; these things must pass, through education, from generation to generation. . . .

. . . It's possible that if we don't take the time, our children, taught as they have been to doubt, will live the consequences of not knowing what they may safely believe. (William J. Bennett, "Let's Bring Back Heroes," *Newsweek,* 15 August 1977, p. 3.)

Captain Moroni provides young and old with the kind of hero the world so critically needs—a hero who deserves to be emulated. He possessed personal characteristics that set him apart as a remarkable individual. The prophet Mormon recognized the rare values found in Captain Moroni's life and experience and generously chose to share them with us in our day and time.

Perhaps Mormon chose the name Moroni for his son—who concluded the Book of Mormon record—because he considered Captain Moroni to be so exceptional.

Captain Moroni—and we might well call him "General," since he was the chief captain over many other captains—taught us much about the inestimable values that must be preserved even if it means fighting a defensive war to protect them with our very lives: "Inasmuch as ye are not guilty of the first offense, neither the second, ye shall not suffer yourselves to be slain by the hands of your enemies. And again, the Lord has said that: Ye shall defend your families even unto bloodshed. Therefore for this cause were the Nephites contending with the Lamanites, to defend themselves, and their families, and their lands, their country, and their rights, and their religion." (Alma 43:46–47.)

Moroni did not delight in going to war and being involved in the shedding of blood. In fact, he avoided war as far as possible, but when it came to defending basic rights and freedoms, we read: "The Nephites were inspired by a better cause, for they were not fighting for monarchy nor power but they were fighting for their homes and their liberties, their wives and their children, and their all, yea, for their rites of worship and their church" (Alma 43:45). Captain Moroni "delighted in the saving of his people from destruction" (Alma 55:19).

He was always willing to allow the Lamanites to call a halt to the fighting, to forgive them and allow them to return to their homes even on the mere promise that they would not come to war again. Moroni taught the Nephites "never to raise the sword except it were against an enemy, except it were to preserve their lives" (Alma 48:14).

Brother Hugh Nibley insightfully records:

> The idea of total victory was alien to him—no revenge, no punishment, no reprisals, no reparations, even for an aggressor who had ravaged his country. He would send the beaten enemy home after the battle, accepting their word for good behavior or inviting them to settle on Nephite lands, even when he knew he was taking a risk. Even his countrymen who fought against him lost their lives only while opposing him on the field of battle: There were no firing squads, and conspirators and traitors had only to agree to support his popular army to be reinstated. . . .
>
> . . . By all means, let us take Captain Moroni for our model and never forget what he fought for—the poor, outcast and despised; and what he fought against—pride, power, wealth and ambition; or how he fought—as the generous, considerate and magnanimous foe, a leader in every sense. ("Leadership Versus Management," *BYU Today*, February 1984, pp. 16–19, 45, 46.)

Moroni was a believer and a defender of the truth. He appreciated the fact that Alma, his sons, and others had gone "forth among the people, to declare the word unto them," and that "they preached the word, and the truth, according to the spirit of prophecy and revelation; and they preached after the holy order of God by which they were called" (Alma 43:1–2).

Once that peaceful message of truth had been established, Moroni was willing to take up the sword if necessary against all who would rob the people of the right to believe and practice in peace the faith they had adopted.

The prophet Mormon, in his abridgement and through the example and experience of Captain Moroni, lets us know today of the types of problems that bring difficulties upon society and those that should be avoided: "For it has been their quarrelings and their contentions, yea, their murderings, and their plunderings, their idolatry, their whoredoms, and their abominations . . . which brought upon them their wars and their destructions" (Alma 50:21).

Additional character and personality traits of Captain Moroni that merit mention and emulation include the following:

1. *He had prepared himself throughout his early years* so that at age twenty-five he was qualified and trusted enough to be appointed leader of all the armies of the Nephites (see Alma 43:17).

2. *He was compassionate and wise.* He did not delight in bloodshed, as has been mentioned. At the earliest indications that his enemies were weakening or willing to stop the conflict, he would call a halt to the battle. He was magnanimous in forgiveness, but, as in the case of the confrontation with Zarahemnah, he was firm for the right (see Alma 44:1–20). Moroni was vitally concerned for the welfare of his people, and particularly for those who fought under his leadership. He worked diligently to assure that they were well armed, trained, and prepared for war (see Alma 43:18–21). He built up defenses of stone walls, forts, and banks of earth to help secure his people (see Alma 48:7–10; see also 49:6, 18–20; 50:1–4).

3. *He was spiritual and sensitive to ecclesiastical leadership.* He sought, obtained, and followed the counsel of the prophet Alma (see Alma 43:23–26). He delighted in doing good, in preserving his people, and in keeping the commandments of God (see Alma 48:16).

4. *He was intelligent.* He used a variety of tactics and strategies to defeat his enemies (for example, see Alma 43:27–35). Even some modern military leaders have indicated that Moroni's military skills were obvious and ingenious.

5. *He was a leader who surrounded himself with good and able people.* "Helaman and his brethren were no less serviceable unto the people than was Moroni; for they did preach the word of God, and they did baptize unto repentance all men whosoever would hearken unto their words" (Alma 48:19).

6. *He demonstrated great leadership ability, including charisma,*

and was able to rally a people to the title of liberty (see Alma 46:13). In Moroni's day "there never was a happier time among the people of Nephi" (Alma 50:23). His leadership likely inspired the two thousand stripling warriors who were led into battle so successfully by Helaman (see Alma 53, 56–57).

7. *He knew the value of organization and labor.* He knew that when he caused the Lamanite prisoners to work, it was easier to guard them (see Alma 53:5). A parallel might be that when we are busy, it is easier to guard ourselves against the influences of the adversary.

8. *He was family-oriented.* The Nephite armies would not take prisoners of women and children. When the opportunity came to exchange prisoners with the Lamanites, Moroni would not exchange except on the condition that a Nephite man *and* his wife and children would be freed for each Lamanite prisoner exchanged (see Alma 54:11).

9. *He was a man of courage.* He personally scaled the wall of a Lamanite city and directed his men to a victory through remarkable valor and strategy (see Alma 62:20–23). His type of courage is reminiscent of that portrayed by James Butler Bonham:

> [He] was a courier who left the Alamo during the siege and rode to Goliad, 95 miles away, to plead for reinforcements. . . . The commander at Goliad could offer no troops. At that moment, Bonham knew that the Alamo was doomed. But he turned around, fought his way back through the Mexican Army and rejoined his comrades to fight to a certain death.
>
> . . . The hoofbeats of Bonham's ride express it much better. They leave us with the lingering and essential challenge: *who among modern heroes would have made that return trip?* (Axthelm, "Heroes," p. 45; emphasis added.)

Captain Moroni was the type of courageous hero who very likely "would have made that return trip."

This Moroni is a heroic ideal and model for our times. He is one whose life and characteristics should be understood by the older and taught to the younger so that they will never be able to say honestly that they do not have a hero worthy of emulation. He is one who taught us powerfully of those values—those priceless blessings—worth fighting and even dying for.

Captain Moroni was a believer in Christ and defended His cause. He followed the example of the Savior's development and "increased in wisdom and in stature, and in favour with God and man" (Luke 2:52). Of him it has been recorded: "Yea, verily, verily I say unto you, if all men had been, and were, and ever would be, like unto Moroni, behold, the very powers of hell would have been shaken forever; yea, the devil would never have power over the hearts of the children of men" (Alma 48:17).

Our young people today need heroes who go beyond the popular musicians, comedians, great athletes, the rich, and the famous. They, and all of us, need to know of people like Captain Moroni, whose influence will live long after the applause of those who are currently popular has faded away.

May we all emulate his example.

13

Elder John K. Carmack

Pahoran: Wartime Statesman, Defender of Freedom

To understand chief judge and governor Pahoran we must link his life and activities with Captain Moroni. Often we find it necessary to link important historic persons with another person, sometimes by spotlighting one in contrast with another, sometimes because activities of the two persons are inextricably linked. In the cases of Pahoran and Moroni, their mutual public service causes the joinder. Examples of other historic linkage include Winston Churchill and Adolph Hitler as important war leaders whose values and motives contrasted sharply; Ulysses S. Grant and Robert E. Lee, generals linked both by contrast in styles and by virtue of their assignments as opposing military commanders during joint involvement in the American Civil War; and Dwight D. Eisenhower and George C. Marshall, perhaps a close parallel to the Moroni-Pahoran tie in that Marshall as U.S. Army chief of staff appointed and supervised Eisenhower, who commanded D-Day in the field.

Book of Mormon students agree that Captain Moroni was a brave man possessing faith, courage, military brilliance, and unexcelled character—a towering figure. Not only did he save the Nephite nation from destruction during wars of attrition with the Lamanites, who were bent on destroying or subjugating them, but he cleansed the Nephite inner vessel by quelling domestic insurrection. Moroni's example strengthens our courage and deepens our commitment to important values.

Moroni's towering stature tends to overshadow another

great man—chief judge Pahoran. Pahoran's conduct and spirit in the face of extreme provocation teaches us how to react during threatening situations and also teaches us about freedom's priceless value, the vital role of the rule of law in governing people, and the absolute necessity of preserving and defending decisions made by the voice of the people.

PAHORAN'S IMMEDIATE CHALLENGES

Immediately upon becoming chief judge and governor of the Nephite nation, Pahoran confronted daunting circumstances. It had been only five years since his nation had victoriously concluded a frightening war with the Lamanites, thanks to the courage exhibited by Nephite armies and their leaders, Moroni foremost among them. With the war concluded, Moroni did not stand idly by but immediately set about fortifying Nephite cities that had proved vulnerable to attack. He understood that a strong nation was not only less vulnerable but also less likely to be attacked. In the aftermath of the terrible struggle, the Nephites had become stronger and wiser. Peace returned to the land but a new test was on the horizon—the transition from one chief judge to his successor. This transition would provide a stern test for the democratic selection process and the rule of law by judges in place of kings.

Over twenty years had transpired since the Nephites instituted a simple kind of democracy, its key element being election of judges chosen "by the voice of this people" (Mosiah 29:25). King Mosiah, the architect of this new form of government, had explained that these judges would administer "the laws which have been given you by our fathers, which are correct, and which were given them by the hand of the Lord" (Mosiah 29:25).

The reign of elected judges bound by the word of the Lord and governed by laws inspired by God began at Mosiah's death. Mosiah had admonished his people that safety lay in freedom and "do[ing] your business by the voice of the people" (Mosiah 29:26). The position of judge required a combination of judicial and executive service. Anticipating the importance of transition from one chief judge to another, Mosiah established procedures to elect new judges. He also anticipated the need for a means of removing unrighteous judges. Nephites elected judges by assembling the scattered Nephite people "together in bodies throughout the land, to cast in their voices concerning who should be their judges, to judge them according to the law which had been given them; and they were exceedingly rejoiced because of the liberty which had been granted unto them" (Mosiah 29:39).

The first Nephite assemblages elected Alma as their first chief judge. When he later stepped down to spend his full time regulating the Church as the presiding high priest, "Alma delivered up the judgment-seat to Nephihah" (Alma 4:20). The record is insufficient to determine whether Alma appointed Nephihah or held elections. Nephihah saw the people through many wars, including the before-mentioned Lamanite war. As was clear throughout Nephite history, when the people repented of their evil ways—disunity, murder, plunder, idolatry, whoredoms, and other abominations—the Lord made good His promise that keeping the commandments would bring prosperity.

At the conclusion of the Lamanite war, the Nephites experienced a time of happiness, interrupted with a land ownership and boundary dispute between the lands of Morianton and Lehi. Eventually Morianton, as the leader of his faction, fled northward with his followers rather than submit to the law, intending to gather strength sufficient to gain his will by force. Nephite captain Teancum headed them off, restoring unity to the land.

Nephihah died and his son Pahoran "was appointed to fill the judgment seat, in the stead of his father; yea, he was appointed chief judge and governor over the people" (Alma 50:39). We assume his appointment meant election in the manner the Nephites employed as described above.

We have set the stage for the days of trouble and challenge Pahoran faced as governor over his people. He took office in the Nephite way "with an oath and sacred ordinance to judge righteously, and to keep the peace and the freedom of the people, and to grant unto them their sacred privileges to worship the Lord their God, yea, to support and maintain the cause of God all his days, and to bring the wicked to justice according to their crime" (Alma 50:39). We notice the explicit and direct obligations Pahoran undertook as chief judge and governor. No modern official has a similar charge. His responsibilities were akin to those given judges and kings in ancient Israel. The oath administered to the chief judge obligated him to:

—Judge righteously
—Keep peace and freedom intact
—Guard the privilege of worshipping God
—Support and maintain the cause of God
—Bring the wicked to justice according to their crimes

As in ancient Israel, spiritual and temporal duties intermingled. We don't know who administered the sacred ordinance or of what it consisted, but likely the high priest of the Church officiated in some kind of formal anointing as prophets did for kings in Israel. Pahoran took office at the end of the twenty-fourth year of the reign of judges instituted by King Mosiah. Little did he realize what he would face, and almost immediately. Perhaps for most of us it is well that we don't know much in advance about the trials we must face.

KING-MEN REJECT FREEDOM

Pahoran had reason to hope for peace and tranquility. The Nephites had settled the problem with Morianton, and the Lamanites, nursing their fairly recent defeat, were quiet. The people seemed happy, but some among them wanted to alter the law under which they lived. They presented a petition to Pahoran demanding that he replace the system of rule by judges by instituting, once again, a kingdom in its place. Pahoran rejected their petition, causing a warm dispute and division among the people. Those fomenting disunity called themselves "king-men." Those siding with Pahoran in retaining their freedom and participation in government called themselves "freemen." Pahoran placed the issue before the people, according to their governmental system. The people decided in favor of Pahoran and the freemen, silencing the king-men for the time. The quest for a kingdom, however, remained the king-men's goal and ambition. They determined to wrest power and authority over the people from Pahoran, convinced that their "high birth" gave them the right and ability to reign.

Ancient Israelite Parallel

We recall a similar time during the prophet Samuel's era when the elders of Israel counseled together, came to Samuel, and demanded, "Make us a king to judge us like all the nations" (1 Samuel 8:5). Samuel, displeased, prayed to the Lord, who answered, "Hearken unto the voice of the people in all that they say unto thee: for they have not rejected thee, but they have rejected me, that I should not reign over them" (1 Samuel 8:7).

Samuel told the people what the Lord had said, then warned them explicitly against their course of action, explaining what would happen if they followed it:

> [Your king] will take your sons, and appoint them for himself, for his chariots, and to be his horsemen; and some shall run before his chariots.
>
> And he will appoint him captains over thousands, and captains over fifties; and will set them to ear his ground, and to reap his harvest, and to make his instruments of war, and instruments of his chariots.
>
> And he will take your daughters to be confectionaries, and to be cooks, and to be bakers.
>
> And he will take your fields, and your vineyards, and your oliveyards, even the best of them, and give to his servants. (1 Samuel 8:11–14.)

Samuel continued his explanation of the future their insistence on having a king would induce, but "the people refused to obey the voice of Samuel; and they said, Nay; but we will have a king over us. . . . And the Lord said to Samuel, Hearken unto their voice, and make them a king." (1 Samuel 8:19, 22.)

The king-men's desire for a king was similar in motivation to Israel's desire, but the voice of the majority of the Nephites went the opposite way—against the king-men's demand. Had they been just and equitable people who merely differed in their opinions about public policy, that would have concluded the matter. Sadly, the story of the king-men does not end with the people's rejection of their demand, which had tragic results for all concerned.

While this internal dissension transpired among the Nephites, Amalickiah, the Lamanite king, having sworn to drink the blood of Moroni, gathered a "wonderfully great army" and once again commenced a war to subjugate and destroy the Nephites (Alma 51:9–11). The king-men, having lost the contest in the Nephite assemblages, sought to take advantage of the new war by refusing to participate in defending their nation. Moroni, angry at the new internal danger, sought and gained governmental authority to compel the king-men by giving them a choice: either defend the country against the invading Lamanites or be slain. In a brief civil war, during a critical time for the nation's safety, Moroni quashed the rebellion. Amalickiah, taking advantage of the internal problems Moroni faced, attacked and captured a number of Nephite cities by the eastern seashore. Thus did Pahoran's fragile reign as chief judge commence.

Moroni now faced renewed hostilities with the Lamanites, simultaneously on two fronts near the east and west seas. The war threatened the lives and freedom of all Nephites. On the west, Helaman aided Antipus by leading a unique army consisting of two thousand sons of the people of Ammon, who had been converted during the Lamanite missions. The Nephites fought valiantly and their leaders led them brilliantly, and although replacement soldiers slowed to a trickle and the government sent insufficient provisions, they met with much success. When Moroni learned about the circumstances in the west, he sent an epistle to Pahoran, requesting that soldiers be sent to strengthen Helaman's forces. Shortly thereafter the Lamanites conquered the city of Nephihah, prompting Moroni to send Pahoran another epistle—this one castigating him for his neglect of his armies.

Moroni demanded to know why the government was indifferent to the armies' needs on both fronts. They needed men, swords, cimeters, and provisions. In his view, Pahoran, as governor, was responsible to supply and replenish their armies. In his letter Moroni queried, "Can you think to sit upon your thrones in a state of thoughtless stupor, while your enemies are spreading the work of death around you? Yea, while they are murdering thousands of your brethren." (Alma 60:7.)

Warming to his writing task, Moroni broached his worst fear: that the governor himself, and other leaders, was seeking authority and was a traitor. Or, he continued, perhaps Pahoran was just indolent and had forgotten the commandments of God and his duties as governor. Then Moroni threatened to clean house in these words: "God has said that the inward vessel shall be cleansed first, and then shall the outer vessel be cleansed also" (Alma 60:23). He threatened to come with an army and cleanse the center of government. He would, he concluded, find if any had a spark of freedom remaining and would stir them up against the central government, adding, "I do not fear your power nor your authority, but it is my God whom I fear" (Alma 60:28).

PAHORAN'S ANSWER REVEALS HIS CHARACTER

A person's deepest values and true character surface under stress. We would know virtually nothing about the chief judge had he not presided during his nation's time of peril and had the documents Mormon included in his abridgement not been preserved. But in those documents we discover the richness of Pahoran's character and the basic forms and values underlying the Nephite governmental structure.

Pahoran answered Moroni's scathing epistle without a trace of bitterness or defensiveness. An ordinary person, having been placed in Pahoran's devastating position and then wrongly blamed for creating it, would have automatically responded: "Why are you blaming me, after all I've been through? Find someone else to shoulder this responsibility. I'm through!" Pahoran, to his distinct credit, said, "I do not joy in your great afflictions, yea, it grieves my soul. But behold, there are those who do joy in your afflictions, yea, insomuch that they have risen up in rebellion against me, and also those of my people who are freemen." (Alma 61:2–3.)

He continued, explaining the insurrection by the king-men who had persuaded numerous others to join their disloyal and power-seeking conspiracy. Their action had forced Pahoran to flee for refuge with as many men as he could persuade into the land of Gideon. Instead of quitting, Pahoran had sent proclamations to all parts of the nation, asking freemen to join him in defending freedom and avenging the king-men's wrongs. From Zarahemla, the king-men sent word to the Lamanite king that they would cooperate in his plan to subjugate and destroy the Nephites, provided the Lamanites would recognize their king and his territory.

Pahoran responded further to Moroni's angry epistle, "You have censured me, but it mattereth not; I am not angry, but do rejoice in the greatness of your heart" (Alma 61:9). He explained that he did not seek power, but merely retention of his judgment seat to preserve the rights and liberty of his people. "My soul standeth fast in that liberty in the which God hath made us free" (Alma 61:9). He then stated that he was one with Moroni in resisting wickedness and defending their land even to bloodshed. He verified that he had no territorial or other personal ambitions, that he would have had no part in shedding Lamanite blood if they had stayed in their own lands. He was God's servant, and if God asked that the Nephites subject themselves to bondage under the Lamanites, he would even do that. His trust was in God, and he was certain that if they did their part, God would deliver them out of the hands of their enemies as He had delivered Israel so many times.

Nearing the conclusion of his epistolary reply, and illustrating that the Nephite civil governor was in control of the military, Pahoran shifted from his explanatory role into his commander-in-chief role by ordering Moroni to leave the eastern front in the hands of Lehi and Teancum and come speedily with a few men to join him in cleansing the inner Nephite vessel. He should, Pahoran ordered, delegate to Lehi and Teancum "power to conduct the war in that part of the land, according to the Spirit of God, which is also the spirit of freedom which is in them" (Alma 61:15). He had sent some provisions to them and now intended to go against the king-men in the strength of God according to their faith. With Moroni's help, he said, "We will put an end to this great iniquity" (Alma 61:18).

The epistle affords a peek into Pahoran's heart as he concluded his outstanding reply: "I do joy in receiving your epistle, for I was somewhat worried concerning what we should do, whether it should be just in us to go against our brethren. But ye have said, except they repent the Lord hath commanded you that ye should go against them." (Alma 61:20.) He then asked Moroni to "strengthen Lehi and Teancum in the Lord; tell them to fear not, for God will deliver them, yea, and also all those who stand fast in that liberty wherewith God hath made them free" (Alma 61:21).

When Moroni received Pahoran's impressive reply to his blistering epistle, he "was filled with exceedingly great joy because of the faithfulness of Pahoran, that he was not also a traitor to the freedom and cause of his country" (Alma 62:1). But he mourned because of the traitors' iniquity to their nation and to God. Details of the rest of the story remain for others to recall to our minds. Moroni lifted the standard of liberty, raised an additional army, and restored Pahoran to his rightful seat as chief judge. On his part Pahoran saw the war through. He also reestablished and regulated the laws of their nation and arranged for the people to appoint new judges to administer them. His public service and troubles successfully concluded, Pahoran died in peace.

PAHORAN'S LEGACY

Pahoran judged the Nephites in the pattern King Mosiah established. His turbulent years provided a rich legacy of knowledge and insight about good government, righteous reaction in the face of extreme provocation, and insight into Nephite society. This legacy includes the following points:

1. Even in those ancient days prior to Christ's birth, the Nephites had established a simple and effective rule of law to govern themselves. Those laws applied evenly in all parts of the Nephite nation. Judges, even the chief judge and governor, were subject to that law. Thus Nephites enjoyed a government of laws, not one ruled by the whims of autocratic and power-seeking judges and bureaucrats.

2. Nephite laws were basically God's laws, undoubtedly patterned after the law of Moses. When righteously administered, the government relied on the Spirit of the Lord and faith to guide the Nephite leaders.

3. That faith included the ancient Mosaic belief that God could and would deliver their enemies into their hands if they

acted with righteous impulses. Students of the Old Testament will recognize that Israel knew and accepted the concept that God would deliver enemies into the hands of righteous men and women. Once recognizing that basic Israelitish belief, one sees it throughout the Old Testament. Moses' law even excused killing another person if the accused could show that "God delivered him [the enemy] into his hand" (Exodus 21:13). Knowing this deeply held tenet of Israel helps us understand David's words shouted to the Philistines: "I come to thee in the name of the Lord of hosts, the God of the armies of Israel, whom thou hast defied. This day will *the Lord deliver thee into mine hand*; and I will smite thee, and take thine head from thee." (1 Samuel 17:45–46; emphasis added.) Pahoran, in that faith, promised that God would deliver Lehi and Teancum (see Alma 61:21).

One more comment on this point is in order. When we find Pahoran, Moroni, and other Nephites speaking and acting as Israelites, and espousing concepts that are pure law-of-Moses practices and tenets, that builds our faith that we are dealing here with a true record of an Israelite branch. This evidences the truth of Joseph Smith's consistent assertion that he translated plates that Moroni delivered to him.

4. The impulse to replace judges chosen by the people with kings is an evil impulse, but one apparently deeply ingrained in Jacob's later family. Freedom and participation by people in choosing their leaders are God-given rights. God justifies people in defending those rights when attacked by enemies, even if in the process they must shed blood. In modern times, referring to the Revolutionary War fought to defend the right of self-rule in America, God justified those involved in redeeming "the land by the shedding of blood" (D&C 101:80). Freedom is a sacred strand of Jesus Christ's gospel.

5. In general, without condoning modern misguided antigovernment and vigilante actions by individuals and groups, God justifies people in defending themselves, their lands, their possessions, and their families when attacked by aggressors. The Lord assured Pahoran through Moroni that God justified their defensive war against the Lamanites, and also their military action against the traitorous king-men. Dozens of obvious modern examples of defensive wars come to mind. We could also cite examples of wars carried beyond that principle with

disastrous consequences. We'll leave those applications to the reader. The balance between right and wrong is delicate and subtle, but with prophetic guidance and God's inspiration righteous men always discover the right course of action.

6. People can decide serious questions if government officials have sufficient faith in democracy to consult them; they will seldom go wrong en masse. Methods of removing corrupt or out-of-touch officials without bloodshed should be practiced by all governments and are necessary to assure peaceful transitions between administrations.

7. When faced with an angry accusation, Pahoran teaches us by example that a wise and great man tries to learn from the accusation, greets it calmly and thoughtfully, and acts according to righteous spiritual impulses.

We thank Alma for preserving a fragment of Nephite documentary history, thus allowing us to know a great chief judge and governor named Pahoran. In the process we also learn about the Lord's will concerning freedom's value, occasions when God justifies a nation in defending its citizens even if the defense requires bloodshed, the operation of the law of Moses in ancient Nephite civilization, the importance of the rule of law, and how great people operate under stress.

14

Elder Richard G. Scott

Nephi,
Son of Helaman

Much can be learned by careful study of a prophet's life. By analyzing the principles embodied in his pattern of living and identifying the resultant strengths and capacities, each one of us can obtain keys to a more purposeful, productive, enjoyable life.

The devoted, exemplary service of Nephi, the son of Helaman, provides an opportunity to learn from a powerful servant of the Lord truths that are enduring and applicable to a wide variety of circumstances. He lived in a time of great upheaval when the foundations of society were undermined and shaken. He faced intense criticism, adversity, and opposition. Many of these challenges exist in varying degrees in our world today. His successful efforts to overcome them can help us learn patterns for greater attainment and fulfillment.

What were the attributes that characterized the life of this impressive prophet of God and allowed him to be of such power and influence? They can be identified by studying the Book of Mormon references to this fearless prophet of the Lord. Some strengths are explicitly mentioned in the record, while others can be discerned by pondering his life in the context of his world and his personal commitment to serve the Lord. There follows a selection of some of his noble traits with a brief summary of the scriptural references wherein these attributes are revealed.

The Blessing of Righteous Parentage

Nephi descended from a line of elect prophets. While not specifically mentioned, it is obvious that each of these servants had most capable, devoted wives, as evidenced in the training and commitment of their children. Nephi descended from Alma, the Nephite prophet and founder of the Church; and his son Alma the Younger, the high priest and first chief judge; and his son Helaman, a prophet and military commander. His son, also named Helaman, was Nephi's father. The scriptures show how this Nephi and his wife nurtured their son Nephi, who was so righteous that he was privileged to become one of the twelve Nephite disciples. When the Savior called their son Nephi as a disciple, He gave him the power to baptize, including the authority to perform that ordinance for the other eleven disciples (see 3 Nephi 11:18–20; 19:4, 11–12).

The life of the prophet Nephi, son of Helaman, illustrates the powerful effect righteous parents have in establishing a foundation upon which their children can grow, serve, and bless other lives by testifying of specific teachings of the prophets and the Savior:

> And it came to pass that [Helaman] had two sons. He gave unto the eldest the name of Nephi, and unto the youngest, the name of Lehi. *And they began to grow up unto the Lord.* (Helaman 3:21; emphasis added.)

> Helaman died, and his eldest son Nephi began to reign in his stead. And it came to pass that he did fill the judgment-seat with justice and equity; yea, *he did keep the commandments of God, and did walk in the ways of his father.* (Helaman 3:37; emphasis added.)

Parents can learn much from how Nephi's father, Helaman, carefully instructed his sons in doctrine, bearing personal witness of critically important truths. Today children so taught will remember and be blessed by such patient teaching. They will become part of the foundation upon which the Lord will continue to build His kingdom:

> For they remembered the words which their father Helaman spake unto them. . . .

Behold, my sons, I desire that ye should remember to keep the commandments of God; and I would that ye should declare unto the people these words. Behold, I have given unto you the names of our first parents who came out of the land of Jerusalem; and this I have done that when you remember your names ye may remember them; and when ye remember them ye may remember their works; and when ye remember their works ye may know . . . that they were good.

Therefore, my sons, I would that ye should do that which is good. . . .

. . . Behold I have somewhat more to desire of you, which desire is, that ye may not do these things that ye may boast, but that ye may . . . lay up for yourselves a treasure in heaven, . . . that ye may have that precious gift of eternal life. . . .

O remember . . . the words which king Benjamin spake unto his people; . . . that *there is no other way nor means whereby man can be saved, only through the atoning blood of Jesus Christ,* who shall come; yea, remember that he cometh to redeem the world.

And remember also the words which Amulek spake, . . . that the Lord surely should come to redeem his people, but that he should not come to redeem them *in* their sins, but to redeem them *from* their sins.

And he hath power given unto him from the Father to redeem them from their sins because of repentance; therefore he hath sent his angels to declare the tidings of the conditions of repentance, which bringeth unto the power of the Redeemer, unto the salvation of their souls.

And now, my sons, remember, remember that it is upon the rock of our Redeemer, who is Christ, the Son of God, that ye must build your foundation; that when the devil shall send forth his mighty winds, yea, his shafts in the whirlwind, yea, when all his hail and his mighty storm shall beat upon you, it shall have no power over you to drag you down to the gulf of misery and endless wo, because of the rock upon which ye are built, which is a sure foundation, a foundation whereon if men build they cannot fall. (Helaman 5:5–12; emphasis added.)

VALIANT MISSIONARY

Nephi and his impressive brother, Lehi, whose service earned him Mormon's respect as being not "a whit behind [Nephi] as to things pertaining to righteousness" (Helaman

11:19), were fearless, valiant, tireless missionaries. The lasting beneficial effect of parental instruction is evident in the lives of these devoted servants: "And they did remember his words; and therefore they went forth, *keeping the commandments of God,* to teach the word of God among all the people of Nephi" (Helaman 5:14; emphasis added). They testified in Bountiful, Gid, Mulek, and the other southern Nephite cities and from there taught the Lamanites in Zarahemla. Their consistent labors yielded these results:

> They did confound many of those dissenters who had gone over from the Nephites, insomuch that they came forth and did confess their sins and were baptized unto repentance, and immediately returned to the Nephites to endeavor to repair unto them the wrongs which they had done.
>
> And it came to pass that Nephi and Lehi did preach unto the Lamanites with such great power and authority, for they had power and authority given unto them that they might speak, and they also had what they should speak given unto them—
>
> Therefore they did speak unto the great astonishment of the Lamanites, to the convincing them, insomuch that there were eight thousand of the Lamanites who were in the land of Zarahemla and round about baptized unto repentance, and were convinced of the wickedness of the traditions of their fathers. (Helaman 5:17–19.)

FAITH IN JESUS CHRIST

Nephi and Lehi carried their missionary zeal into the land of Nephi, where dwelt a hardened core of the Lamanites. There they were cast into prison. There follows an account of how the unshakable faith in Jesus Christ of Nephi and Lehi resulted in the enduring conversion of these Lamanites who witnessed the miraculous events that unfolded. Encircled as if by fire after suffering days without food, these missionaries observed that the Lamanites were afraid to carry out their plan to slay them. Their hearts took courage and they began to speak, saying:

> Fear not, . . . it is God that has shown unto you this marvelous thing, in the which is shown unto you that ye cannot lay your hands on us to slay us.

. . . When they had said these words, the earth shook exceedingly, and the walls of the prison did shake as if they were about
to tumble to the earth; but behold, they did not fall. And behold,
they that were in the prison were Lamanites and Nephites who
were dissenters.

. . . They were overshadowed with a cloud of darkness, and an
awful solemn fear came upon them.

And it came to pass that there came a voice as if it were above
the cloud of darkness, saying: Repent ye, repent ye, and seek no
more to destroy my servants whom I have sent unto you to declare
good tidings.

. . . They heard this voice, and beheld that it was not a voice of
thunder, neither was it a voice of a great tumultuous noise, but behold, it was a still voice of perfect mildness, as if it had been a whisper, and it did pierce even to the very soul. (Helaman 5:26–30.)

The trembling of the earth and prison increased, and the
voice continued to teach unspeakable truths. The Lamanites
could not flee because of the intense darkness that surrounded
them. They were paralyzed with fear. Aminadab, a former
Nephite who had dissented from the Church, was moved to repentance. He interpreted the miraculous events to the others as
Nephi and Lehi conversed with angels. The others pleaded for
release, and Aminadab responded:

You must repent, and cry unto the voice, even until ye shall have
faith in Christ, who was taught unto you by Alma, and Amulek,
and Zeezrom; and when ye shall do this, the cloud of darkness
shall be removed from overshadowing you.

And it came to pass that they all did begin to cry unto the
voice of him who had shaken the earth; yea, they did cry even
until the cloud of darkness was dispersed.

. . . They saw that they were encircled about, yea every soul,
by a pillar of fire.

And Nephi and Lehi were in the midst of them; yea, they were
encircled about; yea, they were as if in the midst of a flaming fire,
yet it did harm them not, neither did it take hold upon the walls of
the prison; and they were filled with that joy which is unspeakable
and full of glory.

And behold, the Holy Spirit of God did come down from
heaven, and did enter into their hearts, and they were filled as if
with fire, and they could speak forth marvelous words.

And it came to pass that there came a voice unto them, yea, a pleasant voice, as if it were a whisper, saying:

Peace, peace be unto you, because of your faith in my Well Beloved, who was from the foundation of the world.

And now, when they heard this they cast up their eyes as if to behold from whence the voice came; and behold, they saw the heavens open; and angels came down out of heaven and ministered unto them.

And there were about three hundred souls who saw and heard these things; and they were bidden to go forth and marvel not, neither should they doubt.

And it came to pass that they did go forth, and did minister unto the people, declaring throughout all the regions round about all the things which they had heard and seen, insomuch that the more part of the Lamanites were convinced of them, because of the greatness of the evidences which they had received. (Helaman 5:41–50.)

The miraculous events that occurred in this prison came from the faith these servants had in Jesus Christ, and the prompting of the Spirit to them. The result was in the fulfillment of the will of the Lord. The exercise of faith in Jesus Christ does not always result in miracles. However, it invariably brings inspiration and power to the individual who, through righteousness and obedience, qualifies for those blessings. Obedience and faith in the Savior result in quiet miracles of change, helping those who practice the teachings of the Savior to gain a fulness of life and be effective in helping others enjoy similar blessings.

Nephi came to recognize that political office, even that of chief judge, would not be as powerful as the word of God in counteracting the corruption, injustice, and evil that plagued his nation. So he left that office and spent the rest of his life in the difficult but vital labor of moving from place to place among the Lamanites and Nephites, testifying of their wickedness and of the redeeming power of the gospel of Jesus Christ. He grew in stature and capacity while steadfastly facing the terribly difficult task of bearing witness to a rebellious generation.

He spoke with power and clarity, unmistakably singling out transgression, falsehood, iniquity, and corruption. Yet his genuine concern for the souls of the wicked, and his sincere desire to save them from the consequences of their disobedience of

God's commandments, led him to pour out his heart to Father in Heaven for their benefit. His compassion was a powerful, motivating influence in his continuing ability to face seemingly overwhelming odds in his prophetic ministry.

He identified those things which take men from the path of truth and happiness, as illustrated by these scriptures:

> The devil has got so great hold upon your hearts.
>
> Yea, how could you have given way to the enticing of him who is seeking to hurl away your souls down to everlasting misery and endless wo?
>
> O repent ye, repent ye! Why will ye die? Turn ye, turn ye unto the Lord your God. . . .
>
> O, how could you have forgotten your God in the very day that he has delivered you?
>
> . . . It is to get gain, to be praised of men, yea, and that ye might get gold and silver. And ye have set your hearts upon the riches and the vain things of this world. . . .
>
> And for this cause wo shall come unto you except ye shall repent. . . .
>
> Yea, wo shall come unto you because of that pride which ye have suffered to enter your hearts, which has lifted you up beyond that which is good because of your exceedingly great riches!
>
> Yea, wo be unto you because of your wickedness and abominations!
>
> And except ye repent ye shall perish; yea, even your lands shall be taken from you, and ye shall be destroyed from off the face of the earth. (Helaman 7:15–17, 20–22, 26–28.)

Then, in the humility of a true prophet:

> I do not say that these things shall be, of myself, . . . but behold, I know that these things are true because the Lord God has made them known unto me, therefore I testify that they shall be (Helaman 7:29).

As is ever the case, the evil leaders among the people sought to stir up anger by using craftily phrased false accusations against a righteous man who spoke the truth. Although threatened, Nephi continued to speak as directed by the Holy Spirit, declaring that the chief judge had been murdered by his brother. That accusation led to a series of events that caused five men who had believed Nephi's words to be cast in prison and accused of murdering the chief judge. Nephi was also sought as an accomplice. While staunchly defended by the five converts, he was nonetheless bound and brought before the multitude. Further inspiration came to Nephi. While directly rebuking the evil leaders, he declared who murdered the chief judge and how to confirm it. Through pure inspiration resulting from his faith, righteousness, and obedience, he was led in what to say. The true murderer of the chief judge, Seezoram—his brother, Seantum—confessed. Nephi's fearless defense of truth and his confrontation with the forces of iniquity gained many believers who recognized him as a prophet. Some even felt he was a god, for he could read the thoughts of their hearts.

The Book of Mormon then teaches a most impressive lesson concerning how we can learn truth: "And it came to pass that Nephi went his way towards his own house, pondering upon the things which the Lord had shown unto him" (Helaman 10:2). As is characteristically the case, that pondering opened a channel of communication that brought additional understanding and truth to Nephi. In this particular instance, because of Nephi's valiant testimony it allowed the Lord to confer upon him the sealing power. He later used that power to bring many of the Nephites and Lamanites to repentance and salvation.

And it came to pass as he was thus pondering in his heart, behold, a voice came unto him saying:

Blessed art thou, Nephi, for those things which thou hast done; for I have beheld how thou hast with unwearyingness declared the word, which I have given unto thee, unto this people. And thou hast not feared them, and hast not sought thine own life, but *hast sought my will, and to keep my commandments.*

And now, because thou hast done this with such unwearyingness, behold, I will bless thee forever; and I will make thee mighty in word and in deed, in faith and in works; yea, even that all things shall be done unto thee according to thy word, for thou shalt not ask that which is contrary to my will. . . .

Behold, I give unto you power, that whatsoever ye shall seal on earth shall be sealed in heaven; and whatsoever ye shall loose on earth shall be loosed in heaven. (Helaman 10:3–5, 7; emphasis added.)

The singular strength of Nephi's character is revealed by how he responded to the singular blessings which came because Nephi was willing to subject his will to the will of his Father and because of his determination to keep the commandments of God. The Lord clarified that He could trust Nephi with this extraordinary power because he would not ask that which was contrary to His will. That is, he would use the power only as directed by the Spirit. The next verse depicts the extraordinary, willing obedience of Nephi at a time when his life had been threatened; he had been bound, been falsely accused, and suffered enough to have certainly earned a rest:

> And now behold, I command you, that ye shall go and declare unto this people, that thus saith the Lord God, who is the Almighty: Except ye repent ye shall be smitten, even unto destruction.
>
> And behold, now it came to pass that when the Lord had spoken these words unto Nephi, *he did stop and did not go unto his own house, but did return* unto the multitudes who were scattered about upon the face of the land, and began to declare unto them the word of the Lord which had been spoken unto him, concerning their destruction if they did not repent. (Helaman 10:11–12; emphasis added.)

Oh, that we could be that obedient, setting aside our own convenience, when necessary, for the benefit of others!

Thus began another series of Nephi's valiant missionary efforts, with the obedient testifying of truth against a hardened nation that rejected him, caused him great suffering, and even sought to take his life. Conditions worsened and there was great bloodshed among the people that became more aggravated over a two-year period. Nephi was prompted to plead for the people, saying: "O Lord, do not suffer that this people shall be destroyed by the sword; but O Lord, rather let there be a famine in the land, to stir them up in remembrance of the Lord their God, and perhaps they will repent and turn unto thee. And so it was done, according to the words of Nephi. And there was a great famine upon the land, among all the people of Nephi. . . . And the work of destruction did cease by the sword but became sore by famine." (Helaman 11:4–5.)

The severe famine continued for two more years, affecting all the Lamanites and the Nephites, including Nephi. The greatest loss of life, however, was among the more wicked part of the people. Then "the people saw that they were about to perish by famine, and they began to remember the Lord their God; and they began to remember the words of Nephi. And the people began to plead with their chief judges and their leaders, that they would say unto Nephi: Behold, we know that thou art a man of God, and therefore cry unto the Lord our God that he turn away from us this famine, lest all the words which thou hast spoken concerning our destruction be fulfilled." (Helaman 11:7–8.)

Observing that the remaining people had repented and were humbled in sackcloth, Nephi went before the Lord, saying:

> O Lord, behold this people repenteth; and they have swept away the band of Gadianton from amongst them insomuch that they have become extinct, and they have concealed their secret plans in the earth.
>
> Now, O Lord, because of this their humility wilt thou . . . let thine anger be appeased in the destruction of those wicked men whom thou hast already destroyed. . . .
>
> . . . And cause that this famine may cease in this land. . . .
>
> . . . Send forth rain upon the face of the earth, that she may bring forth her fruit, and her grain in the season of grain.
>
> O Lord, thou didst hearken unto my words when I said, Let there be a famine, that the pestilence of the sword might cease; and I know that thou wilt, even at this time, hearken unto my words, for thou saidst that: If this people repent I will spare them. (Helaman 11:10–14.)

The Lord heard His servant's supplication and caused the famine to cease, but not until the following year. This event illustrates that the Lord hears our pleas immediately but then answers when, in His wisdom, we will benefit the most from His response.

> The Lord did turn away his anger from the people, and caused that rain should fall upon the earth, insomuch that it did bring forth her fruit in the season of her fruit. And it came to pass that it did bring forth her grain in the season of her grain.

> And behold, the people did rejoice and glorify God, and the whole face of the land was filled with rejoicing; and they did no more seek to destroy Nephi, but they did esteem him as a great prophet, and a man of God, having great power and authority given unto him from God. (Helaman 11:17–18.)

Nephi continued throughout the remainder of his life to teach courageously the truth. There was a four-year period of peace and then, because of disobedience, the return of suffering and death from transgression.

UNWAVERING OBEDIENCE

The hallmark of the life of this wonderful prophet Nephi was his unwavering obedience to the commandments of God. That consistent willingness to subject his personal desires to the will of the Lord and to conform his life to sacred truth made him a powerful, productive source of help to others, immensely enriching their lives. His life was made most worthwhile under singularly negative circumstances. This valiant prophet was greatly regarded by the righteous people and unusually blessed by the Lord. He may have been taken home in a special way, as these passages suggest:

> And Nephi, the son of Helaman, had departed out of the land of Zarahemla, giving charge unto his son Nephi . . . concerning the plates of brass, and all the records which had been kept, and all those things which had been kept sacred from the departure of Lehi out of Jerusalem. . . . And whither he went, no man knoweth. (3 Nephi 1:2–3.)

> [He] did not return to the land of Zarahemla, and could nowhere be found in all the land" (3 Nephi 2:9).

Nephi lived in a time of tremendous upheaval and dissension when morals and standards were abandoned, government had disintegrated, and Gadianton robbers ruled the land, yet he remained faithful and engendered faith in others willing to hear the message of Jesus Christ. He taught with power. He was fearless in proclaiming truth no matter what opposition he encountered. When Satan applied more pressure he became more determined in living and acting righteously. He perfected his ability to be led by the Spirit and followed its direction without hesitation. His fearlessness came from a righteous heart. He possessed great humility and compassion. He blessed others with a knowledge of truth. His total faith in Jesus Christ allowed him to be protected and empowered to do good. He taught us how to pray for an answer when we urgently need it. He showed those who hold the priesthood how to exercise that sacred authority properly.

In describing this period, Mormon crystallized the effect of righteous teaching on the people in this way:

> Thus we may see that the Lord is merciful unto all who will, in the sincerity of their hearts, call upon his holy name.
>
> Yea, thus we see that the gate of heaven is open unto all, even to those who will believe on the name of Jesus Christ. . . .
>
> Yea, we see that whosoever will may lay hold upon the word of God, which is quick and powerful, which shall divide asunder all the cunning and the snares and the wiles of the devil, and lead the man of Christ in a strait and narrow course across that everlasting gulf of misery which is prepared to engulf the wicked. (Helaman 3:27–29.)

I love this prophet. I humbly testify that Nephi's greatness came from his humility, his unflinching obedience, and his firmly rooted faith in Jesus the Christ. When truth was taught, he listened carefully and obeyed it consistently. May our study and pondering of the example of this admirable servant of the Lord enrich us with a desire to be more submissive when tested, more obedient when tempted, more forgiving when falsely accused, and more resolute in our faith in the Master.

15

Elder Andrew W. Peterson

Samuel the Lamanite

For me, one of the great exclamation points in the Book of Mormon is the story of Samuel the Lamanite! We read about Samuel in the book of Helaman, chapters 13 to 16.

Who was Samuel? In the *Encyclopedia of Mormonism* we read:

> Samuel the Lamanite was the only Book of Mormon prophet identified as a Lamanite. Apart from his sermon at Zarahemla (Helaman 13–15), no other record of his life or ministry is preserved. . . .
>
> Approximately five years before Jesus' birth, Samuel began to preach repentance in Zarahemla. After the incensed Nephite inhabitants expelled him, the voice of the Lord directed him to return. Climbing to the top of the city wall, he delivered his message unharmed, even though certain citizens sought his life (Helaman 16:2). Thereafter, he fled and "was never heard of more among the Nephites" (Helaman 16:8). (*Encyclopedia of Mormonism*, s.v. "Samuel the Lamanite.")

The prophet Mormon, who lived near the close of the Book of Mormon time line of a thousand years, was commanded to abridge and compile the records. Guided by the Spirit, Mormon chose what would be included. He said, "But behold, a hundredth part of the proceedings of this people, yea, the account of the Lamanites and of the Nephites, and their wars, and contentions, and dissensions, and their preaching, and their prophecies, and their shipping and their building of ships, and their building of temples, and of synagogues and their sanctuaries, and their righteousness, and their wickedness, and their murders, and their robbings, and their plundering, and all manner of abominations and whoredoms, cannot be contained in this work" (Helaman 3:14).

As Mormon abridged the records and finalized what would be preserved, he did so knowing that it would bless future generations. Mormon was impressed that the record and prophecies of Samuel the Lamanite needed to be included.

Samuel the Lamanite is "noted chiefly for his prophecies about the birth of Jesus Christ, [and] his prophetic words, which were later examined, commended, and updated by the risen Jesus (3 Nephi 23:9–13), were recorded by persons who accepted him as a true prophet and even faced losing their lives for believing his message (3 Nephi 1:9)." (*Encyclopedia of Mormonism,* s.v. "Samuel the Lamanite.")

Careful study of chapters 13–15 of Helaman provides powerful points of doctrine to ponder. As we study them, let us ask ourselves these questions: Why are these chapters included in the Book of Mormon? What principles do we learn from them? How will we implement and live these principles so as to bless lives and be obediently focused?

May I share three thoughts, upon which I will elaborate in the sections that follow:

1. Whate'er Thou Art, Act Well Thy Part
2. Daily Walls to Climb
3. Following Living Prophets

WHATE'ER THOU ART, ACT WELL THY PART

These words inspired President David O. McKay while serving as a missionary in Scotland. He said:

Peter G. Johnson and I were walking around Stirling Castle in Scotland. I was discouraged, I was just starting my first mission. I had been snubbed that day in tracting. I was homesick, and we walked around the Stirling Castle, really not doing our duty, and as we re-entered the town I saw a building, half-finished, and to my surprise, from the sidewalk I saw an inscription over the lintel of the front door, carved in stone. I said to Brother Johnson, "I want to go over and see what that is." I was not more than half way up the pathway leading to it, when that message struck me, carved there: "What e'er thou art, act well thy part." As I rejoined my companion and told him, do you know what man came into my mind first? The custodian at the University of Utah, from which I was just graduated. I realized that I had as great a respect for that man as I had for any professor in whose class I had sat. He acted well his part. I recalled how he helped us with the football suits, how he helped us with some of our lessons, for he was a university graduate himself. Humble, but to this day I hold respect for him. (In Conference Report, October 1954, p. 83.)

Samuel teaches us likewise to do our best. His name is a powerful reminder. Samuel humbly refers to himself as Samuel *a* Lamanite (see Helaman 13:5). But other references refer to him as Samuel *the* Lamanite (see Helaman 14:1; 16:1; 3 Nephi 1:5; 23:9). Perhaps he achieved this title prior to his ministry to the Nephites. A great work of conversion had occurred among the Lamanites. Samuel's influence may have been so profound that even among his people he was called Samuel the Lamanite. Perhaps Mormon, in reading through the records, was so impressed with a Lamanite called of God by an angel, fearless and determined to fulfill his calling, worthy of communicating the word of God as it was revealed to his mind and heart, that he titled this prophet Samuel the Lamanite. We do not know, nor is it important. But we can apply the principle in our lives that touched President McKay and elevated Samuel to *the* Lamanite.

Whatever we want to do, or are called to do, we should strive to do to the best of our ability. Whether it be "within the walls of our own home" as President Harold B. Lee taught (in Conference Report, April 1973, p. 130), at our place of employment, pursuing our educational goals, fulfilling a Church calling, or rendering service within the community, Samuel reminds us that we should do our best.

Suppose our Church calling is as an elder's quorum president or as a counselor in a ward Primary presidency. Rather than striving to be remembered as John, an elder's quorum president, or Jane, a Primary counselor, we are inspired by Samuel's words to remember the Savior's invitation proffered to the

Nephites forty years after Samuel prophesied on Zarahemla's city wall: "Therefore, what manner of men ought ye to be? Verily I say unto you, even as I am." (3 Nephi 27:27.) Here is the ultimate invitation to "act well thy part."

DAILY WALLS TO CLIMB

"But behold, the voice of the Lord came unto him, that he should return again, and prophesy unto the people whatsoever things should come into his heart. And it came to pass that they would not suffer that he should enter into the city; therefore he went and got upon the wall thereof, and stretched forth his hand and cried with a loud voice, and prophesied unto the people whatsoever things the Lord put into his heart." (Helaman 13:3–4.)

Samuel bravely delivered his message! When denied entrance to Zarahemla he climbed upon the wall of the city. Perhaps he was familiar with the story of Nephi and the brass plates (see Alma 18:36–38; 63:11–12). Nephi said unto his father: "I will go and do the things which the Lord hath commanded, for I know that the Lord giveth no commandments unto the children of men, save he shall prepare a way for them that they may accomplish the thing which he commandeth them" (1 Nephi 3:7). "And I was led by the Spirit, not knowing beforehand the things which I should do. Nevertheless I went forth." (1 Nephi 4:6.) Likewise, Samuel went forth and found his way upon the wall.

There are daily walls to climb in our own lives. They present themselves most often as invitations for growth: the daily challenges of parenting, a difficult assignment at work, a new calling in the Church, a sacrament meeting or stake conference talk to present, a lesson to be given in priesthood meeting or Relief Society.

I well remember my first morning of tracting as a new missionary in Cordoba, Argentina. My senior companion knocked on the first door and presented, what seemed to me, a very impressive door approach in fluent Spanish. The next door was mine! The walls of Zarahemla could not have seemed any higher than the short distance from the sidewalk to the front door. In spite of my limited Spanish, my faith, prayers, and a desire to learn and obey sustained me as I "climbed upon my wall" that morning.

When temptations present themselves, as surely they do, we must climb upon the daily walls of life and learn to say no.

No! When tempted to break the Word of Wisdom.

No! When tempted to break the law of chastity.

No! When tempted to be dishonest.

No! When tempted by pornography, questionable videos, movies, or music.

No! When tempted to pay less than a full tithing.

And so on.

Soon, as we stand upon the walls of solid fundamental gospel principles and look temptation in the eye and say "No!" it will become easier and easier to stand firm, and "virtue [will] garnish [our] thoughts unceasingly; then shall [our] confidence wax strong in the presence of God; and the doctrine of the priesthood shall distil upon [our] soul as the dews from heaven" (D&C 121:45).

As we climb our daily walls, Samuel the Lamanite teaches us to not fear: "But as many as there were who did not believe in the words of Samuel were angry with him; and they cast stones at him upon the wall, and also many shot arrows at him as he stood upon the wall; but the Spirit of the Lord was with him, insomuch that they could not hit him with their stones neither with their arrows" (Helaman 16:2).

Our own modern-day living prophet and president, Gordon B. Hinckley, likewise teaches us not to fear. He has said, "We have nothing to fear. God is at the helm. He will overrule for the good of this work. He will shower down blessings upon those who walk in obedience to His commandments. Such has been His promise. Of His ability to keep that promise none of us can doubt." ("This Is the Work of the Master," *Ensign,* May 1995, p. 71.)

FOLLOWING LIVING PROPHETS

In abridging the records of the Nephites, Mormon has blessed us with historical insight into the Book of Mormon as to the importance of living prophets. Such is the case with Samuel the Lamanite.

As the book of Alma closes, a great war has ended between the Lamanites and the Nephites (see Alma 62). Captain Moroni turns command of the Nephite army over to his son, Moronihah. Pahoran, the chief judge, returns to the judgment seat. And Helaman, the son of Alma the Younger, returns to teaching the gospel and administering the affairs of the Church throughout the land.

> Therefore, Helaman and his brethren went forth, and did declare the word of God with much power unto the convincing of many people of their wickedness, which did cause them to repent of their sins and to be baptized unto the Lord their God.
>
> And it came to pass that they did establish again the church of God, throughout all the land.
>
> Yea, and regulations were made concerning the law. And their judges, and their chief judges were chosen.
>
> And the people of Nephi began to prosper again in the land, and began to multiply and to wax exceedingly strong again in the land. And they began to grow exceedingly rich.
>
> But notwithstanding their riches, or their strength, or their prosperity, they were not lifted up in the pride of their eyes; neither were they slow to remember the Lord their God; but they did humble themselves exceedingly before him.
>
> Yea, they did remember how great things the Lord had done for them, that he had delivered them from death, and from bonds, and from prisons, and from all manner of afflictions, and he had delivered them out of the hands of their enemies.
>
> And they did pray unto the Lord their God continually, insomuch that the Lord did bless them, according to his word, so that they did wax strong and prosper in the land. (Alma 62:45–51.)

These events happened after the year 60 B.C. Fifty-four years later, in 6 B.C., Samuel the Lamanite climbed on top of the walls of Zarahemla. There would not have been a need for Samuel to do this if the Nephites had continued in their remembrance of the Lord, following the words of the prophets.

Fifty-four years earlier:

— "They were not lifted up in the pride of their eyes."
— "Neither were they slow to remember the Lord."
— "They did humble themselves."

—"They did remember how great things the Lord had done for them."

—"They did pray unto the Lord their God continually."

—"The Lord did bless them . . . so that they did wax strong and prosper."

Is there application in these teachings for us today?

Samuel delivered the message the Lord put in his heart (see Helaman 13:3). He said to the Nephites of Zarahemla:

> Behold ye, the people of this great city, and hearken unto my words; yea, hearken unto the words which the Lord saith; for behold, he saith that ye are cursed because of your riches, and also are your riches cursed because ye have set your hearts upon them, and have not hearkened unto the words of him who gave them unto you.
>
> Ye do not remember the Lord your God in the things with which he hath blessed you, but ye do always remember your riches, not to thank the Lord your God for them; yea, your hearts are not drawn out unto the Lord, but they do swell with great pride, unto boasting, and unto great swelling, envyings, strifes, malice, persecutions, and murders, and all manner of iniquities.
>
> For this cause hath the Lord God caused that a curse should come upon the land, and also upon your riches, and this because of your iniquities.
>
> Yea, wo unto this people, because of this time which has arrived, that ye do cast out the prophets, and do mock them, and cast stones at them, and do slay them, and do all manner of iniquity unto them, even as they did of old time.
>
> And now when ye talk, ye say: If our days had been in the days of our fathers of old, we would not have slain the prophets; we would not have stoned them, and cast them out.
>
> Behold ye are worse than they; for as the Lord liveth, if a prophet come among you and declareth unto you the word of the Lord, which testifieth of your sins and iniquities, ye are angry with him, and cast him out and seek all manner of ways to destroy him; yea, you will say that he is a false prophet, and that he is a sinner, and of the devil, because he testifieth that your deeds are evil.
>
> But behold, if a man shall come among you and shall say: Do this, and there is no iniquity; do that and ye shall not suffer; yea, he will say: Walk after the pride of your own hearts; yea, walk after the pride of your eyes, and do whatsoever your heart desireth—and if

a man shall come among you and say this, ye will receive him, and say that he is a prophet. (Helaman 13:21–27.)

What a stirring reminder to the Nephites, and to us, about appropriate regard for prophets and their timely inspired invitations and exhortations!

Samuel the Lamanite strongly reminded the Nephites that they had become casual and neglectful in living basic principles of the gospel. Living prophets of our dispensation have likewise reminded us to be firm and steady in the faith (see Helaman 6:1).

Samuel said, "Ye do not remember the Lord your God in the things with which he hath blessed you" (Helaman 13:22). President John Taylor said, "Do you have prayers in your family? . . . And when you do, do you go through the operation like the grinding of a piece of machinery, or do you bow in meekness and with a sincere desire to seek the blessing of God upon you and your household? That is the way that we ought to do, and cultivate a spirit of devotion and trust in God, dedicating ourselves to him, and seeking his blessings." (*The Gospel Kingdom*, sel. G. Homer Durham [Salt Lake City: Bookcraft, 1943], p. 284.)

Samuel said, "Ye do always remember your riches" (Helaman 13:22). President Marion G. Romney said, "Tithing is a debt which everyone owes to the Lord for his use of the things that the Lord has made and given to him to use. It is a debt just as literally as the grocery bill, or a light bill, or any other duly incurred obligation. As a matter of fact, the Lord, to whom one owes tithing, is in a position of a preferred creditor. If there is not enough to pay all creditors, he should be paid first. Now I am sure you will have a little shock at that, but that is the truth. Other creditors of tithe-payers, however, need to have no cause to worry, for the Lord always blesses the person who has faith enough to pay his tithing so that his ability to pay his other creditors is not thereby reduced." (Marion G. Romney, *The Blessings of an Honest Tithe*, Brigham Young University Speeches of the Year [Provo, Utah, 5 November 1968], p. 4.)

Samuel said, "Your hearts are not drawn out unto the Lord, but they do swell with great pride" (Helaman 13:22). President Ezra Taft Benson said, "Pride is the universal sin, the great vice. . . . It was essentially the sin of pride that kept us from establishing Zion in the days of the Prophet Joseph Smith. It was the same sin of pride that brought consecration to an end among the Nephites. Pride is the great stumbling block to Zion. I repeat: Pride *is* the great stumbling block to Zion." (In Conference Report, April 1989, pp. 6, 7; emphasis in original.)

As a prophet, Samuel the Lamanite predicted:

> And four hundred years shall not pass away before I will cause that they shall be smitten; yea, I will visit them with the sword and with famine and with pestilence.
>
> Yea, I will visit them in my fierce anger, and there shall be those of the fourth generation who shall live, of your enemies, to behold your utter destruction; and this shall surely come except ye repent, saith the Lord; and those of the fourth generation shall visit your destruction. (Helaman 13:9–10.)

Mormon saw the literal fulfillment of this prophecy given by a living prophet of earlier times:

> Behold, four hundred years have passed away since the coming of our Lord and Savior.
>
> And behold, the Lamanites have hunted my people, the Nephites, down from city to city and from place to place, even until they are no more; and great has been their fall; yea, great and marvelous is the destruction of my people, the Nephites. (Mormon 8:6–7.)

The story of Samuel the Lamanite, a living prophet in the eighty-sixth year of the reign of the judges (6 B.C.), in full context of the Book of Mormon teaches us the importance of listening to and obeying living prophets.

Listen to what President Harold B. Lee said about following living prophets:

> When the Church was first organized, in fact, the day on which it was organized, the Lord was speaking to the Church. He didn't mean just the six members that were then the constituted number of the Church: he was speaking about the President of the Church, who was the Prophet Joseph Smith at that time. And this is what he said [cites D&C 21:4–6].
>
> We have some tight places to go before the Lord is through with this church and the world in this dispensation, which is the

last dispensation, which shall usher in the coming of the Lord. The gospel was restored to prepare a people ready to receive him. The power of Satan will increase; we see it in evidence on every hand. There will be inroads within the Church. There will be, as President Tanner has said, "Hypocrites, those professing, but secretly are full of dead men's bones." We will see those who profess membership but secretly are plotting and trying to lead people not to follow the leadership that the Lord has set up to preside in this church.

Now the only safety we have as members of this church is to do exactly what the Lord said to the Church in that day when the Church was organized. We must learn to give heed to the words and commandments that the Lord shall give through his prophet, "as he receiveth them, walking in all holiness before me; . . . as if from mine own mouth, in all patience and faith." (D&C 21:4–5.) There will be some things that take patience and faith. You may not like what comes from the authority of the Church. It may contradict your social views. It may interfere with some of your social life. But if you listen to these things, as if from the mouth of the Lord himself, with patience and faith, the promise is that "the gates of hell shall not prevail against you; yea, and the Lord God will disperse the powers of darkness from before you, and cause the heavens to shake for your good, and his name's glory." (D&C 21:6.) (In Conference Report, October 1970, p. 152.)

Further we read, in the Conference Report of October 1897, the words of President Wilford Woodruff:

I will refer to a certain meeting I attended in the town of Kirtland in my early days. At that meeting some remarks were made that have been made here today, with regard to the living oracles and with regard to the written word of God. The same principle was presented, although not as extensively as it has been here, when a leading man in the Church got up and talked upon the subject, and said: "You have got the word of God before you here in the Bible, Book of Mormon, and Doctrine and Covenants; you have the written word of God, and you who give revelations should give revelations according to those books, as what is written in those books is the word of God. We should confine ourselves to them." When he concluded, Brother Joseph turned to Brother Brigham and said, "Brother Brigham I want you to take the stand and tell us your views with regard to the written oracles and the written word of God." Brother Brigham took the stand, and he took the Bible, and laid it down; he took the Book of Mormon, and laid it down; and he took the Book of Doctrine and Covenants, and laid it down before him, and he said: "There is the written word of God to us, concerning the work of God from the beginning of the world, almost, to our day." "And now," said he, "when compared with the living oracles those books are nothing to me; those books do not convey the word of God direct to us now, as do the words of a Prophet or a man bearing the Holy Priesthood in our day and generation. *I would rather have the living oracles than all the writing in the books.*" That was the course he pursued. When he was through, Brother Joseph said to the congregation: *"Brother Brigham has told you the word of the Lord, and he has told you the truth."* (In Conference Report, October 1897, pp. 22–23; emphasis added.)

I am grateful for Samuel the Lamanite, a great exclamation point in the Book of Mormon! May his example and his words inspire us to act upon proven principles of righteousness.

16

Elder Spencer J. Condie

Mormon: Historian, General, Man of God

If ever there lived a person who resisted and withstood the evil influence of a depraved world to become a worthy servant of the Lord, this person was Mormon. He was named after his father and after the land of Mormon, where Alma had baptized his flock of newly converted Saints in the waters of Mormon (see Mormon 1:5; 3 Nephi 5:12; Mosiah 18:4–9). Except for one respite of four years and another period of ten years of peace, most of Mormon's life was lived against a background of unrelenting bloodshed and preparation for war (see Mormon 1:12; 3:1).

It is not uncomon for children who are robbed of their carefree youth and adolescence by an environment of wickedness, such as that experienced by Mormon, to quickly mature beyond their years. Ammaron, the Nephite record-keeper, perceived ten-year-old Mormon to be "a sober child" who was "quick to observe" (Mormon 1:2). Thus, Ammaron gave him the charge to go to the land of Antum when he became twenty-four years old, and there in a hill called Shim he was to retrieve the sacred plates containing the record of his people.

When Mormon was eleven his family moved to Zarahemla just as preparations were being made for a war against the Lamanites. After a series of raging battles, "peace settled in the land" for about four years (Mormon 1:12). It was during this pause in warfare, at age fifteen, that Mormon "was visited of the Lord, and tasted and knew of the goodness of Jesus" (Mormon 1:15).

Much like young Joseph Smith after his experience in the Sacred Grove, Mormon "did endeavor to preach" and to share his wondrous spiritual experiences, but he "was forbidden to preach unto them, because of the hardness of their hearts" (Mormon 1:16–17).

Mormon, like Nephi from whom he descended, was large in stature, and at a time when the innocence of youth was lost in war, at age fifteen he was called upon to lead all the armies of the Nephites (see Mormon 2:1–2). Their enemies were not confined to the traditional foe, the Lamanites, but also included the Gadianton robbers among the Lamanites (see Mormon 1:18; 2:8).

Eventually, for a brief moment in history, "the Nephites began to repent of their iniquity" (Mormon 2:10), and as Mormon saw their mourning his heart rejoiced, assuming "that they would again become a righteous people" (Mormon 2:12). But his joy was short-lived, as closer observation revealed that "their sorrowing was not unto repentance" but rather resulted because the Lord would not allow them "to take happiness in sin" (Mormon 2:13; see also Alma 41:10; Helaman 13:38). Mormon added that "my heart has been filled with sorrow because of their wickedness, *all my days*" (Mormon 2:19; emphasis added).

Notwithstanding an occasional victory on the battlefield, Mormon sadly acknowledged that "the strength of the Lord was not with us; yea, we were left to ourselves . . . therefore we had become weak like unto our brethren" (Mormon 2:26).

In A.D. 350 a treaty was reached with the Lamanites, and for the next ten years there was peace in the land. It was perhaps during this decade, when Mormon was in his forties, that he was able to do a large part of the extensive editing of the plates he recovered from the hill Shim.

This challenging abridgement of all the plates from Mosiah through the book bearing his own name covered a period of five centuries. To link the small plates of Nephi to his own abridgement of the subsequent record, he inserted "The Words of Mormon," in which he expressed some degree of frustration that he could not write "the hundredth part" of the things of his people (Words of Mormon 1:5; see also Jacob 3:13; Helaman 3:14; 3 Nephi 5:8; 26:6).

With such rigorous editing, Mormon's imprint is felt throughout his entire abridgement. And yet it is obvious that he did not superimpose his own writing style on the various books he abridged. Sophisticated computer-assisted statistical analysis of the unique phrases used by different authors conclusively demonstrates the multiple authorship of the Book of Mormon (see Wayne A. Larsen and Alvin C. Rencher, "Who Wrote the Book of Mormon? An Analysis of Wordprints," in *Book of Mormon Authorship: New Light on Ancient Origins,* ed. Noel B. Reynolds and Charles D. Tate [Provo, Utah: Brigham Young University Religious Studies Center, 1982], pp. 157–88). Nor did Mormon's extensive editing obfuscate the chiastic style of writing used by various authors of the books contained in the complete work. A chiasm is a form of inverted, symmetrical parallelism found in such passages as 1 Nephi 15:9–11; 1 Nephi 17:36–39; 2 Nephi 25:24–27; 2 Nephi 29:13; Mosiah 3:18–19; Mosiah 5:10–12; Alma 36; and Alma 41:13–15. Notwithstanding extensive abridgement, many of these precious passages have remained in the characteristic form of the chiasmus. (See John W. Welch, "Chiasmus in the Book of Mormon," *New Era,* February 1972, pp. 6–11; Welch, "A Book You Can Respect," *Ensign,* September 1977, pp. 45–48; Welch, "Chiasmus in the Book of Mormon," in *Book of Mormon Authorship,* ed. Reynolds and Tate, pp. 33–52. See also Noel B. Reynolds, "Nephi's Outline," in *Book of Mormon Authorship,* pp. 53–74.)

THIRD NEPHI

Of all the books between and including Mosiah and Mormon, the editing impress of Mormon is perhaps the greatest in the sacred writings of 3 Nephi. Mormon discloses his identity in four different verses throughout this particular book (see 3 Nephi 5:12, 20; 26:12; 28:24), which contains the account of the Savior's visit to the ancient Nephites and His instruction to them. Twice Moroni bemoans the fact that not even "a hundredth part" of the teachings of Jesus were included in this part of the record (3 Nephi 5:8; 26:6). Nevertheless, there are truly many plain and precious parts which have been retained for our inspiration and guidance.

Prior to the Savior's appearance among the Nephites, the people heard His voice following the destruction and three days of darkness which covered the land: "Behold, I am Jesus Christ the Son of God" (3 Nephi 9:15). He taught them that He would no longer accept their sacrifices and burnt offerings, but commanded them that they should "offer for a sacrifice unto me a broken heart and a contrite spirit" (3 Nephi 9:19–20).

He then appeared to them and taught them the proper mode of baptism and the importance of receiving the Holy Ghost (see 3 Nephi 11). The Lord then delivered a sermon sharing much of the content of the Sermon on the Mount, found in Matthew chapters five through seven (see also 3 Nephi 12–14). Included in this discourse are the Beatitudes, which President Harold B. Lee described as the "constitution for a perfect life" (Harold B. Lee, *Decisions for Successful Living* [Salt Lake City: Deseret Book Co., 1973], pp. 54–62). Slight yet profound additions were made in the Book of Mormon version of the Beatitudes which greatly illuminate our understanding. The changes are italicized in these examples:

— "Yea, blessed are the poor in spirit *who come unto me,* for theirs is the kingdom of heaven" (3 Nephi 12:3; compare Matthew 5:3).

— "And blessed are all they who do hunger and thirst after righteousness, for they shall be filled *with the Holy Ghost*" (3 Nephi 12:6; compare Matthew 5:6).

The Savior testified that He is Jehovah of the Old Testament as He declared: "Behold, I am he that gave the law, and I am he who covenanted with my people Israel" (3 Nephi 15:5).

The seventeenth chapter of 3 Nephi is one of the most supernal accounts of the Savior's ministry found anywhere in the scriptures. He compassionately taught the ancient Nephites and invited them to bring forth those who were sick and afflicted, and He healed them all. In gratitude the multitude "did bathe his feet with their tears." (3 Nephi 17:9–10.) He then prayed to His Father in behalf of the house of Israel, and "the eye hath never seen, neither hath the ear heard, before, so great and marvelous things as [they] saw and heard Jesus speak unto the Father" (3 Nephi 17:14–17).

The multitude was filled with joy, and this caused the Savior Himself to weep. He then "took their little children, one by one, and blessed them," and angels descended from heaven and "encircled those little ones about, and they were encircled about with fire; and the angels did minister unto them." (3 Nephi 17:21–24.) The sublime spirit and language of this chapter eloquently testify of the Savior's love and mercy and compassion toward all of our Heavenly Father's children.

The Savior then instituted the sacrament, and after calling twelve disciples, He delegated to them the task of teaching the multitude (see 3 Nephi 18–19). Christ taught the people of the scattering and gathering of Israel, of the New Jerusalem, and of the Second Coming and the day of judgment. He further taught them the law of tithing and of the Spirit of Elijah and the turning of hearts of children to their fathers. (See 3 Nephi 20–26.) Jesus Christ also instructed them that His church should bear His name (see 3 Nephi 27:8).

He then posed the penetrating question "What manner of men ought ye to be?" answering with the high expectation: "Verily I say unto you, even as I am" (3 Nephi 27:27). Before He departed, He granted the desire of three of His disciples that they would "never taste of death" (3 Nephi 28:4–12).

Elder Jeffrey R. Holland has surmised that "it is possible that some of the passages Mormon gives us were not taken from any written record but were revealed directly to him" (Jeffrey R. Holland, "Mormon: the Man and the Book, Part 2," *Ensign*, April 1978, p. 58). This would certainly not be outside the realm of possibility for such a prophet, seer, and revelator as Mormon to clarify certain passages under inspiration, much as did the Prophet Joseph Smith during his inspired translation of the Bible.

One question often raised about Mormon's abridgement is, why is 4 Nephi such a brief book, with only four pages covering a period of 285 years? A corollary question is, if, during the first 166 years after the visit of Christ to the Nephites, "there could not be a happier people" (4 Nephi 1:16), why do we not have a much more detailed record of their recipe for righteousness?

A partial answer may be found in the fact that 3 Nephi *does* contain this recipe for righteousness. Fourth Nephi then records the natural consequences of righteousness, as "they did walk after the commandments which they had received from their Lord and their God," and "there was no contention in the land, because of the love of God which did dwell in the hearts of the people" (4 Nephi 1:3, 12, 15).

An additional explanation of Mormon's brief abridgement of the extended period of righteousness while elaborating on the gruesome details of depravity in his own record can be found in the words of Nephi, who said in an earlier era: "Behold, if ye were holy I would speak unto you of holiness; but as ye are not holy, and ye look upon me as a teacher, it must needs be expedient that I teach you the consequences of sin" (2 Nephi 9:48).

Although not even "the hundredth part" of the history of this people was contained in the final record, Mormon preserved the doctrinal richness and purity of the central doctrine of the gospel: the atonement of Jesus Christ. Virtually every prophet throughout the entire Book of Mormon taught of Christ's infinite love, compassion, and mercy, and of His great intercession in paying the price of sin upon conditions of our personal repentance (see 1 Nephi 11; 2 Nephi 2, 9; Jacob 1; Enos; Jarom; Mosiah 3–5, 15; Alma 7, 42; Helaman 5; 3 Nephi 9–15; Mormon 9; Ether 12; Moroni 7–8).

Those prophets who lived before the Savior's birth testified with great certitude, persuading the people "to look forward unto the Messiah, and believe in him to come as though he already was" (Jarom 1:11). Those prophets living after His earthly ministry testified of the reality of His divine atoning sacrifice, His death, and His resurrection, and extended the invitation to "come unto Christ, and be perfected in him" (Moroni 10:32).

It is also interesting to note certain repetitive events which Mormon included in his abridgement. One such category of events is the appearance of three anti-Christs: Sherem in circa 544–421 B.C. (see Jacob 7), Nehor in circa 91 B.C. (see Alma 1), and Korihor in 74 B.C. (see Alma 30). We can only surmise that the inclusion of at least three anti-Christs instead of only one is to underscore Satan's pervasive use of anti-Christs, with their much learning and flattery and sign-seeking. Mormon's inclusion of three different anti-Christs makes the reader much more aware and vigilant than might have been the case if only one fleeting example had been included.

An inspiring example of repetition is found in the missionary labors of Ammon and Aaron as they taught the gospel to King Lamoni and his father, respectively (see Alma 18, 22). The first three verses of Alma 17 explain that successful missionaries who desire to have "the spirit of prophecy, and the spirit of revelation" and who would teach "with power and authority of God" must search the scriptures diligently and give themselves to much prayer and fasting.

Ammon's teaching of Lamoni and Aaron's teaching of Lamoni's father are dual demonstrations of the Spirit's role in teaching the gospel. Their independent use of questions to build relationships of trust, and their bearing of powerful yet brief testimonies to resolve concerns, underscores the importance of certain tried-and-true principles of proselyting. The similarity in their messages also underscores the importance of systematically teaching the gospel "line upon line."

Still another recurrent theme throughout the entire Book of Mormon is the Lord's repeated promise that "inasmuch as ye shall keep my commandments ye shall prosper in the land" (2 Nephi 1:20; see also 1 Nephi 2:20; 4:14; 2 Nephi 1:20; 4:4; Jarom 1:9; Omni 1:6; Alma 9:13; 36:1, 30; 38:1; 50:20; Helaman 4:15).

The best explanation for justifying what was repeatedly included or excluded in Mormon's abridgement is found in his own words: "And I do this . . . according to the workings of the Spirit of the Lord which is in me" (Words of Mormon 1:7).

BACK TO THE BATTLE

Meanwhile, back on the battlefield, weary of unrelenting war, Mormon refused to continue leading his people "because of their wickedness and abomination" (Mormon 3:11). The Lord commanded him to "stand as an idle witness" of the events that transpired (Mormon 3:16). During this time of personal disengagement from warfare, Mormon shared the observation that "it is *by the wicked that the wicked are punished*" (Mormon 4:5; emphasis added).

After obtaining all the records remaining in the hill Shim for safekeeping, Mormon repented of his previous oath and agreed to once again lead the Nephite armies, though his heart was obviously not in the task (see Mormon 5:1–2). All too often in the history of the world, battles begin with certain rules and boundaries protecting the civilian population, but as hatred mounts, sheer killing, though wicked enough, gives way to additional acts of depravity. Mormon records that the Lamanites had sacrificed the Nephite women and children unto idols (see Mormon 4:15, 21).

Somewhat apologetic for depicting "an awful scene of blood and carnage," Mormon explained that he dared not "give a full account . . . that ye might not have too great sorrow because of the wickedness of this people" (Mormon 5:8–9).

Mormon lamented the fact that his people "were once a delightsome people, and they had Christ for their shepherd" (Mormon 5:17). As the end drew near and the Nephite battalions fell by the tens of thousands, Mormon cried in eloquent anguish: "O ye fair ones, how could ye have departed from the ways of the Lord! O ye fair ones, how could ye have rejected that Jesus, who stood with open arms to receive you! Behold, if ye had not done this, ye would not have fallen. But behold, ye are fallen, and I mourn your loss." (Mormon 6:17–18.)

Mormon's own record concludes with a testimony to the "remnant of the house of Israel," inviting them to repent of their sins and to believe in Jesus Christ (Mormon 7:1–5). He further testifies that the sacred record of the Nephites confirms the truth of the record of the Jews, or, in other words, that the Book of Mormon and the Bible testify of each other and of the truth of the gospel of Christ (see Mormon 7:8–9).

DOCTRINAL CONTRIBUTIONS

Although Mormon's editorial influence is felt throughout the Book of Mormon, he himself contributed only seven chapters in his own book (Mormon 1–7) and three chapters in the book of Moroni (Moroni 7–9). But notwithstanding his modest brevity, Mormon made some extremely important doctrinal contributions, among which are the following:

Judgment. Questions are sometimes raised regarding the relationship between the twelve Apostles in the land of Jerusalem and the twelve disciples whom Jesus chose from among the Nephites. Mormon makes it clear that the twelve tribes of Israel will be judged by the Twelve in Jerusalem. The remnant of Lehi will be judged by the twelve Nephite disciples, and they in turn "shall be judged by the other twelve whom Jesus chose in the land of Jerusalem." (Mormon 3:18–19.)

Scattering and gathering. Mormon prophesied that after the people of that day had "been driven and scattered by the Gentiles, behold, then will the Lord remember the covenant which he made unto Abraham and unto all the house of Israel" (Mormon 5:20). The exponential growth of the Church in the lands peopled by the descendants of father Lehi attests to the fulfillment of Mormon's prophecy.

Intent of the heart. We are greatly indebted to Moroni for including in his own benedictory record a sermon which his father had "taught them in the synagogue" (Moroni 7:1). Against a life-long background of violence and bloodshed, Mormon addressed "the peaceable followers of Christ" (Moroni 7:3), emphasizing the importance of righteous works and of offering gifts and prayers to the Lord with "real intent of heart" (Moroni 7:6). He further taught that "every thing which inviteth and enticeth to do good, and to love God, and to serve him, is inspired of God" (Moroni 7:13).

Spirit of Christ. A profound teaching by Mormon is that "the Spirit of Christ is given to every man, that he may know good from evil; wherefore, I show unto you the way to judge; for every thing which inviteth to do good, and to persuade to believe in Christ, is sent forth by the power and gift of Christ; wherefore ye may know with a perfect knowledge it is of God" (Moroni 7:16).

Ministering angels. Ministering angels are a central part of the restoration of the gospel. Angels also played a crucial role throughout the entire Book of Mormon, in reproving Laman and Lemuel (see 1 Nephi 3:29), through interpreting Lehi's dream to Nephi and showing him other visions (see 1 Nephi 11:14–14:29), by ministering to Jacob (see Jacob 7:5), in providing the words of King Benjamin's stirring benedictory message (see Mosiah 3:2; 4:1; 5:5), by getting Alma the Younger and the sons of Mosiah back on track (see Mosiah 27:1–15), through leading Alma to Amulek (Alma 8:14–21), and ministering daily unto Nephi the son of Nephi (see 3 Nephi 7:18), to cite but a few examples. Now, against a backdrop of utter hopelessness, Mormon asks the question "Have miracles ceased?" (Moroni 7:29.) He then emphatically answers his own query: "Nay; for it is by faith that miracles are wrought; and it is by faith that angels appear and minister unto men" (Moroni 7:37).

Faith, hope, and charity. Some thoughtless individuals have criticized the Book of Mormon on the grounds that certain teachings seem to have been plagiarized from the Bible. Commonly cited examples are the Sermon on the Mount, as found in both Matthew 5 and 3 Nephi 12, and Mormon's eloquent exegesis on charity in Moroni 7, which closely approximates 1 Corinthians 13:4–8.

Humble followers of Christ understand the process whereby God speaks to His children on earth through living prophets. These prophets record these divine messages, and they are known to us as scriptures. Because numerous prophets have lived throughout the ages in different parts of the earth, it is not only possible, it is to be expected that the divine messages will be repeated over and over again. Throughout the four Gospels it is interesting to note the number of times the Savior himself introduced His teachings by reciting scriptures from the Old Testament, saying, "It is written . . ." (see Matthew 4:4, 6, 7, 10; 21:13; 26:24, 31; Mark 1:2; 7:6; 9:12–13; 11:17; 14:21, 27; Luke 4:4, 8, 10; 7:27; 19:46; 20:17; 22:37; 24:46; John 6:31, 45; 8:17; 10:34; 12:14; 15:25).

Mormon, much like the Apostle Paul, wrote that "charity suffereth long, and is kind, and envieth not, and is not puffed up, seeketh not her own, is not easily provoked, thinketh no evil, and rejoiceth not in iniquity but rejoiceth in the truth, beareth all things, believeth all things, hopeth all things, endureth all things" (Moroni 7:45). Mormon then adds the sublime definition of charity as "the pure love of Christ" (Moroni 7:47). After defining charity, Mormon then performs a magnificent service to every person who will ever read the Book of Mormon—he tells us in detail *how* we may obtain this pure love of Christ: "Wherefore, my beloved brethren, pray unto the Father with all the energy of heart, that ye may be filled with this love, which he hath bestowed upon all who are true followers of his Son, Jesus Christ; that ye may become the sons of God; that when he shall appear we shall be like him, for we shall see him as he is; that we may have this hope; that we may be purified even as he is pure" (Moroni 7:48).

If the diplomats of warring nations understood and followed Mormon's admonition, the world would be spared the scourge of war. If married couples perpetually pleaded for and practiced charity, the world would be spared the devastation of broken homes and hearts. If all those whose lives have been scarred by abuse would pray with all the energy of their hearts for the pure love of Christ, their burdens would be lifted and their hearts would be filled with love. Charity, the pure love of Christ, is acquired only through great effort on our part. After praying with great energy of heart, then comes the promise: we will be filled with love.

This single verse is one of the most profound statements found in holy writ. If this succinct prescription were truly followed, much of the misery of the human condition would be alleviated. It is well to note that Mormon writes of our need to become "purified even as [Christ] is pure" (Moroni 7:48). Generally, purity is equated with virtue and chastity and the avoiding of lustful thoughts and lascivious actions. But in this context, Mormon emphasizes the fact that purity also includes the indispensability of charity, the pure love of Christ. A heart that is filled with love has no room for envy, contention, revenge, discouragement, hatred, or fear, for a heart filled with love is full. The atonement of Jesus Christ is the miracle of forgiveness, and if we would be forgiven we must forgive others (see D&C 64:9–10).

Infant baptism. We are very fortunate that Moroni preserved and included his father's epistle on infant baptism, a discourse found nowhere else in such clarity. To lay aside all disputations, as moved upon by the Holy Ghost, Mormon powerfully declared: "Listen to the words of Christ, your Redeemer, your Lord and your God. Behold, I came into the world not to call the righteous but sinners to repentance; the whole need no physician, but they that are sick; wherefore, little children are whole, for they are not capable of committing sin." (Moroni 8:8.)

Speaking with great boldness, he further taught that "he that saith that little children need baptism denieth the mercies of Christ, and setteth at naught the atonement of him and the power of his redemption" (Moroni 8:20). Concluding his exegesis on baptism, he taught that "the first fruits of repentance is baptism; and baptism . . . bringeth remission of sins . . . [which] bringeth meekness, and lowliness of heart; and because of meekness and lowliness of heart cometh the visitation of the Holy Ghost, which Comforter filleth with hope and perfect love" (Moroni 8:25–26).

Enduring to the end. Ever the prophet-general, even though "the Spirit of the Lord [had] ceased striving" with those with whom he had labored so long (Moroni 9:4), Mormon wrote his son that "notwithstanding their hardness, let us labor diligently; for if we should cease to labor, we should be brought under condemnation; for we have a labor to perform whilst in this tabernacle of clay, that we may conquer the enemy of all righteousness, and rest our souls in the kingdom of God" (Moroni 9:6).

As both a general and a prophet, Mormon had spoken sharply to his people on various occasions in very clear and unmistakable terms, but in his farewell blessing to his son we readily capture the tenderness of this mighty man of God:

"My son, be faithful in Christ; . . . may Christ lift thee up, and may his sufferings and death, and the showing his body unto our fathers, and his mercy and long-suffering, and the hope of his glory and of eternal life, rest in your mind forever" (Moroni 9:2).

17

Elder Cecil O. Samuelson Jr.

The Brother of Jared

The ministry of the brother of Jared, one of the key Book of Mormon prophets, occurs quite early in the historical chronology of God's dealings with his prophets, but the account of his experiences is found near the end of the Book of Mormon as it is presently compiled. Wherever its location, however, this record assumes great prominence because of the contributions made by and through Jared's brother. His experiences were remarkable, even unique, and his faith was unexcelled by any mortal of whom we know.

What we understand about the brother of Jared is largely recorded in Moroni's abridgement of the twenty-four plates containing the history of the Jaredite nation, which we currently have as the book of Ether. We know that he was "a large and mighty man, and a man highly favored of the Lord" (Ether 1:34). We know that Jared and his brother, their families, and a few others began their recorded odyssey at the time the Lord showed his displeasure with the tower of Babel and those who erected it. We even know the real name of the brother of Jared—Mahonri Moriancumer—through the Prophet Joseph Smith, although it is not directly found in the book of Ether itself (see "The Jaredites," *The Juvenile Instructor*, 1 May 1892, p. 282).

These few details are of interest and importance in establishing the context of the truths acquired by and from the brother of Jared, and particularly for the applications that should be relevant to our own lives. His specific name, his physical stature, and even his unique relationship with his brother Jared are not nearly as important to us, however, as are the characteristics that he demonstrated and the lessons from the Savior that he learned—tutorials from which we can also benefit if we, as he, choose to ponder (see 2 Nephi 4:15), search (see Jacob 7:23), liken the scriptures unto ourselves (see 1 Nephi 19:23), and incorporate them into our own lives. As Elder Neal A. Maxwell has explained, experiences such as those of the brother of Jared can even become a part of our own "enlarged . . . memory" (Alma 37:8) and bring us, proportionate to our own preparation, the same spiritual blessings as were brought to the brother of Jared by his righteous faith and strivings.

At least two questions about the brother of Jared appropriately might be asked. First, why did the Lord respond to and treat the brother of Jared as He did? Second, why does the Lord allow us to have access to several of His remarkable interactions with the brother of Jared when many other uniquely sacred specifics (see Ether 4:4–7) have been withheld from us?

The first question could be partially addressed by examining a number of the characteristics or traits demonstrated by the brother of Jared which clearly found favor with the Lord. A reasonable response to the second question might be that the experiences of the brother of Jared not only were important to him but also are necessary and significant for all who wish to "come unto Christ" (Moroni 10:32). The lessons learned by the brother of Jared were obviously essential for the safe arrival of the people of the Jaredite nation in the new world and also are highly significant in our own journeys toward eternal life with our Heavenly Father. These profound truths, evidence of the benevolence of Deity, bear witness of the promise "that every good gift cometh of Christ" (Moroni 10:18).

Because of the dramatic impact of the visions of the brother of Jared and the miracles in which he was involved, it is easy to understand why we might be tempted to focus on the sensational alone in our studies of Moroni's abridgement. We must remember, however, that these spectacular events did not occur capriciously in a vacuum or even because of real needs of the Jaredite people alone; these remarkable experiences occurred because they were faithfully invited and even earnestly pleaded for and earned. It seems fair to observe that the brother of Jared was focused primarily on obtaining lights for barges and that he learned almost serendipitously eternal truths about the nature of Jesus and especially about himself in the process. As is so often the case, Mahonri Moriancumer received so much more from the Lord than he thought he had asked for or needed.

Before focusing solely on the positive characteristics and dispositions of this "large and mighty man" which were clearly so pleasing to the Lord, it is important to remember that the brother of Jared was a mortal man like the rest of us and therefore not yet perfect in his striving, although his heart and mind seemed to be fundamentally right. Moroni's account in the book of Ether does not provide all of the details, and yet it appears that Mahonri Moriancumer and his brother were, if not directly involved, at least in the vicinity at the time the Tower of Babel was erected. Clearly, there was enough proximity that Jared was concerned that the language of his family might be confounded by the Lord, as was being done with the language of those who had been directly involved in this apostate activity (see Ether 1:33–37).

After repenting, praying for forgiveness, and receiving wonderful blessings, including direct communication with the Lord, the people of Jared came in their travels to a beautiful resting place, where they remained for the space of four years. Apparently during this time the brother of Jared and, by implication, the rest of Jared's people neglected to call on the Lord as they had been commanded (see Ether 2:13–14).

Because of the brevity of the abridged record, all of the details of the peaceful and apparently comfortable four years Jared's party spent on the seashore are not available. One might wonder whether the brother of Jared and those with him really did not pray at all during that four-year period or whether their efforts at prayer had become routine and perfunctory, as they were quite comfortable with their satisfactory circumstances and the apparent lack of impending doom or crisis. Had they merely not remembered to really "call upon the name of the Lord" (Ether 2:14) with the intent, feeling, power, and concentration necessary to make their petitions meaningful? We do know that in spite of their neglect, whether absolute or relative, "the Lord came again unto the brother of Jared, and stood in a cloud and talked . . . for the space of three hours . . . and chastened him because he remembered not to call upon the name of the Lord" (Ether 2:14).

Whatever the specifics, we do know that "the brother of Jared repented of the evil which he had done, and did call upon the name of the Lord for his brethren who were with him" (Ether 2:15). We do know that the Lord graciously forgave the brother of Jared and his family but with the clear caution that they should not commit this sin again, with the stunning reminder, "My Spirit will not always strive with man" (Ether 2:15).

As we consider the brother of Jared and the clearly responsive attention that he received from the Lord, we might profitably consider some of his characteristics or traits that seem to have facilitative functions in the Lord's interactions with him. While there are others that might be mentioned, several seem worthy of our consideration and emulation as we attempt to better understand the Messiah and His expectations for us:

1. Mahonri Moriancumer consistently acted in faith. Not only did he have faith in his own abilities, those of his brother, and perhaps others, he had an even more profound and fundamental faith in the Lord and in His capacity to answer prayers and provide whatever assistance was needed, after he had done all that he could do himself. The Lord explained to him that "because of thy faith thou hast seen that I shall take upon me flesh and blood; and never has man come before me with such exceeding faith as thou hast; for were it not so ye could not have seen my finger" (Ether 3:9).

2. Although willing to be completely dependent on and responsive to the word of the Lord, the brother of Jared provides clear evidence that he also carefully analyzed and thoughtfully examined the dilemmas that faced him. While he fully exerted his faith in the capacity of the Lord to help him solve his challenges, he likewise proposed solutions to those problems to the Lord and asked for His assistance after he had done all that he could do alone (see Ether 3:4).

3. Not only did he respond to requests from Jared and others, he often accepted their counsel and advice, when appropriate, with respect to how he should function and act (see Ether 1:38–39).

4. Even though he on occasion had obvious deficiencies that led to rebuke, he clearly and most often regularly prayed to the Lord to express praise and gratitude for blessings received (see Ether 6:9) and to ask specifically for blessings that were needed. His consistency pleased the Lord, and his prayers were answered because of the "long time" he had cried unto the Lord (Ether 1:43).

5. Not only did he pray, he expected answers to his prayers (see Ether 3:12). As he listened for and to the answers to his petitions, his sensitivity to those communications increased as well as his capacity to receive instruction from the Lord.

Why, we might ask, did the Lord speak to the brother of Jared for three hours? At least part of the answer is that the brother of Jared obviously continued to listen to the teaching, instruction, and counsel that he was receiving. He surely paid attention when he received answers he expected, such as when the stones were lighted (see Ether 3:6). He also paid attention, however, when he learned more than he had asked, such as when he learned that the Lord to whom he prayed was Jesus Christ, the Savior and Creator of the world, and that the brother of Jared and, indeed, all mankind were created after the Savior's image (see Ether 3:14–15). He even paid attention when he received instructions seemingly not related to his specific request, such as when he was told to gather flocks and families and begin the epic journey to the promised land (see Ether 1:40–42).

6. He repented (see Ether 2:15). When the brother of Jared was chastened for his forgetfulness about calling upon the name of the Lord, there is no evidence that he resisted this rebuke or did anything other than immediately resolve to modify his behavior and his obedience in more appropriate ways. Mahonri Moriancumer was a man who significantly learned from his mistakes and took steps so that they would not be repeated.

7. He regularly followed the Lord's commandments and followed through. Even when receiving directions and instructions that might have seemed audacious or impossible to fulfill, the brother of Jared seemed dogged in his determination to accomplish the work he had been given. He was much like Nephi in his absolute confidence that the Lord would provide the means to fulfill any assignments he had received (see 1 Nephi 3:7), and he also was resolute in his pursuit of his duties.

What are some of the other lessons that we learn from the experiences of the brother of Jared? While many might be identified, several that are fundamental to our essential faith and knowledge are helpfully expanded in the scriptural account of the experiences of this great prophet-leader.

Nowhere in the scriptures is a clearer account given of the nature of the spirit body of the Lord Jesus Christ and, indeed, of the characteristics of our own spirits. The brother of Jared not only saw the finger of the antemortal Jesus Christ but indeed perceived His entire spirit body (see Ether 3:6, 13). Understanding the premortal godhood of Jesus Christ together with our own spiritual identities prior to our births in the flesh is a great blessing and advantage. These insights breaching traditional boundaries were the direct result of the brother of Jared's nonboundaried faith.

The absolute recognition that both seemingly small and courageously mighty prayers are answered by the Lord, if asked in true and deep faith, is clearly demonstrated by the experiences of the brother of Jared. The encounters of this prophet with Jesus Christ give evidence that the Lord reveals what is needed but usually not much more. Once blessings or specific acts of assistance are rendered by the Lord, more should not be expected until that portion which is received is appropriately and adequately used and applied. President Joseph Fielding Smith commented on this principle: "I would like to call your attention to one thing in the Book of Mormon. The Lord has promised us greater knowledge, greater understanding than we find in the Book of Mormon, when we are prepared to receive it. When the brother of Jared went upon the mount to have the Lord touch stones to give them light to light their way across the great ocean, the Lord revealed to him the history of this world from the beginning to the end. We do not have it." (In Conference Report, October 1961, p. 19.) We do need to consider, individually and collectively, what we must do if we wish to qualify, as did the brother of Jared, for the Lord to "show [us] all things" (Ether 3:26).

One of the compelling truths taught by the account of the brother of Jared's experiences is that this record is really not just about Mahonri Moriancumer, or even his extended family, but rather more fundamentally about Jesus Christ Himself. The account of the experiences of the brother of Jared with the Lord clarifies and expands our understanding of the physical and spiritual characteristics and the character of the premortal Messiah. The reality of His role in the creation under the direction of the Father, as well as His interest and involvement in things both obviously great and ostensibly modest, is born witness of by these episodes. Limitations placed on the interactions of the Lord with men in the flesh are not imposed by the Savior but rather most often result from the unwillingness of people to pay the price for greater involvement with the Lord.

After the Jaredites spent almost one year in their barges and miraculously reached the promised land, the abridged record covering the period from their arrival in their new homeland to the death of Jared and his brother is brief and almost cryptic. In the last days of the mortal lives of these great sibling leaders, they called their people together to "number them" (Ether 6:19) and to grant any last wishes to them before these prophet-fathers went to their graves.

To the distress of these faithful patriarchs, that which was requested was that they appoint a king over the emerging nation. The response of the brother of Jared was direct and clear: "Surely this thing leadeth into captivity" (Ether 6:23). Unfortunately, Jared, respecting both the agency and wishes of the people but not the inspired counsel of his brother, instructed their people that they should choose from their sons who might be king (see Ether 6:24). All of the sons save one declined, and Orihah was anointed king (see Ether 6:27). In spite of Orihah's goodness and the proximate prosperity of the people, in time the last recorded prophecy of the brother of Jared was fulfilled, and their civilization, together with their sacred blessings, was lost.

In 1966, Elder Harold B. Lee used the experiences of the brother of Jared to illustrate how the blessings of heaven are received:

> The Lord gave to the brother of Jared, that great prophet, a blueprint of the ships that he was to construct, by which he was to take his people across large bodies of water to a promised land. As he surveyed these and began to build, he faced two problems: (1) no provision was made for ventilation and (2) there was no light. The ventilation problem was solved rather simply by having holes

at proper places that could be opened and closed; but the matter of light was one that he could not quite solve. So the brother of Jared cried to the Lord, saying, ". . . behold, I have done even as thou hast commanded me; and I have prepared the vessels for my people, and behold there is no light in them. Behold, O Lord, wilt thou suffer that we shall cross this great water in darkness?" (Ether 2:22.)

Notice how the Lord dealt with this question. He said to the brother of Jared, "What will ye that I should do that ye may have light in your vessels?" (Ether 2:23.)—as much as to say, "Well, have you any good ideas? What would you suggest that we should do in order to have light?" And then the Lord said, "For behold, ye cannot have windows, for they will be dashed to pieces; neither shall ye take fire with you, for ye shall not go by the light of fire. . . ."

Then the Lord went away and left him alone. It was as though the Lord were saying to him, "Look, I gave you a mind to think with, and I gave you agency to use it. Now you do all you can to help yourself with this problem; and then, after you've done all you can, I'll step in to help you."

The brother of Jared did some thinking. Then he gathered up sixteen stones, molten out of rock, and carried them in his hands to the top of the mount called Shelam, where he cried unto the Lord, "O Lord, thou hast said that we must be encompassed about by the floods. Now behold, O Lord, and do not be angry with thy servant because of his weakness before thee; for we know that thou art holy and dwellest in the heavens, and that we are unworthy before thee; because of the fall our natures have been evil continually; nevertheless, O Lord, thou hast given us a commandment that we must call upon thee, that from thee we may receive according to our desires." (Ether 3:2.)

Now, what is he doing? He is confessing his sins before he asks again. He has come to the conclusion that before he is worthy to seek a blessing he must keep the basic laws upon which the blessings he seeks are predicated.

Then he says, "Behold, O Lord, [I know that] thou hast smitten us because of our iniquity, and hast driven us forth, and for these many years we have been in the wilderness; nevertheless, thou hast been merciful to us. O Lord, look upon me in pity, and turn away thine anger from this thy people. . . ." (Ether 3:3.) The brother of Jared is confessing the sins of the people, because the blessing he wants is not just for himself; it is for his whole people. Having done all that he knew how to do, he came again with a specific request and said: [cites Ether 3:4–6]. . . .

This is the principle in action. If you want the blessing, don't just kneel down and pray about it. Prepare yourselves in every conceivable way you can in order to make yourselves worthy to receive the blessing you seek. ("How to Receive a Blessing from God," *Improvement Era*, October 1966, pp. 862–63, 896.)

The brother of Jared has much to teach us about obtaining God's blessings and about the tremendous power of our personal faith in the Lord. His remarkable experiences and his exemplary discipleship reveal many of the keys to successful living and help us understand the will of the Lord in our own lives. Moroni's abridgement of these ancient Jaredite records—particularly his inclusion of words describing the devoted service of this inspired prophet, the brother of Jared—clearly charts how we must live if we wish to fully understand and enjoy all the sublime truths and blessings promised by the Lord to those who love and follow Him.

18

Elder Monte J. Brough

The Prophet Ether:
Man of the More Excellent Hope

A good man, whom I love, awoke one morning to find his wife suffering with a serious heart attack. He immediately summoned emergency medical help and then attempted resuscitation to restore her breathing. In the frantic few moments before help could arrive, it became apparent that her life was gone and that his attempts were futile. The deep grief and the enormous feelings of loss were almost more than he could comprehend. His emotions ranged from deep sorrow to anger and then questioning. He repeatedly expressed his lack of understanding for this event and questioned the kindness or caring wisdom of Heavenly Father in allowing his wife's death.

In trying to be of some modest assistance, his friends and family members recalled to him the great plan of happiness, which provides answers to these difficult experiences. My friend cried that if the Lord would reveal to him that the plan was true, then he could more easily accept the event of his wife's death.

I was immediately reminded of Moroni's commentary after abridging part of the record of the Jaredites. Moroni was particularly impressed by the stories of the Jaredite prophets that demonstrate to the reader examples of faith and diligence. It was the life of Ether that prompted Moroni to say: "And now, I, Moroni, would speak somewhat concerning these things; I would show unto the world that faith is things which are hoped for and not seen; wherefore, dispute not because ye see not, for ye receive no witness until after the trial of your faith" (Ether 12:6).

In other words, we learned together during that day of deep distress that we must first endure the trials of our faith, and then the witness of truth will come. This pattern of trial and then witness is repeated over and over again in each of our lives. My friend was inspired by Moroni's commentary and has responded to his trials in a wonderful manner. True to Ether's life and Moroni's promise, the witness has come to this good man, whom I love, in a most profound and important way.

This deeply personal experience prompted me to become very interested in the man who inspired Moroni in such a tender way. Ether was a hero to Moroni and has also become one to me.

One sleepless night, while serving as a mission president, I was greatly concerned about the condition of the mission. There was a need to provide some inspiration and motivation for the missionaries, but I was at a loss as to what or how I might provide it. Again my thoughts were turned to the prophet Ether because of his example of diligence and inspiration during his missionary experience. I love learning and studying about Ether because his life demonstrates qualities which I personally desire for myself, such as his supreme ability to concentrate during his service as a missionary:

> And Ether was a prophet of the Lord; wherefore Ether came forth in the days of Coriantumr, and began to prophesy unto the people. . . .
> . . . For he truly told them of all things, from the beginning of man; and that after the waters had receded from off the face of this land it became a choice land above all other lands, a chosen land of the Lord; wherefore the Lord would have that all men should serve him who dwell upon the face thereof. . . .
> Behold, Ether saw the days of Christ, and he spake concerning a New Jerusalem upon this land. (Ether 12:2; 13:2, 4.)

That night I was impressed that a study of the life of Ether might provide the inspiration which was needed for our mission. Every missionary in the Church would do well to emulate this great prophet who understood the rigors of missionary work and performed at such a high level. Ether "could not be restrained because of the Spirit of the Lord which was in him. For he did cry from the morning, even until the going down of the sun." (Ether 12:2–3.)

As a mission president, I found that this example of hard work and diligent effort was among the finest available. We challenged every missionary to learn to be an "Ether" because the Spirit of the Lord could make it possible for each of them to "not be restrained." Many of our missionaries did gain this level of spirituality which "could not be restrained," and thus were blessed with faith and results which had not been previously enjoyed. This, of course, resulted in a higher level of work even from early morning until late in the evening.

A tragic automobile accident claimed the life of a close relative, who was a beautiful thirty-year-old mother of four little boys. At the time of the accident, the eldest boy was six years old and the youngest was still a nursing baby of only a few months. The loss of a young mother is certainly one of the most tragic mortal conditions we can experience. During these significant trials, we often attempt to build a rationale which might explain these tragic losses. Yet as we come to understand, we realize that the experience of having trials and tribulations is part of the great plan for Heavenly Father's children. Remembering my love of Ether, I again referred a grieving husband and father to the Jaredite prophet for solace.

Ether was not immune from the tribulations of the world. His missionary work was essentially without positive results, and certainly was not productive. "For . . . they rejected all of the words of Ether" (Ether 13:2). Further, "they esteemed him as naught, and cast him out; and he hid himself in the cavity of a rock by day, and by night he went forth . . . viewing the destructions which came upon the people" (Ether 13:13–14). He did not cease his efforts and the exercise of his faith, even as he observed the disastrous lack of positive results from his work: "It came to pass that Coriantumr repented not, neither his household, neither the people; and the wars ceased not; and they sought to kill Ether, but he fled from before them and hid again in the cavity of the rock" (Ether 13:22).

For those of us who try to understand the great loss of our loved ones, we may compare our lot with that of Ether. We don't know exactly what happened to Ether's family. The record is silent as to his brothers and sisters and his wife and children, if any. We know little about his own household except that he was a son of Coriantor, who traced his genealogy back to Jared. Ether recorded that Coriantor died after begetting him, having spent his entire life in some form of captivity. Ether records that his great-grandfather Ethem "was wicked in his days" (Ether 11:11). Ether's grandfather Moron also "did that which was wicked before the Lord" (Ether 11:14).

Ether obviously came from difficult circumstances in his home, with somewhat of a "wicked" environment imposed on the household of his extended family. It is likely that he had little contact with his imprisoned or deceased father during the years of his youth. Somehow I envision a faithful and loving mother who accepted responsibility for her son because of her husband's captivity and untimely death. I know of several faithful men and women who have also lost their fathers early in life. It is a great loss to lose a parent at a young age. Yet many who have done so were taught important principles by their other parent, which resulted in a deep and abiding testimony of the gospel. The abridged record of Ether does not disclose the influence of a wonderful mother or even much detailed information regarding Ether's own immediate family. We are left to wonder about the family's conditions during Ether's youth.

Of Ether's personal life, we know that he was possessed of an unwavering faith and testimony of the Lord. The record does teach that the loss and destruction of his people, and possibly members of his own family, was so enormous that Ether was left alone. None of his own immediate or extended family survived the tragic civil war that resulted in the death and destruction of an entire people. No person among all of the people would repent and listen to the voice of this great spiritual giant. "For behold, they rejected all the words of Ether" (Ether 13:2).

Ether must have deeply sorrowed for the complete loss of this entire people, including any friends and family members. These loved ones could have been lost through the wickedness of the great civil war or through silent, innocent death.

It was Ether's enormous faith in difficult conditions that inspired Moroni and can also inspire us. It was the constant condition of trials and tribulation that framed the life of this great man of faith. Much of what we know about Ether is from the inspiration that came to Moroni while reading and abridging the record of the Jaredites. Some of the most inspiring principles were summarized by Moroni, with the conditions of the Jaredites and particularly the life conditions and writings of the prophet Ether as the context for his thoughts. Moroni, as a student of Ether, recognized that a belief in God is essential to the reality of a better world for every person. One should remember Moroni's words about hoping for a better world: "Wherefore, whoso believeth in God might with surety hope for a better world, yea, even a place at the right hand of God, which hope cometh of faith, maketh an anchor to the souls of men, which would make them sure and steadfast, always abounding in good works, being led to glorify God" (Ether 12:4).

Ether, as my personal mentor of some years, has helped me understand how hope, which "cometh of faith, maketh an anchor" to my soul. It is this hope for a better world that is the foundation of the great plan of happiness. This profound hope—not yet complete faith—is part of the process of bringing stability into our lives. We can look to many of those we know and love for examples of spiritual stability. These are they who have sufficient faith to make an anchor to their souls. We will find this stability most with those who are "always abounding in good works," which will make them "sure and steadfast." Ether was a model of good works, which becomes a testament to his anchor of faith. He was steadfast, never wavering but always appropriately anxious to glorify God.

As Moroni continued to learn and be inspired about Ether and his fellow Jaredites, he became overwhelmed by his inability to convey the power of their words—a feeling experienced by other Book of Mormon record-keepers relative to their writings. Many of us, as we face the challenges in our own lives (even I as I write this chapter), are possessed with these same feelings. Through Moroni, the Lord provided a revelation which surely applies to us all: "And if men come unto me I will show unto them their weakness. I give unto men weakness that they may be humble; and my grace is sufficient for all men that humble themselves before me; for if they humble themselves before me, and have faith in me, then will I make weak things become strong unto them." (Ether 12:27.)

The story of Ether was powerful enough to remind Moroni

of the eternal nature of hope. Hope is both a predecessor and a derivative of faith. One may not be able to know or testify about things which are not seen, but one surely can have strong and significant hope. Neither Moroni nor Ether despaired or were much discouraged about the conditions and consequences of their lives. Each was given a deep and abiding faith in the mission of the Lord Jesus Christ. The following is what Ether's words inspired Moroni to say about hope, which must precede and grow into "a more excellent hope:" "And I also remember that thou hast said that thou hast prepared a house for man, yea, even among the mansions of thy Father, in which man might have a more excellent hope; wherefore man must hope, or he cannot receive an inheritance in the place which thou hast prepared" (Ether 12:32).

In facing tragedy, it is instructional to observe those who have complete and total faith in the reality of the mansions of our Father. This faith does result in a testimony of Jesus Christ and the process of the Atonement. "Man must hope, or he cannot receive" the blessing of the great plan of happiness, which provides peace and understanding for mortal mankind. It is this "more excellent hope" that allows us to accept whatever trial or test comes to us.

As each of us faces personal tragedy, we can have a much better acceptance of the final results because of the prophet Ether's example. Even the last words written and recorded by Ether are instructional and helpful in our personal lives. One can feel the great accord and peace which was manifest during his final mortal days: "Now the last words which are written by Ether are these: Whether the Lord will that I be translated, or that I suffer the will of the Lord in the flesh, it mattereth not, if it so be that I am saved in the kingdom of God. Amen." (Ether 15:34.)

19

President Gordon B. Hinckley

Moroni

From my window I frequently look at the figure of Moroni on the tallest tower of the Salt Lake Temple. He has been there since 6 April 1892, the date on which the capstone was laid before the largest crowd ever assembled in Salt Lake City up to that time. When the capstone was placed, thousands of voices joined in shouting, "Hosanna to God and the Lamb." Later that day the statue was placed on top of the capstone.

Today, strangers who see him wonder who he is. Some think the gleaming figure represents Gabriel, the biblical angel sent to Daniel, to Zacharias, and to Mary. Others are simply puzzled.

But he is no puzzle to us. He is a symbol of the restoration of the gospel in this the dispensation of the fulness of times. He was guardian and deliverer of the golden plates, the translation of which became the Book of Mormon, another witness of the Lord Jesus Christ. We regard his coming as fulfillment of the vision of John the Revelator: "And I saw another angel fly in the midst of heaven, having the everlasting gospel to preach unto them that dwell on the earth, and to every nation, and kindred, and tongue, and people, saying with a loud voice, Fear God, and give glory to him; for the hour of his judgment is come: and worship him that made heaven, and earth, and the sea, and the fountains of waters" (Revelation 14:6–7).

Of all the characters who walk the pages of the Book of Mormon, none stands a greater hero, save Jesus only, than does Moroni, son of Mormon.

He was skilled as the commander of an army of ten thousand warriors. He was concise as an editor and historian. He was prophetic in speaking of his own and future generations. He was a man who walked alone for years, a fugitive from his enemies who were unrelenting in their pursuit. Moroni was military commander, prophet-historian, the last of the Nephite survivors.

He was a direct descendant of Nephi. He grew up in the household of his remarkable father, Mormon. His father had witnessed the glorious flowering of the Nephite nation when "the whole face of the land had become covered with buildings, and the people were as numerous almost, as it were the sand of the sea" (Mormon 1:7). Mormon had also witnessed the abject decay of that civilization. It became a season when wickedness prevailed throughout the entire land "and the work of miracles and of healing did cease because of the iniquity of the people. And there were no gifts from the Lord, and the Holy Ghost did not come upon any, because of their wickedness and unbelief." (Mormon 1:13–14.)

Moroni was a witness of this decay. The Nephites became embroiled in wars with the Lamanites, wars that were to result in their annihilation.

He cried out to his people: "Who can stand against the works of the Lord? Who can deny his sayings? Who will rise up against the almighty power of the Lord? Who will despise the works of the Lord? Who will despise the children of Christ? Behold, all ye who are despisers of the works of the Lord, for ye shall wonder and perish." (Mormon 9:26.)

There came into his hands the record of the Jaredites written on the twenty-four plates discovered by the people of Limhi in the days of King Mosiah. From these plates, he chronicled the rise and fall of the Jaredites from the time of the Tower of Babel, their remarkable voyage across the sea to the promised land, the declaration of the Lord to them concerning this promised land, their subsequent prosperity, their ensuing wickedness, and their ultimate total destruction.

In the depravity of his own people he doubtless saw history repeating itself. He knew that destruction would also come to them if they persisted in their evil course. He raised his voice in warning. But they paid no attention.

In the eventual terrible slaughter which occurred between the Lamanites and the Nephites, he watched the destruction of 230,000 Nephite warriors, including his own ten thousand. He was a witness to that awful carnage when the Nephite men, with their wives and children, saw "the armies of the Lamanites marching towards them; and with that awful fear of death which fills the breasts of all the wicked, did they await to receive them" (Mormon 6:7). He was a witness to their destruction until only twenty-four of his people were left in all the land. All but him eventually were hunted down and destroyed. His father was among those slain. Moroni wrote: "I even remain alone to write the sad tale of the destruction of my people. But behold, they are gone. . . . And whether they will slay me, I know not." (Mormon 8:3.)

While wandering as a lonely fugitive, Moroni added to his father's record. His words ring with pathos: "I would write . . . if I had room upon the plates, but I have not; and ore I have none, for I am alone. My father hath been slain in battle, and all my kinsfolk, and I have not friends nor whither to go. . . . And behold, the Lamanites have hunted my people, the Nephites, down from city to city and from place to place, even until they are no more; and great has been their fall; yea, great and marvelous is the destruction of my people, the Nephites." (Mormon 8:5, 7.)

Who can sense the depth of his pain, the poignant loneliness that constantly overshadowed him as he moved about, a fugitive relentlessly hunted by his enemies? For how long he actually was alone we do not know, but the record would indicate that it was for a considerable period. His conversation was prayer to the Lord. His companion was the Holy Spirit. There were occasions when the Three Nephites ministered to him. But with all of this, there is an element of terrible tragedy in the life of this man who became a lonely wanderer.

In his chronicle of the Jaredites he interjects a farewell to the Gentiles and also to his own people whom he loved. He speaks of the time when we shall all "meet before the judgment-seat of Christ. . . . And then shall ye know that I have seen Jesus, and that he hath talked with me face to face, and that he told me in plain humility, even as a man telleth another in mine own language, concerning these things." (Ether 12:38–39.)

He wrote his last testament in the book which carries his name and which concludes the Nephite record. He wrote as one with a certain knowledge that his record would eventually come to light. He expressed the hope that perhaps a few more things might be of worth unto his brethren the Lamanites, in some future day (see Moroni 1:4).

He repeated some of the teachings of his noble father, writing: "But behold, that which is of God inviteth and enticeth to do good continually; wherefore, every thing which inviteth and enticeth to do good, and to love God, and to serve him, is inspired of God. . . . For behold, the Spirit of Christ is given to every man, that he may know good from evil; wherefore, I show unto you the way to judge; for every thing which inviteth to do good, and to persuade to believe in Christ, is sent forth by the power and gift of Christ; wherefore ye may know with a perfect knowledge it is of God." (Moroni 7:13, 16.)

In the final chapter of his own composition he bore testimony of the record of his people and categorically promised that those who would read it could know by the power of the Holy Ghost of its truth.

No other book contains such a promise. If Moroni had written nothing else, this promise in his concluding testimony would mark him forever as an eloquent witness of eternal truth. For, said he, "by the power of the Holy Ghost ye may know the truth of all things" (Moroni 10:5).

In his final words of declaration he spoke with measured certainty concerning the record which should lie for centuries in the Hill Cumorah, to come forth as a voice from the dust: "And I exhort you to remember these things; for the time speedily cometh that ye shall know that I lie not, for ye shall see me at the bar of God; and the Lord God will say unto you: Did I not declare my words unto you, which were written by this man, like as one crying from the dead, yea, even as one speaking out of the dust?" (Moroni 10:27.)

To us of this time he wrote a ringing final challenge: "And again I would exhort you that ye would come unto Christ, and lay hold upon every good gift, and touch not the evil gift, nor the unclean thing. And awake, and arise from the dust, O Jerusalem; yea, and put on thy beautiful garments, O daughter

of Zion; and strengthen thy stakes and enlarge thy borders forever, that thou mayest no more be confounded, that the
covenants of the Eternal Father which he hath made unto thee,
O house of Israel, may be fulfilled." (Moroni 10:30–31.) These
were his words of benediction.

Centuries passed. Then came the dawning of the last and
final dispensation, the dispensation of the fulness of times. The
God of heaven and His Beloved Son, the Lord Jesus Christ, appeared to the boy Joseph Smith, opening a new age of gospel
truth and priesthood authority.

In continuation of this process of restoration there followed
on the night of September 21, 1823, a return to earth of this same
Moroni. When Joseph had retired and was calling upon the Lord
in prayer, his room grew light, "lighter than at noonday," and
there appeared at his bedside a personage standing in the air. He
was dressed in robes of exquisite whiteness. (See Joseph
Smith–History 1:30–31.)

This resurrected being introduced himself as Moroni and
called the boy Joseph by name, saying "that he was a messenger
sent from the presence of God, . . . that God had a work for
[Joseph] to do; and that [his] name should be had for good and
evil among all nations, kindreds, and tongues, or that it should
be both good and evil spoken of among all people" (Joseph
Smith–History 1:33).

He spoke of the ancient record written on gold plates, and of
their contents. He declared that the means for translating them
were buried with the plates in a nearby hill. He quoted from
scripture and instructed the young man in other ways.

He appeared to the boy again the next day. He directed him
to the Hill Cumorah, the burial place of the plates, and there met
him each year through a period of four years. He finally delivered the ancient record to the youthful prophet.

That translated record, the Book of Mormon, is here today,
available for all to handle. It has come as a voice speaking from
the earth in testimony of the divinity of the Lord Jesus Christ. It
goes hand in hand with the Bible as another witness of the
Redeemer of the world.

Terrible was Moroni's ordeal in life as he witnessed the
decay of his civilization and the total destruction of his people.

Terrible was his loneliness as he wandered, a fugitive, the last of his race. Glorious has been his return to earth as a resurrected being, a testament to this and succeeding generations of the truths of the ancient record, and of its validity for us and all people as another witness of the Lord Jesus Christ.

20

Elder Carlos E. Asay

Golden Threads of the Book of Mormon

As the foregoing chapters of this book attest, the Book of Mormon is a volume of holy scriptures written by many men who enjoyed the spirit of prophecy and revelation. It is a record of the ancient inhabitants of America opened by Nephi, the son of Lehi, who fled Jerusalem with his family about six hundred years before Christ. And it is a record closed by Moroni, the son of Mormon, who remained alone to write the sad tale of the destruction of his people in approximately 400 A.D. This exciting account, which spans more than a thousand years of history, brings to the stage of human drama a large cast of mighty leaders who wrote things pleasing unto God with the intent of persuading all mankind "to come unto the God of Abraham, and the God of Isaac, and the God of Jacob, and be saved" (see 1 Nephi 6:3–6).

A Tapestry of Truths

The "things of God," or things of great worth unto the children of men, included in the Book of Mormon constitute the fulness of the gospel of Jesus Christ. For example, Lehi taught, "Redemption cometh in and through the Holy Messiah; for he is full of grace and truth" (2 Nephi 2:6). Nephi wrote concerning the need to keep the commandments (see 1 Nephi 3:7; 17:3, 50–51). Jacob recorded, "For this intent have we written these things, that they may know that we knew of Christ, and we had a hope of his glory many hundred years before his coming; and not only we ourselves had a hope of his glory, but also all the holy prophets which were before us" (Jacob 4:4). Hence, the provocative question, "Why not speak of the atonement of Christ, and attain to a perfect knowledge of him?"—a statement made more than four centuries before the Savior's birth in Bethlehem (Jacob 4:12). Enos told of his wrestle before God and the remission of his sins (see Enos 1:1–5). A dying King Benjamin admonished his people to love, serve, become saints, and seek salvation through the name of Christ. His teachings had such a powerful effect upon the people that they returned to their homes having "no more disposition to do evil, but to do good continually." (See Mosiah 2-5.) Abinadi, the martyr, would not deny the commandments of God; thus, he sealed the truth of his words by suffering death by fire (see Mosiah 17:20). Alma recalled how his bitter pains of sin were replaced by exquisite joy through repentance and reliance upon the Son of God, who would atone for the sins of the world (see Alma 36:17–22). Each of the prophets mentioned above and many more wove into the tapestry of the Book of Mormon precious strands of truth that make it a powerful and enduring volume of sacred writings known as another testament of Christ.

We might compare the Book of Mormon to a colorful Oriental carpet of intricate arabesque design woven by several skilled weavers. Each weaver, or prophet, in his appointed time sat at the loom and tied the yarn following a pattern provided by the Master Weaver. Slowly, but progressively, the weavers pulled the yarn, tied the knots, and cut the strings. Row by row and string by string the spiritual craftsmen painstakingly made their contributions, some lengthy and some short. In the end, a beautiful piece of godly handiwork emerged, even a marvelous work and a wonder.

THREE GOLDEN THREADS

To add brilliance, value, and meaning to the tapestry, the prophets were inspired to weave into the record three prevailing themes, or golden threads, if you will. One golden thread is an *invitation* extended to all mankind, "Come unto Christ" (Omni 1:26). The second is a timeless *warning* to avoid "hardness of heart" and "blindness of mind" (see Alma 13:3–4). Number three is a *promise* made by the Lord that has never been rescinded. It is, "Inasmuch as ye shall keep my commandments ye shall prosper in the land; but inasmuch as ye will not keep my commandments ye shall be cut off from my presence" (2 Nephi 1:20).

One who examines carefully the Book of Mormon will discover that the three golden threads cited above (invitation, warning, and promise) hold together the teachings of the ancient prophets, just as golden threads may hold together the fabric of a precious rug. They appear early in the account of the Nephites, well before Lehi and his family reach the land of promise. They are seen in the brief books of Jarom and Omni, where very few words are wasted by the record keepers. And they are highlighted toward the end of the record in the books of Ether and Moroni. Whether one simply glances at the tapestry of the book or takes the time to turn over each page and "count the knots per square inch," as he would in assessing the worth of a carpet, the three golden threads shine forth with luster and provide strong cords of continuity for the Book of Mormon.

An Invitation

Throughout His mortal ministry, Christ invited all to follow Him and to do the things they saw Him do. "Come and see" was His entreaty to some (John 1:39; see also 1:46). Others heard Him say, "Come unto me" (Matthew 11:28). He didn't command followership; He invited discipleship. His was not an idle invitation, nor one to be taken lightly.

So it is not surprising that Christ would repeat His invitation in communicating with the "other sheep" who were led away to the Americas (3 Nephi 15:17). Note what Nephi recorded: "He [the Lord] inviteth . . . all to come unto him and partake of his goodness; and he denieth none that come unto him, black and white, bond and free, male and female; and he remembereth the heathen; and all are alike unto God, both Jew and Gentile" (2 Nephi 26:33). Note also what Jacob said about the weight of his calling and the callings of all prophets: "Wherefore we labored diligently among our people, that we might persuade them to come unto Christ, and partake of the goodness of God, that they might enter into his rest" (Jacob 1:7).

From these and many other references found in the Book of Mormon, it can be concluded that the divine invitation would be extended to the entire family of Adam, regardless of time or place or circumstance. But, you might ask, what purpose would such an invitation serve, if it were not accompanied by specific instructions pertaining to our approach Christ-ward? That the Book of Mormon would indeed provide such instructions is implicit in Nephi's statement about the Restoration's impact on latter-day descendants of Lehi: "Wherefore, they shall come to the knowledge of their Redeemer and the very points of his doctrine, _that they may know how to come unto him and be saved_" (1 Nephi 15:14; emphasis added). Thus, the Book of Mormon becomes a "how to" book, a handbook, for all those who sincerely want to return "home to that God who gave them life" (Alma 40:11).

According to the prophet Alma, the process of coming to Christ involves repentance and baptism. Said he: "I speak by way of command unto you that belong to the church; and unto those who do not belong to the church I speak by way of _invitation,_ saying, Come and _be baptized unto repentance,_ that ye also may be partakers of the fruit of the tree of life" (Alma 5:62; emphasis added). Earlier in the same discourse Alma stated: "Behold, he [God] sendeth an _invitation_ unto all men, for the arms of mercy are extended towards them, and he saith: Repent, and I will receive you. . . . Yea, come unto me and bring forth works of righteousness." (Alma 5:33, 35; emphasis added.)

Amaleki associated fasting, prayer, and enduring to the end with our coming unto Christ. He pleaded: "I would that ye should come unto Christ, who is the Holy One of Israel, and partake of his salvation, and the power of his redemption. Yea, come unto him, and offer your whole souls as an offering unto him, and continue in fasting and praying, and endure to the end; and as the Lord liveth ye will be saved." (Omni 1:26.)

Moreover, Amaleki pointed out the necessity of believing in prophesying, revelations, the ministering of angels, the gift of speaking with tongues, the gift of interpreting languages, and in all things which are good, if one hopes to come unto God, the Holy One of Israel (see Omni 1:25).

The Wise Men in the meridian of time came unto the Christ child and presented Him with gifts of gold, frankincense, and myrrh (see Matthew 2:1–12). Following His crucifixion, that same Christ invited the Nephites to come unto Him and present gifts such as "full purpose of heart" (3 Nephi 12:24), strict obedience (see 3 Nephi 12:20), and "a broken heart and a contrite spirit" (3 Nephi 12:19). In fact, He commanded: "Repent, all ye ends of the earth, and come unto me and be baptized in my name, that ye may be sanctified by the reception of the Holy Ghost, that ye may stand spotless before me at the last day" (3 Nephi 27:20). And in a similar command that the Lord instructed Mormon to write specifically to the Gentiles, Christ told them to repent and come unto Him, "that ye may be numbered with my people who are of the house of Israel" (3 Nephi 30:2).

It is significant, I believe, that Moroni would repeat the divine invitation toward the close of the Nephite record and speak of the grace of God, love of God, and perfection in Christ. He said: "Come unto Christ, and be perfected in him, and deny yourselves of all ungodliness; and if ye shall deny yourselves of all ungodliness, and love God with all your might, mind and strength, then is his grace sufficient for you, that by his grace ye may be perfect in Christ; and if by the grace of God ye are perfect in Christ, ye can in nowise deny the power of God" (Moroni 10:32).

There are those who scoff at the idea of coming unto Christ. Consequently, they refuse the divine invitation extended by a loving God through ancient and modern prophets. Such people do this because they lack faith, and love the pleasures of the world more than the joys that can come from the more enduring and spiritual aspects of living. But, however loath one may be to come unto Christ, he is doing so every day that he lives: each day brings us closer to death and one step nearer the time when we shall stand before Christ at that great judgment day, whether we are ready or not. For it is written, "Ye must all stand before the judgment-seat of Christ, yea, every soul who belongs to the whole human family of Adam; and ye must stand to be judged of your works, whether they be good or evil" (Mormon 3:20). Hence, the pleading invitation, "O then, my beloved brethren, come unto the Lord, the Holy One. Remember that his paths are righteous. Behold, the way for man is narrow, but it lieth in a straight course before him, and the keeper of the gate is the Holy One of Israel; and he employeth no servant there; and there is none other way save it be by the gate; for he cannot be deceived, for the Lord God is his name." (2 Nephi 9:41.)

Those who have rejected Christ and procrastinated the day of their repentance will reap the bitter consequences (see Mormon 9:1–5). That is why Mormon cried out to a fallen people, "O ye fair ones, how could ye have rejected that Jesus, who stood with open arms to receive you!" (Mormon 6:17.) On the other hand, those who have found the path and inched their way forward during their mortal lives by repenting, being baptized, denying themselves of all ungodliness, and so on will rejoice as Enos did: "And I soon go to the place of my rest, which is with my Redeemer; for I know that in him I shall rest. And I rejoice in the day when my mortal shall put on immortality, and shall stand before him; then shall I see his face with pleasure, and he will say unto me: Come unto me, ye blessed, there is a place prepared for you in the mansions of my Father." (Enos 1:27.)

A WARNING

Along with the divine invitation "Come unto me," a kind and loving Father in Heaven has always issued warnings to His children. This fact is verified in the history of the Nephites. God warned Lehi and his family to flee Jerusalem so that they would not be destroyed or carried away captives into another land. He later warned Nephi and his righteous followers to separate themselves from those who sought their lives. Through the prophet Jacob, He warned the people against fornication and lasciviousness. And, during a time of war, He promised a group that if they were faithful in keeping the commandments He would warn them to flee or to prepare for battle, according to their danger. We would not expect anything less than frequent and timely warnings from a benevolent Deity whose continuing concern has been and will always be the welfare of His sons and daughters on earth.

We do, therefore, find in the Book of Mormon multiple instances wherein God issues warnings to both the Nephites and the Lamanites. However, the one warning that stands out above all the rest and which is repeated over and over again—constituting the second golden thread woven into the tapestry of the Book of Mormon—is this: *Avoid hardness of heart and blindness of mind.*

Alma made reference to some priests who were ordained to teach the people. It was said that they were "called and prepared from the foundation of the world according to the foreknowledge of God, on account of their exceeding faith and good works." Unfortunately, others lost their privileges because they rejected "the Spirit of God *on account of the hardness of their hearts and blindness of their minds.*" So it is understandable that Alma and all of the other prophets were inspired to issue stern warnings against those twin conditions of the soul that deprive men and women the full privileges and blessings of the gospel of Jesus Christ. (Alma 13:1–4; emphasis added.)

On this subject the author has written elsewhere: "Blindness of mind is really spiritual darkness. It is a condition or state of mind that alienates people, young or old, from godly matters. Those who suffer from this awful condition fail to see the hand of providence manifest in the affairs of mankind. They believe only in that which can be seen and felt and hefted. In effect, a dark curtain of unbelief has been drawn over their minds, causing them to see little or no purpose in their being.

"Much like the sightless man who cautiously makes his way down the street tapping his cane to identify the hazards that lie ahead, the person 'blind of mind' stumbles awkwardly through life. Every step is tentative; each roadblock is almost insurmountable; and progress is painfully slow at best. Of such people it is said they 'have eyes to see and see not.'. . .

". . . Hardness of heart is a gradual, subtle illness and not a massive heart attack that comes with little or no warning. It begins with the breaking of a single law. It grows layer by layer as more and more commandments are flaunted and as one thus becomes less and less able to distinguish between right and wrong. Then, as time lapses and rebellion increases, the once gentle and feeling heart becomes an impenetrable flint. No one is more hardened in character than he who has, without repenting, transgressed the laws of God." (*The Road to Somewhere* [Salt Lake City: Bookcraft, 1994], pp. 9–10, 11.)

In the book of Mosiah, we read: "Now the eyes of the people were blinded; *therefore* they hardened their hearts against the words of Abinadi. . . . And king Noah hardened his heart against the word of the Lord, and he did not repent of his evil doings." (Mosiah 11:29; emphasis added.) This scripture suggests that blindness of mind is the antithesis of faith and that hardness of heart is the opposite of good intentions and good works. Moreover, it is seen that these two spiritual maladies are inter-related like high cholesterol and a heart attack—the one leading to the other.

Whenever the Spirit of the Lord is offended and withdrawn, the people suffer hardness of heart and blindness of mind (see Ether 15:19). Whenever the veil of unbelief is drawn closed between God and man, hardness of heart and blindness of mind are the awful results (see Ether 4:15). Whenever people succumb to the temptations of the devil, their minds become blinded and their hearts hardened (see 1 Nephi 12:17).

Both blindness of mind and hardness of heart, according to the Apostle Paul, alienate individuals from the life of God. Said he: "This I say therefore, and testify in the Lord, that ye henceforth walk not as other Gentiles walk, in the vanity of their mind, having the understanding darkened, being alienated from the life of God through the ignorance that is in them, because of the blindness of their heart: who being past feeling have given themselves over unto lasciviousness, to work all uncleanness with greediness" (Ephesians 4:17–19).

It is significant that one prophet referred to the righteous as those "who believed in the *warnings* and the revelations of God" (2 Nephi 5:6; emphasis added), whereas the wicked were those who turned a deaf ear to the warnings of the prophets.

A depraved and degenerate nation overcome with hardness of heart and blindness of mind was described by Mormon as being "without principle, and past feeling" (Moroni 9:20). Such is the fate of all nations, ancient or modern, that wander in unbelief and wallow in the works of the flesh.

With an eye to our day, an angel of the Lord issued this warning through the prophet Nephi:

> Therefore, wo be unto the Gentiles if it so be that they harden their hearts against the Lamb of God.

For the time cometh, saith the Lamb of God, that I will work a great and a marvelous work among the children of men; a work which shall be everlasting, either on the one hand or on the other—either to the convincing of them unto peace and life eternal, or unto the deliverance of them to the hardness of their hearts and the blindness of their minds unto their being brought down into captivity, and also into destruction, both temporally and spiritually, according to the captivity of the devil, of which I have spoken. (1 Nephi 14:6–7.)

Only the foolish will ignore this warning—this golden thread woven into the Book of Mormon—knowing that if they do believe, repent, and follow after righteousness "it shall be well with them" (1 Nephi 14:5).

A PROMISE

The third golden thread, or prevailing theme, that runs from the beginning to the end of the Book of Mormon is well expressed by father Lehi. Said he: "I . . . have obtained a *promise*, that inasmuch as those whom the Lord God shall bring out of the land of Jerusalem shall keep his commandments, they shall prosper upon the face of this land; and they shall be kept from all other nations, that they may possess this land unto themselves. And if it so be that they shall keep his commandments they shall be blessed upon the face of this land, and there shall be none to molest them, nor to take away the land of their inheritance; and they shall dwell safely forever." (2 Nephi 1:9; emphasis added.)

Other prophets who trailed Lehi knew of this promise and mentioned it often to their people. For instance, Jarom reported a victory over his enemies and explained: "And thus being prepared to meet the Lamanites, they did not prosper against us. But the word of the Lord was verified, which he spake unto our fathers, saying that: Inasmuch as ye will keep my commandments ye shall prosper in the land." (Jarom 1:9.)

King Benjamin spoke of the constancy of God's word. He said: "And behold, all that he requires of you is to keep his commandments; and he has promised you that if ye would keep his commandments ye should prosper in the land; and he never doth vary from that which he hath said; therefore, if ye do keep his commandments he doth bless you and prosper you" (Mosiah 2:22).

Alma personalized the promise when he pleaded with his son: "O remember, remember, my son Helaman, how strict are the commandments of God. And he said: If ye will keep my commandments ye shall prosper in the land—but if ye keep not his commandments ye shall be cut off from his presence." (Alma 37:13.)

One Book of Mormon passage associates faith with the promise: "And this was their faith, that by so doing God would prosper them in the land, or in other words, if they were faithful in keeping the commandments of God that he would prosper them in the land; yea, warn them to flee, or to prepare for war, according to their danger" (Alma 48:15).

A most impressive description of man's tendency to forget the promise or take it for granted during the "good times" is provided in the book of Helaman. Here Mormon refers to the cycle of prosperity to ease to rebellion to suffering to repentance and back again to prosperity—a cycle which seems to be the pattern that most men and women follow:

> And thus we can behold how false, and also the unsteadiness of the hearts of the children of men; yea, we can see that the Lord in his great infinite goodness doth bless and prosper those who put their trust in him.
>
> Yea, and we may see at the very time when he doth prosper his people, yea, in the increase of their fields, their flocks and their herds, and in gold, and in silver, and in all manner of precious things of every kind and art; sparing their lives, and delivering them out of the hands of their enemies; softening the hearts of their enemies that they should not declare wars against them; yea, and in fine, doing all things for the welfare and happiness of his people; yea, then is the time that they do harden their hearts, and do forget the Lord their God, and do trample under their feet the Holy One—yea, and this because of their ease, and their exceedingly great prosperity. (Helaman 12:1–2.)

Any student of the Book of Mormon is intrigued by the linkage between the promise and reference to lands of promise.

Nephi was assured by the Lord that he and his people would be led to a "land of promise . . . , a land which is choice above all other lands" (1 Nephi 2:20). In answering Enos's prayers, the Lord referred to the land given to Enos and his people as "a holy land" (Enos 1:10). Nephi claimed that God leads "away the righteous into precious lands" (1 Nephi 17:38). And, with an eye to our modern day, Jacob stated: "And now, my beloved brethren, I have read these things that ye might know concerning the covenants of the Lord that he has covenanted with all the house of Israel—that he has spoken unto the Jews, by the mouth of his holy prophets, even from the beginning down, from generation to generation, until the time comes that they shall be restored to the true church and fold of God; when they shall be gathered home to the lands of their inheritance, and shall be established in all their lands of promise" (2 Nephi 9:1–2).

As mentioned previously, the promise given and repeated over and over again to the Nephite people during the course of many centuries has never been rescinded. It is a simple and plain statement: "Inasmuch as ye shall keep the commandments of God ye shall prosper in the land" (Alma 36:30). It may be applied to individuals, families, or nations, because blessings are promised those who obey the commandments of the Lord, and a curse or forfeiture of blessings is the lot of the disobedient (see Deuteronomy 11:26–28).

CONCLUSION

Those who study the Book of Mormon carefully will appreciate the three golden threads woven into the fabric of its pages. The invitation, warning, and promise appear over and over again like the recurring melody of a composer's masterpiece. Yet the messages of the book—a book regarded as "the keystone of our religion" and as a book that will draw us "nearer to God" (Introduction to the Book of Mormon)—do not come to life until we "liken all scriptures unto us, that it might be for our profit and learning" (1 Nephi 19:23).

Insert yourself into the scriptures and assume that God's spokesman is speaking directly to you when he invites: "And now, my beloved brethren, I would that ye should come unto

Christ, who is the Holy One of Israel, and partake of his salvation, and the power of his redemption. Yea, come unto him, and offer your whole souls as an offering unto him, and continue in fasting and praying, and endure to the end; and as the Lord liveth ye will be saved." (Omni 1:26.)

Assume that the Lord is addressing you face-to-face when He warns, "If ye will not harden your hearts, and ask me in faith, believing that ye shall receive, with diligence in keeping my commandments, surely these things shall be made known unto you" (1 Nephi 15:11).

Pretend that you are Helaman and you hear your father express the Lord's promise: "But behold, my son, this is not all; for ye ought to know as I do know, that inasmuch as ye shall keep the commandments of God ye shall prosper in the land; and ye ought to know also, that inasmuch as ye will not keep the commandments of God ye shall be cut off from his presence. Now this is according to his word." (Alma 36:30.)

Three "golden threads" of eternal truth are woven into the fabric of the Book of Mormon and must be woven into the fabrics of our lives. Such may be done if we—

- Accept the *invitation* in good faith,
- Heed the *warning* given and act accordingly,
- And claim the *promised* blessings by living righteously.

Index

— A —

Aaron (brother of Ammon), 123, 174
Abinadi, dealings with King Noah,
   69–72
   influence of, on Alma the Elder,
     81–82, 88
   teachings of, 72–78
Accountability, 64
Adoption to Christ, 76–77
Alma the Elder, Abinadi's influence
   on, 72, 81–82, 88
   example of, 79–80, 96–97
   founded the Church, 85–87
   as governor, 90–92
   legacy of, 87–89
   as a missionary, 82–84
   as persevering parent, 92–94
   as a teacher, 94–96
Alma the Younger, on baptism, 204
   became first chief judge, 87, 136
   confronted by Zeezrom, 112–14
   conversion of, 92–94, 99–102
   is defended by Zeezrom, 116–17
   and Lehi, 16–18
   pleads with son Helaman, 210
   rebukes Zeezrom, 114–15
   seed metaphor and tree of life,
     25–29

teaches Amulek, 107, 109
wayward youth of, 98–99
Amaleki, 204
Amalickiah, 139
Aminadab, 119, 149–50
Ammaron, 168
Ammon, faith of, 125–27
   as hero, 121
   missionary experiences of, 122–27
   rehearsed King Benjamin's
     words, 66
   taught by the Spirit, 174
Ammonihah, 103–4, 109, 112–13
Amulek, angel appears to, 106–7
   is confronted by Zeezrom, 112–14
   is defended by Zeezrom, 116–17
   rebukes Zeezrom, 108–9
Amulon, 91
Ananias, 118
Angel(s), appears to Alma the
   Younger, 93, 99–100, 103–4
   appears to Amulek, 106–7
   conversed with Nephi and Lehi
     in prison, 149
   issued warning through Nephi,
     208–9
   ministering, 176–77
   taught King Benjamin, 63–64
Anti-Christs, 25, 32–33, 173

Anti-Nephi-Lehi, 110, 116, 125
Antipus, 139
Arnold, Matthew, *Sohrab and Rustum*, 68
Atonement, Mormon preserved doctrine of, 173
  taught by Jacob, 44
  taught by King Benjamin, 64
  taught by Nephi, 9, 13
  See also Jesus Christ

— B —

Babel, tower of, 180, 182
Baptism, 83–84, 204
  of infants, 178–79
Baptism of Finau (story), 51–54
Benjamin, King, 59–67
Bennett, William J., on heroes, 128–29
Benson, Ezra Taft, on pride, 164–65
Blessings, and laws, 2
  seeking and obtaining, 186–88
Blindness of mind, 207–9
Bonham, James Butler, 132
Brass plates, 3
Brother of Jared, and blessings, 186–88
  characteristics of, 183–84
  details of life on twenty-four plates, 180
  Jesus Christ appears to, 182–83, 185–86

— C —

Callings, acceptance of, 1
Carpet metaphor, 202
Charity, 177–78
Chastity, 41
Church of Christ, established by Alma the Elder, 85–87
Clark, J. Reuben, on giving, 104
Condescension of God, 22–23
Conversion, of Alma the Elder, 81–82
  of Alma the Younger, 92–94

of Amulek, 107
  of King Benjamin's people, 64–65
  and the seed, tree, and fruit, 29
Coriantor, 192
Coriantumr, 191
Courage, 132

— D —

David, King, 143

— E —

Enduring to the end, 179
Enos, concern for others, 55–56, 83
  effort of, 50
  gratitude of, 48–49
  humility of, 49
  persistence of, 47, 55–58
  taught by Jacob, 95
Ephraim, tribe of, 10
Ethem, 192
Ether, influence on Moroni, 193–94
  as a missionary, 190–91
  Moroni's commentary on, 189–90
  trials of, 191–92

— F —

Faith, of Ammon, 125–27
  of Nephi (son of Helaman), 148–55
  of Zoramites, 26
Fathers, 59, 92–94
Fear, 161
Finau's baptism (story), 51–54
First Presidency, on the Father and the Son, 74
Forgiveness, 50–51
Freedom, 129–30, 143
  See also Liberty, religious
Fruit of tree, symbolism of, 23–24

— G —

Gadianton robbers, 155, 169
Gratitude, 48–49

— H —

Heart, hardness of, 207–9
    intent of, 176
Helam, 84
Helam, land of, 90, 94
Helaman (son of Alma), returns to
    teaching, 162
    stripling warriors of, 95, 139
Helaman (son of Helaman), on
    Christ, 33
    taught sons, 146–47
Heroes, 128–29
Hill Cumorah, 198, 199
Hinckley, Gordon B., on fear, 163
    on his parents, 95
Holland, Jeffrey R., on Mormon, 172
Holy Ghost, 198
Humility, of Enos, 49
    of Zoramites, 26
Hunter, Howard W., on concern for
    others, 55

— I —

Idolatry, 175
Invitation of prophets, 24, 203–6
Iron rod, 19–20
"Iron Rod, The" (hymn), 12
Isaiah, writings of, Jacob draws on,
    36
    Nephi draws on, 6–7, 42–43
    technique for reading, 73
Ishmael, sons of, 4
Israel, terrain and climate of, 3–4
Israel, house of, Jacob's theme of,
    35–38
    scattering and gathering, 176

— J —

Jacob (brother of Nephi), afflictions
    of, 34–35
    anointed by Nephi, 5
    becomes Nephite prophet, 6
    concern of, for others, 38–42
    confronted by Sherem, 32–33

covenantal theme of, 35–38
    taught Enos, 95
    testifies of Christ, 42–46
    on wisdom, 2
Jared, brother of. *See* Brother of Jared
Jaredites, 189
Jerusalem, Lehi sends sons to, 3–4
Jesus Christ, in Abinadi's teach-
    ings, 73–78
    adoption to, 76–77
    appears to brother of Jared,
        182–83
    as the Father, 74–75
    image of, in countenance, 29
    invitation to come to, 24, 203–6
    Jacob testifies of, 42–46
    in King Benjamin's sermon,
        62–64
    ministry among Nephites, 170–72
    in Nephi's teachings, 9, 12–15, 79
    spirit body of, 185
    spirit of, 176, 198
    tree of life symbol of, 21–22
    truths about, in brother of Jared's
        experience, 185–86
    visits Mormon, 168–69
    See also Atonement
Johnson, Peter G., 158–59
Joseph (brother of Nephi), afflic-
    tions of, 34
    anointed by Nephi, 5
Judges, system of, 112, 135–37
Judgment, 175–76

— K —

Kimball, Spencer W., on repen-
    tance, 101
    on service, 104–5
    on teaching parents, 94–95
King-men, 137–42
Korihor, 173

— L —

Laban, plates of, 3
Laman and Lemuel, in Lehi's
    dream, 19, 20

resisted father's counsel, 3–4
taught by Lehi, 95
Lamoni, King, 125, 174
Law of Moses, 73, 142–43
Laws, and blessings, 2
Leadership, 131
Lee, Harold B., on brother of Jared,
       186–88
    on following living prophets,
       165–66
    "within walls of our home," 159
Lehi, and Alma the Younger, 16–18
    dreams of tree of life, 18–20
    as man of God, 8
    obeyed and honored by Nephi,
       3–4
    taught Laman and Lemuel, 95
    in the wilderness, 34–35
Lehi (son of Helaman), prison ex-
       perience of, 119, 148–50
    in war, 141, 142
Liberty, religious, 87
    See also Freedom
Limhi, King, 66, 68
Love of God, 21–22

— M —

Mahonri Moriancumer. *See* Brother
       of Jared
Mary, virgin, 22
Maxwell, Neal A., on "enlarged
       memory," 181
McKay, David O., "act well thy
       part," 158–59
Melek, 111
Mind, blindness of, 207–9
Ministering angels, 176–77
Missionary work, of Alma the
       Elder, 82–84
    of Alma the Younger, 102–5
    and Alma's seed metaphor, 26–27
    of Ammon, 120–27
    of Ether, 190–91
    of Nephi (son of Helaman),
       147–48, 153–55

Mormon, abridges records, 157–58,
       169–70
    in battle, 174–75
    childhood of, 168–69
    doctrinal contributions of, 175
    his editing influence on 3 Nephi,
       170–74
    origin of name, 88–89
    saw destruction of Nephites, 165
    taught Moroni, 96
Mormon, place of, 83–84, 88–89
Moron, 192
Moroni, abridges records, 180
    appears to Joseph Smith, 199
    on Ether, 189–90
    as record keeper, 197–98
    saw destruction of Nephites,
       196–97
    as student of Ether, 192–94
    as symbol, 195
    taught by Mormon, 96
    writes about Ammon, 121, 125
Moroni, Captain, defends Nephite
       freedom, 129–30
    and Pahoran, 134–35, 139–42
    personality traits of, 131–33
    as true hero, 128–29
    turns command over to
       Moronihah, 162
Moronihah, 162
Moroni statue, 195
Moses, law of, 73, 142–43
Mosiah, established judicial sys-
       tem, 135–36
    sons of, 83, 92, 115
    trained by father, 59
Mothers, taught stripling warriors,
       96

— N —

Natural man, 65
Nehor, 173
Nephi (son of Helaman), doctrinal
       contributions of, 175–79
    his faith in Jesus Christ, 148–55

as missionary, 147–48
obedience of, 155–56
parentage of, 146–47
prison experience of, 119, 148–50
Nephi (son of Lehi), commanded to
    build a ship, 5–6
    example of, 1–2
    humility of, 8
    in Lehi's dream, 19, 20
    literacy of, 6–7
    as man of God, 8–12
    obeys and honors Lehi, 3–4
    on pressing forward, 62
    as record keeper, 4–5, 7
    saw vision of Christ, 11, 12
    saw vision of tree of life, 20–25
    teachings centered on Christ, 9,
        12–15, 79
Nephi, Third (book), 170–74
Nephihah, 102, 136
Nibley, Hugh, on Captain Moroni,
    130
Nicodemus, 21
Noah, King, 69–72, 81, 91

— O —

"O" exclamation, 43–44
Opposition, 34–35, 145, 189–90,
    191–92
Orihah, 186

— P —

Packer, Boyd K., on Nephi's vision
    of Christ, 11
Pahoran, answers Moroni's epistle,
    140–42
    and Captain Moroni, 134–35
    defends government against
        king-men, 137–40
    and judicial system, 135–37
    legacy of, 142–44
Parents, honoring of, 3–4
    righteous teachings of, 95–96,
        146–47

Paul, Apostle, 118
    on Atonement, 23
    on natural man, 65
Persistence, 47, 55–58
Peter, Apostle, on Atonement, 23
    commanded to help others, 102
    on divine nature, 29
    on light, 116
Philistines, 143
Pondering, 152
Poverty, 66
Prayer, 56, 164, 184
Preparation, 131
Pride, 164–65
Promise of Book of Mormon, 209–11
Prophets, in Book of Mormon teach
    fulness of gospel, 201–2
    following the living, 161–67, 177
    invitation of, 24, 203–6

— R —

Record keeping, and King
    Benjamin, 59–60
    and Mormon, 157–58, 169–70
    and Moroni, 180, 197–98
    and Nephi (son of Lehi), 4–5, 7
Repentance, 80, 101–2, 184, 205
Restitution, 101–2
Resurrection, 75–76
Revelation, 11
Rod of iron, 19–20
Romney, Marion G., on tithing, 164

— S —

Salt Lake Temple, 195
Sam (son of Lehi), 19, 20
Samaria, woman of, 22
Samuel, Israelite prophet, 138
Samuel the Lamanite, and living
    prophets, 161–67
    prophecies of, in Mormon's
        abridgement, 157–58
    teaches us to do our best, 158–60
    upon the wall, 160–61

Sariah, 3, 4, 19, 20, 34
Saul. *See* Paul, Apostle
Scripture study, 98
Seantum, 152
Seed, Alma's metaphor of, 25–29
    of Christ, 77
Seezoram, 152
Service, 104–5
Sherem, 32–33, 116, 173
Shim, hill called, 168
Sidom, 117, 118
Smith, Joseph, 199
Smith, Joseph Fielding, on using
    our blessings, 185
Sohrab and Rustum (poem), 68
Stephen, Apostle, 118
Stirling Castle quote, 158–59
Strait and narrow path, 19–20

— T —

Tanner, N. Eldon, on hypocrites, 166
Taylor, John, on prayer, 164
Teancum, 136, 141, 142
Tithing, 164
Tree of life, and Alma's seed
    metaphor, 25–29
  Lehi's dream of, 18–20
  Nephi's vision of, 20–25

— W —

Wall-climbing metaphor, 160–61
Warning in Book of Mormon, 206–9

Wayward children, 92–94, 98–99
Whiteness, symbolism of, 21
Wisdom, 2
Wise men, the, 205
"Wo" exclamation, 41–42, 44
Women, Jacob's concern for, 41
Woodruff, Wilford, on living ora-
    cles, 166–67

— Y —

Young, Brigham, on natural man,
    65
  on reading the scriptures, 98

— Z —

Zarahemla, 85, 86, 92, 97, 109, 141,
    163, 168
Zeezrom, confronts Alma and
    Amulek, 112–14
  conversion of, 115–16
  defends Alma and Amulek,
    116–17
  is healed, 117–18
  is rebuked by Alma, 114–15
  is rebuked by Amulek, 108–9
  serves mission with Amulek,
    111
Zeniff, 68, 85
Zenos's allegory, 37
Zoram, 3, 6
Zoramites, 25–26, 111